HOW TO REBUILD FORD COYOTE ENGINES

COVERS GEN I, II, & III ENGINES

Jim Smart

CarTech®

CarTech®

CarTech®, Inc.
6118 Main Street
North Branch, MN 55056
Phone: 651-277-1200 or 800-551-4754
Fax: 651-277-1203
www.cartechbooks.com

Edit by Bob Wilson
Layout by Connie DeFlorin

ISBN 978-1-61325-851-4
Item No. SA553

Library of Congress Cataloging-in-Publication Data Available

Written, edited, and designed in the U.S.A.
Printed in China
10 9 8 7 6 5 4 3 2 1

DISTRIBUTION BY:

Europe
PGUK
63 Hatton Garden
London EC1N 8LE, England
Phone: 020 7061 1980 • Fax: 020 7242 3725
www.pguk.co.uk

Australia
Renniks Publications Ltd.
3/37-39 Green Street
Banksmeadow, NSW 2109, Australia
Phone: 2 9695 7055 • Fax: 2 9695 7355
www.renniks.com

Canada
Login Canada
300 Saulteaux Crescent
Winnipeg, MB, R3J 3T2 Canada
Phone: 800 665 1148 • Fax: 800 665 0103
www.lb.ca

ACKNOWLEDGMENTS

When I wrote the *Ford Coyote Engines: How to Build Max Performance* book nearly a decade ago, there was still much to be learned about the newest version of Ford's Modular engine family, which was code-named "Coyote." Although I had written plenty about the Modular engines, the Coyote was a fresh look at an exciting and proven Ford mill.

The all-new twin independent variable camshaft timing (Ti-VCT) Coyote showed that Ford product planners and engineers were listening and had taken an extensive look at the Modular engine family regarding what enthusiasts liked and didn't like about this rugged engine. This was the first time in Ford history that a production engine was developed to be a high-performance mill from the start and that it would also be used in F-Series trucks.

When my original Coyote book, *Ford Coyote Engines: How to Build Max Performance*, was written for CarTech and published in 2016, I still had a lot to learn, and I'm am continuing to learn more about what turned out to be the greatest high-performance V-8 that Ford has ever produced. When I was writing that original Coyote book, Mike Delahanty (formerly of Ford Performance) pro-

vided a complete Gen 2 5.0L Ti-VCT dual-overhead-cam (DOHC) Coyote V-8 and most of the parts necessary to conduct dyno testing. Ford Performance allowed me to take the Coyote engine and test in the dynamometer room at JGM Performance Engineering in Valencia, California. The results were remarkable.

We never came close to reaching the limits and potential of the Gen 2 Coyote. The numbers were achieved with a stock bottom end. We dogged the Coyote on the JGM dyno: pulled the heads; swapped cams, intake manifolds, and throttle bodies; tried different headers; and marveled at the power that the engine made with help from BBK Performance, Comp Cams, and Ford Performance.

Ford Performance, Performance Assembly Solutions (PAS), and Roush Performance have invited me to Livonia, Michigan, on two occasions to see how Ford Performance Aluminator crate engines are built. Crate engines have long received a well-deserved bad rap over quality issues. However, Ford's Aluminator Coyote crate engines are a huge exception to this belief because the high standards are OEM in scope.

These Aluminator Coyote crate engines are world class and mass-produced in an intimate shop envi-

ronment, where every engine is produced with strict accountability. Members of the PAS staff talk with each other daily, and issues are discussed and resolved immediately. John Torvinen, Frank Hoffman, and Will Clendenin of PAS have been very supportive through the years.

Jim Grubbs of JGM Performance Engineering (now retired) took on this project initially and became committed to its success. He and his associate at the time, Jeff Latimer, spent weeks preparing JGM's SuperFlow 901 dyno for our Gen 2 engine testing. Ray Herron of Ford Performance's technical support group has been very supportive through the years. We call, and Ford Performance advises.

Ray McClelland of Full Throttle Kustomz (FTK) was kind enough to come to JGM Performance Engineering to custom tune our original Gen 2 Coyote test mule as modifications were made. With McClelland's knowledge and extraordinary tuning abilities, we managed to gain more than 100 hp with simple bolt-on modifications in a naturally aspirated package.

In more recent times, Mike Goodwin of Ford Performance has answered the call with a Gen 3 dual-injection Coyote Aluminator crate engine to play with at Quarter Mile Performance Racing Engines (QMP) and FTK in Los Angeles. QMP has taken the latest rendition of the Coyote engine and bolstered it with H-beam rods, forged pistons, specialized port work, and hotter cams. Then, this engine was shipped to FTK for a workout. McClelland took the QMP Gen 3 Coyote engine and gave it an FTK super tune.

Tim Gilpin at BBK Performance has been endlessly supportive, providing performance parts and technical support. Trent Goodwin at Comp Cams has supported my efforts more times than I can count through the decades, providing cam kits, valvetrain components, and performance parts along the way. Wes Duenkel came to my rescue with needed Coyote build images to help fill in where photo content was lacking. Duenkel's exceptional work provided me with an education on how to improve my own work, which proves that you're never too old to learn. Thanks, Wes.

There is also my longtime friend and cohort in crime, Alan Rebescher of Summit Racing Equipment, who has stood by me through untold numbers of projects over the past 30 years and has again come to my rescue with *Ford Coyote Engines: How to Rebuild*. Alan, I could never have had this much success without you.

A book like this isn't without its issues (meaning differences of opinion), and there are many out there. Although I do have an automotive engine-building background, I am not an engine-building professional. I am the messenger. I take what I learn from engine-building professionals and racers and impart what I learn to you. I invite your thoughts and feedback so that I can better serve you in the future.

I'm grateful for your support.

INTRODUCTION TO THE COYOTE ENGINE

Ford's innovative 5.0L twin independent variable camshaft timing (Ti-VCT) Coyote and the 5.2L flat-plane-crank Voodoo (Shelby GT350) dual-overhead-cam (DOHC) V-8 are the two most advanced overhead-cam V-8 engines that the company has ever produced. "Coyote" was the code name for the Ti-VCT engine, which entered development in 2008. Product planners and engineers began development by examining the Modular single-overhead-cam (SOHC)/DOHC engine family and where improvements needed to be made. There was plenty of room for improvement.

When the Coyote was introduced in 2011 as an all-new, high-performance Mustang GT engine, it appeared that there was no way Ford could do any better than the Gen 1, but it has steadily become better over the past decade. Improvements began in 2015 with the Gen 2 Coyote with Charge Motion Control Valve (CMCV) induction and continued in 2018 with the dual-injection Gen 3 engine. Dual throttle bodies and more significant upgrades have since arrived for 2024 in the Mustang GT.

The Coyote is an easy engine to understand and build because it is produced in one North American plant (Essex, Ontario, Canada) with one block and head casting type. There isn't the confusion of two engine plants with different approaches and parts like there was with the 4.6L and 5.4L Modular engines. However, the more specialized

This inside look at the 5.0L Ti-VCT DOHC Coyote V-8 shows what makes this the most advanced Ford V-8 in history. Conceived as a Detroit-born, high-performance V-8, the Coyote makes more than 450 hp right out of the box and is capable of a 500-plus hp without extensive modifications.

Coyote engines, such as the Predator and Shelby GT350 Voodoo, were assembled at Ford's Romeo, Michigan, engine plant.

The Coyote's firing order (1-5-4-8-6-3-7-2) is different than the 4.6L and 5.4L V-8s. The compression ratios (11.0:1 and 12.0:1) remind me of the 1960s, making the most of its lower displacement and carefully executed valve timing. Imagine being able to do this with 87-octane fuel, although 91-octane fuel is preferable. This innovation comes from twin independent variable cam timing (Ti-VCT), which enables each camshaft to control valve timing based on input from the powertrain control module (PCM).

What makes the Coyote Ti-VCT different from the 4.6L and 5.4L engines are great innovations that make it a more user-friendly engine. If you're considering a Modular engine swap, the 5.0L Ti-VCT DOHC

Gen 2 Coyote Improvements

Improvements to the Gen 2 Coyote (2015–2017) focused on improved breathing characteristics. These improvements, many of which were derived from the lessons learned developing the "Roadrunner" 2012–2013 Mustang Boss 302 Coyote engine, allowed for improved breathing at higher revs. Additional improvements include:

- Larger intake valves
- Larger exhaust valves
- Revised intake camshafts
- Revised exhaust camshafts
- Stiffer valve springs to ensure improved valve action at high RPM
- New cylinder-head castings, including revised ports that provide a straighter path to the valves for less-restrictive intake and exhaust flow and combustion-chamber modifications to accommodate larger valves
- Sinter-forged connecting rods used on the Boss 302 engine for durability at high RPM
- Redesigned piston crowns with deeper cutouts to clear larger valves
- Rebalanced forged crankshaft that supports high-RPM operation
- A new intake manifold featuring CMCVs to partially close off port flow at lower engine speeds. This increases the air charge tumble and swirl for improved air/fuel mixing, resulting in better fuel economy, idle stability, and lower emissions
- On the intake side, variable camshaft timing had new mid-lock phasers, allowing better control of the valve timing over a broader range of engine RPM ■

Gen 3 Coyote Improvements

The Gen 3 Coyote (2018–2023) has been a game changer for this engine family, making it the most advanced Coyote to date. It features dual injection, which consists of port injection and direction injection for power, improved emissions, and reduced fuel consumption. More improvements include:

- Larger bores to allow for larger valves
- Plasma transferred wire arc (PTWA) cylinder bores (as found on the GT350 5.2L Voodoo engine)
- Larger intake valves
- Larger exhaust valves
- Revised, higher-lift intake camshafts
- Revised, higher-lift exhaust camshafts
- Stiffer valve springs to allow a higher maximum RPM of 7,500 rpm
- Stronger cylinder-head castings, including further revised ports from Gen 2, resulting in flow characteristics approaching the CNC ports in the GT350 5.2L Voodoo engine
- Sinter-forged connecting rods carried over from the Boss 302 engine and Gen 2 Coyote
- Higher-compression pistons (12.0:1) with deeper cutouts to clear the larger valves
- A rebalanced, forged crankshaft that supports higher-RPM operation
- A new, revised, higher-flowing intake manifold with the same CMCV feature as introduced on Gen 2
- A dual fuel system (direct injection and port fuel systems, allowing for a higher compression ratio and maximizing performance and fuel efficiency)
- On the intake side, variable camshaft timing mid-lock phasers carried over from Gen 2 engine. The exhaust phasers migrate to an in-cylinder-head oil control valve for better control at all speeds and loads. ■

V-8 is the best way to go if you're going to invest all of this time and expense.

The latest Coyote generation is the Gen 4 for 2024. The Ford Performance engine team brings you the Gen 4 Coyote crate engines and control packs. It will be offering two versions of the current Mustang 5.0L Coyote engine. The Gen 4 engines (M-6007-M50D and M-6007-M50DAUTO) feature dual

Coyote Specifications

Gen 1 (2011–2014) 5.0L Ti-VCT Specifications
- 5.0L Ti-VCT DOHC V-8 (302 ci)
- Code-named "Coyote"
- Bore: 3.630 inches (92 mm)
- Pistons: hypereutectic (high-silicon cast)
- Stroke: 3.650 inches (93 mm)
- Connecting rods: powdered-metal forged
- Crankshaft: forged steel with eight-bolt flange
- Horsepower: 412 at 6,500 rpm
- Torque: 390 ft-lbs at 4,250 rpm
- Redline: 7,000 rpm
- Compression: 11.0:1 (naturally aspirated), 9.0:1 (supercharged)
- Aluminum block with steel cylinder liners
- Aluminum hemispherical four-valve heads
- Variable valve timing (VVT), composite intake/exhaust cams
- Manufactured at Essex, Ontario, Canada
- Intake manifold: composite, 16.5-inch runners
- CMCV flap valves for improved low-end torque and idle quality
- Returnless electronic fuel injection (EFI)
- Coil-on-plug electronic ignition
- Shorty tubular stainless-steel headers
- Oil capacity: 8-quarts with filter change

Gen 2 (2015–2017) 5.0L Ti-VCT Specifications
- 5.0L Ti-VCT DOHC V-8 (302 ci)
- Code-named "Coyote"
- Bore: 3.630 inches (92 mm)
- Pistons: hypereutectic (high silicon cast)
- Stroke: 3.650 inches (93 mm)
- Connecting rods: powdered-metal forged
- Crankshaft: forged steel with eight-bolt flange
- Horsepower: 435 at 6,500 rpm
- Torque: 400 ft-lbs at 4,250 rpm
- Redline: 7,000 rpm
- Compression: 11.0:1 (naturally aspirated), 9.0:1 (supercharged)
- Aluminum block with steel cylinder liners
- Aluminum hemispherical four-valve heads
- VVT, composite intake/exhaust cams
- Manufactured at Essex, Ontario, Canada

- Intake manifold: composite, 16.5-inch runners
- CMCV flap valves for improved low-end torque and idle quality
- Returnless EFI
- Coil-on-plug electronic ignition
- Shorty tubular stainless-steel headers
- Oil capacity: 8-quarts with filter change

5.2L Shelby GT350 Voodoo (2015–2020) Specifications
- 5.2L DOHC V-8 (315 ci)
- Code-Named "Voodoo"
- Bore: 3.700 inches (94 mm)
- Pistons: hypereutectic (high-silicon cast)
- Stroke: 3.660 inches (93 mm)
- Connecting rods: powdered-metal forged
- Crankshaft: forged-steel flat-plane with eight-bolt flange
- Horsepower: 526 at 7,500 rpm
- Torque: 429 ft-lbs at 4,750 rpm
- Redline: 8,000 rpm
- Compression: 12.0:1 (naturally aspirated)
- PTWA sprayed-on cylinder liners
- Aluminum hemispherical four-valve heads
- VVT, composite intake/exhaust cams
- Manufactured at Romeo, Michigan
- Intake manifold: composite, 16.5-inch runners
- Throttle body: 87 mm
- CMCV flap valves for improved low-end torque and idle quality
- Returnless EFI
- Coil-on-plug electronic ignition
- Shorty tubular stainless-steel headers
- Oil capacity: 8-quarts with filter change

Gen 3 (2018–2023) 5.0L Ti-VCT Specifications
- Larger cylinder bores to accommodate larger valves
- PTWA cylinder walls borrowed from the Shelby GT350 5.2L block
- Horsepower: 460 at 7,000 rpm
- Torque: 420 ft-lbs at 4,600 rpm
- Larger intake and exhaust valves
- Revised lift intake and exhaust cams
- Stiffer valve springs to allow for higher maximum revs of 7,500 rpm

80-mm throttle bodies. They make 480 hp at 7,150 rpm and 415 ft-lbs of torque at 4,900 rpm.

Since Ford Performance understands the challenges of packaging dual throttle bodies and dual air-inlet systems, the team developed a single throttle-body alternative for Gen 4 crate engines. The Gen 4X (M-6007-M50H) features a single 80-mm throttle-body intake and produces 460 hp at 7,000 rpm and

- New stronger cylinder-head castings including revised ports from the Gen 2, resulting in better flow experienced from the CNC-ported GT350's 5.2L Voodoo
- Sinter-forged connecting rods carried over from the 2012–2013 Boss 302 engine and Gen 2 Coyote
- Greater compression (12.0:1) from domed pistons with deeper cutouts to clear larger valves
- Improved, balanced forged-steel crankshaft for higher-RPM operation
- A fresh, revised intake manifold with the same CMCV from the Gen 2
- Dual fuel induction with both direct and port fuel injection. This allows for higher compression and clean intake-valve faces, maximizing performance and fuel efficiency.
- On the intake side, variable camshaft timing with mid-lock phasers carried over from the Gen 2. Exhaust cam phasers migrate to an in-head oil-control valve with spring return for better control at all speeds and loads.
- Additional oil return passage in the block for diverted oil from the oil-filter adapter
- Camshaft lift (14 mm) that is greater than the Gen 2
- Exhaust cam number-1 journal is also larger to accommodate seals, which prevent oil leakage from the phaser
- The Gen 2 chain drive uses Gen 2 intake phasers, primary chains, secondary chains, and crank sprocket. The Gen 3 chain driver kit is M-6004-A5018.
- Exhaust phasers (watch spring style) are new for the Gen 3 (no interchangeability with Gen 1 and 2) and attached with a single bolt
- Gen 3 valve springs employ a greater pressure and installed height than Gen 2
- Bridge cooling holes in Gen 3 head gaskets due to greater compression and cylinder pressures

Gen 3 (2020–2022) 5.2L Ti-VCT Predator Specifications
- 5.2L DOHC V-8 (315 ci)
- Bore: 3.700 inches (94 mm)
- Pistons: hypereutectic (high-silicon cast)
- Stroke: 3.660 inches (93 mm)
- Connecting rods: powdered-metal forged

- Crankshaft: forged steel with eight-bolt flange
- Horsepower: 760 at 7,300 rpm
- Torque: 625 ft-lbs at 5,000 rpm
- Redline: 8,000 rpm
- Compression: 12.0:1 (naturally aspirated)
- PTWA sprayed-on cylinder liners
- Aluminum hemispherical four-valve heads
- VVT, composite intake/exhaust cams
- Manufactured at Romeo, Michigan
- Intake manifold: composite, 16.5-inch runners
- Throttle body: 87 mm
- CMCV flap valves for improved low-end torque and idle quality
- Returnless EFI
- Coil-on-plug electronic ignition
- Shorty tubular stainless-steel headers
- Oil capacity: 8 quarts with filter change

Gen 4 (2024) 5.0L Ti-VCT Specifications
- 2024-and-newer Mustang GT
- 5.0 liters (302 ci)
- Compression ratio: 12.0:1
- Horsepower: 480 at 7,150 rpm
- Torque: 415 ft-lbs at 4,900 rpm
- Mahle hard-anodized forged pistons with Grafal low-friction coating
- Manley H-beam connecting rods with ARP 2000 bolts
- Forged-steel crankshaft
- Production 2024 Mustang GT aluminum block
- 2024 production oil pan
- Tuned composite Mustang GT intake manifold with production dual drive-by-wire 80-mm throttle bodies with variable runner control
- Four-valve-per-cylinder aluminum heads with roller finger followers to reduce friction
- Mustang GT production camshafts
- Includes colder-heat-range spark plugs (M-12405-M50A)
- Includes Ford Performance oil filter (M-6731-FL820)
- Includes billet steel gerotor oil pump gears (M-6600-M50A) ■

This photo of the original Gen 1 Ti-VCT was taken when the engine was introduced at the 2010 SEMA Show. The Ti-VCT dual-overhead-cam engine has variable cam timing, which enables each cam to work independently, depending upon demand.

It is challenging to differentiate the Coyote block from a 4.6L block because they have the same deck height and bore spacing. However, the Ti-VCT block has Modular engine architecture with a much more robust block. The Coyote's cooling system has been designed to route coolant around the exhaust-valve seats first and then down through the block instead of the valley, which frees up space for induction and supercharging. Ventilation "chimneys" (arrows) in the block improve crankcase scavenging and free up power.

420 ft-lbs of torque at 4,600 rpm. The Gen 4X Coyote engine requires a unique control pack. The Gen 4 and 4X front-end accessory drive (FEAD) components and alternator kits are a simple carryover from the Gen 3 5.0L Coyote crate engines. The exhaust-flange pattern on the driver-side cylinder head has been changed to match the 5.2L pattern. The passenger-side exhaust flange pattern remains the same as it was on the Gen 3 engine.

The Block

The Coyote block shares the same bore spacing of 3.937 inches (100 mm), deck height of 8.937 inches (227 mm), bellhousing bolt pattern, and external dimensions as the 4.6L SOHC and DOHC engines. The bore size increased to 3.629 inches (92.2 mm) along with an increased stroke of 3.649 inches (92.8 mm), which is still a "square" engine design with an identical bore and stroke.

The Gen 1 and Gen 2 Coyote engines sport a rugged aluminum block with paper-thin iron cylinder liners. Because the Coyote's iron cylinder liners are so thin, this block must be sleeved for all-out racing in the 1,000- to 1,500-plus-hp range. For example, Modular Motorsports offers racers the "Pro Mod" Coyote block with extra-thick ductile-iron cylinder liners that ensure solid block integrity. You can build one of these Pro Mod engines for the street even if you're an avid weekend racer. Bores can be taken as high as 3.700 inches to achieve 5.2 liters.

Improved block architecture holds the Coyote together. The main bearing webs are thicker and heavier, allowing for performance extremes. This means that the Coyote block can stand up to naturally aspirated performance demands, supercharging, nitrous, and direct injection. It can be said with great confidence this block will withstand 1,500-plus hp when sleeved with the thicker ductile-iron cylinder liners.

The Coyote block brings great advances in crankcase ventilation known as "bay to bay" breathing. Ford engineers placed venting in the main webs that is designed to allow the freedom of air scavenging without hurting power. These vents are known as chimneys. The result is a more positive piston-ring seal, which helps efficiency and power. The Modular V-8's cooling tube down the middle of the valley is gone on the Coyote. Instead, coolant is routed through the front

The Coyote's bottom end has a skirted six-bolt-main-cap construction that uses larger bolts than the 4.6L and 5.4L Modular engines. These main caps are a perfect fit and are void of the jackscrews and wedges like the Modular engine has. These caps don't move even under extreme duty, enabling this engine to achieve a 7,000-plus-rpm redline from the factory.

The Coyote's 57-cc, four-valve hemispherical chambers demonstrate how different these heads are from previous Modular castings. However, the valve angle has been significantly revised, not to mention the spacing between valves to achieve less cylinder-head mass and get the intake ports farther away from the crankshaft centerline. The intake valves are 1.460 inches, and the exhaust valves are 1.220 inches. Spark-plug firing tips are in the middle of the chambers.

of the block, leaving plenty of room for exotic induction systems and superchargers.

The Gen 3 Coyote block brought with it great advances in strength. It is an upgraded version of the previous Ford Performance M-6010-M52 and M-6010-M52A 5.2L Coyote aluminum cylinder blocks. It features higher-flow piston cooling jets for improved piston cooling. The rod bolt path is clearance machined into the block. The Gen 3 block employs longer 12-mm cylinder head bolts for greater clamping force, which calls for the longer head-bolt kit (M-6067-M501280) or the head-changing kit from Ford Performance (M-6067-M52B).

The Gen 3 block has improved crankcase windage, larger 94.0-mm bores, and better water jacket flow below cylinder bores, which have been updated with more material for strength. The intake side of the

bore at the deck surface includes a cast-in brace to improve the strength of the cylinder wall and head-gasket sealing. Something new for the Gen 3 block is PTWA spray weld liner coating instead of a steel cylinder sleeve. This high-tech liner provides improved durability and heat transfer, reduced friction, and weight savings compared to Gen 1 and Gen 2 blocks. Gen 3 cylinder bores are finish-honed and ready to assemble, which makes it a bargain over machine work.

All Gen 3 blocks are completely finish-machined, including decks and the main saddles. It sports cross-bolted nodular iron main bearing caps; uses 12-mm cylinder-head bolts; has machined-in provisions for piston oil cooling jets; and includes plugs, dowels, and piston cooling jets. So, the Gen 3 Coyote block is your best choice in terms of strength and advances in design.

Rotating Assembly

The Coyote is fitted with an induction-hardened, fully counterweighted crankshaft (that's virtually indestructible) with an eight-hole flange. Team Coyote chose to stay with the 4.6L Modular engine's main and rod journal dimensions because they have been a proven success during nearly three decades of production in every application imaginable. Instead of traditional tri-metal bearings, aluminum bearings were borrowed directly from the 4.6L engine because of their proven track record as well.

The Coyote engine shares the same connecting-rod dimensions with the 4.6L engine (5.933 inches center to center), but it is not the same rod. The Coyote rod is stronger with 12-point bolt heads. The rod ratio is 1.62:1 for excellent dwell time at each end of the bore. The

Coyote's 5.933-inch cracked rod is a sintered-metal I-beam piece engineered for extreme street and weekend racing duty. However, it is not a rod that will stand up to the severe punishment of supercharging or nitrous.

If you're planning to use a supercharger or nitrous, Manley H-beam rods are mandatory over the stock 5.933-inch rods. While the stock rod will take a lot of punishment, it is pushing your luck to go with anything less than a heavy-duty forged-steel I-beam or H-beam rod if you're going to push the engine to more than 600 hp.

The Coyote is fitted with lightweight hypereutectic pistons with coated skirts for reduced friction and wear. Ford engineers weighed the benefits of forged versus hypereutectic, and hypereutectic won due to its weight and expansion properties. Forged pistons are noisy when cold due to excessive piston-to-cylinder wall clearances, which generated complaints with 4.6L and 5.4L engines. Hypereutectic pistons run quieter because they can run tighter tolerances without cold noise. The Coyote piston will tolerate the extremes of street and weekend race duty and offers durability. However, if you intend to supercharge or use nitrous, you're better off with a forged and coated piston.

Ford opted for oil-cooling jets to keep the pistons running considerably cooler, which improves piston life. This approach also allows for faster warm-up because oil is in direct contact with one of the hottest parts of the engine right from the start. It has been proven by Ford engineers that the crankshaft runs roughly 25°F cooler with the oil jets, which enables this engine to operate on 87-octane fuel andsurvive.Although, 91-octane fuel is recommended.

Clearance issues are critical. Heavy-duty I-beam and H-beam connecting rods may or may not clear the tight confines of the Coyote block. You must first do a mock-up and make sure that everything clears by at least 0.060 to 0.100 inch throughout 360 degrees of crank rotation with all rods and pistons (without rings) installed. Pay close attention to the piston skirt-to-crank counterweight clearances, which can get very tight and is the reason that the Coyote won't accept more than a 3.649-inch (92.5-mm) stroke.

Advanced Cylinder Heads

Ford's Ti-VCT Coyote has an innovative new cylinder-head design that makes the engine less bulky while providing high-RPM breathing. The Ti-VCT's intake ports are free from restrictive tendencies, outflowing even some of the most successful racing cylinder heads in the industry. Intake flow numbers are in excess of 300 cfm.

Ford understood that it needed to spend a lot of time to come up with a cylinder head that could do everything. It had to perform old-fashioned hot-rodding tricks to achieve greater airflow and then jump into areas that these seasoned engineers had never tried before. Coyote engineers had to focus on the distance between the four valves, valve angle, valve-seat revisions, and more. The valve angle had to change to improve valve-to-piston clearances and airflow. Via advanced com-

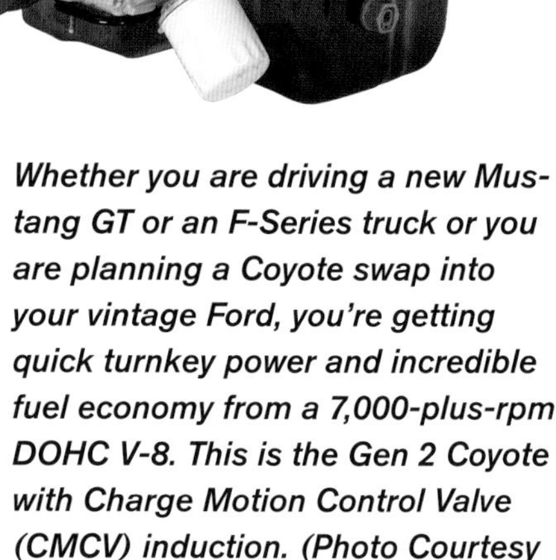

Whether you are driving a new Mustang GT or an F-Series truck or you are planning a Coyote swap into your vintage Ford, you're getting quick turnkey power and incredible fuel economy from a 7,000-plus-rpm DOHC V-8. This is the Gen 2 Coyote with Charge Motion Control Valve (CMCV) induction. (Photo Courtesy Ford Performance)

puter technology, engineers came up with a new cylinder head quickly. Ford revealed that it took extensive development work seven days a week for six months to create a new, more innovative head.

Camshaft and Valvetrain

Rocker arms and valve springs are much smaller to improve efficiency and performance. Place the 4.6L/5.4L and 5.0L Coyote rocker arms and valve springs side by side, and the difference is clear. The Coyote engine does it with less mass and weight. It also enabled Ford to reduce cylinder-head size and width, which reduced overall engine width, making it a more swappable engine.

Ti-VCT can advance/retard valve timing by as much as 50 degrees and do it in 0.2 seconds. This approach offers modest valve timing for the commute and more aggressive valve timing when it's time to pin the throttle. For those who are environmentally conscious, the Coyote doesn't need exhaust gas recirculation (EGR) because valve overlap is increased during certain types of driving, especially deceleration, which reduces hydrocarbon emissions.

To do the complex work of Ti-VCT and other critical functions, Ford's electronic engine control (EEC) was asked to do more than it ever had in its history. The Coyote's computer control is known as the "Copperhead" system. It is a new multichannel system designed to control every aspect of engine and driveline, including Ti-VCT. Instead of a simple on/off system of cam modulation, Ti-VCT advances and retards valve timing on each cam. EEC monitors and controls oil pressure to the cam phasers.

The Coyote's valvetrain system is the most complex cam and valvetrain package that has ever been installed in a Mustang. It is designed to be optimized in all driving conditions. With Ti-VCT, the intake and exhaust cams work independently based on driving demands. Each camshaft is indexed or phased around its centerline by oil pressure. Oil pressure is metered electronically via solenoids and phasers to control cam indexing.

Ti-VCT enables the Coyote to deliver an incredibly wide powerband across RPM ranges while giving the bonus of high-end horsepower, which was never easy to achieve with stationary camshafts. The element that makes the Coyote's Ti-VCT different from the rest of the Ford line is cam torque actuation, which uses valve-spring energy to advance and retard timing more quickly (depending upon engine RPM and driving demands). Instead of a complex, electronically controlled shuttle valve and oiling-system routing, the Coyote's Ti-VCT is a simple on/off solenoid and cam torque does the rest.

The Gen 1 Coyote's valve timing approach changed with the Gen 2 engines (2015–2017). The Gen 2 Coyote went to a different variable valve timing (VVT) phaser on the intake side only.

The Gen 1 Coyote cam timing advanced only on the intake side. The intake cam rested in a more advanced position. The Gen 1 intake cam was parked, depending upon the phaser specifications, anywhere from 133 degrees centerline to 135. The Gen 2 changed where it parked the intake at about 109 degrees advanced. With the Gen 2, the phaser has oil on either side of it to advance and retard, where it would 20 degrees advance and 50 degrees retard. As a result, Ford had to make modifications to where the engine received more oil. This meant changing the head gaskets and oil routing in the heads. It added a restrictor in the main oil gallery to both feed the lash adjusters and get more oil to the phasers.

Induction

The Coyote's sophisticated induction system is the most advanced in Ford's history. It is a composite design, which is mainstream today because it is lighter and has a great heat insulator. It stays cool and keeps the intake charge cooler. It is also easier and cheaper to manufacture. Composite induction systems have been something of a learning curve due to leakage issues, which have hopefully become better with the Coyote.

Induction design and tuning have changed considerably thanks to computer-aided design (CAD) and a lot of engineering time. The Coyote's intake manifold is a single-plane manifold with long intake runners for a broader torque curve. These are long 16.9-inch (430-mm) runners with gentle turns for improved flow. They are carved deep into the valley to allow for a lower hood line. The 80-mm throttle body is

These CMCV actuators for 2015-and-newer (Gen 2 and Gen 3) modulate the intake runner dynamics with one for each cylinder bank. Instead of the CMCVs being plates (as they were on the 4.6L engines), these are flaps that change intake airflow to improve idle quality and low-to-midrange torque. When the throttle is mashed, they move out of the way to improve high-RPM performance.

centered at the front of the engine on top. Another great evolution is a digital mass airflow (MAF) sensor for extremes of fine-tuning as you drive.

The 5.0L Ti-VCT's induction system for 2015–2017 (Gen 2) had CMCV assemblies. The CMCVs are induction "flaps" on the Coyote (closed on start-up to give this engine a smoother idle and better low-to-midrange torque). When it's time to lean on the throttle, these vacuum-controlled CMCV flaps move out of the way to improve high-RPM induction flow.

The Gen 4 Coyote features twin 80-mm throttle bodies in an all-new composite intake manifold. With advances to the Gen 4 Coyote's EEC comes twin throttle actuation. This twin 80-mm throttle-body system includes a dual air-intake box with dual 80-mm throttle bodies. The twin 80-mm throttle bodies enable improved airflow. So, how does this work? It works toward one throttle-body opening at low RPM and a light load. When it is time to get it on, the two throttle bodies work together at wide-open throttle. Just imagine the positive pressure at your backside.

When the 2024 Mustang GT was revealed, Ford said that it tried a single larger throttle body on the 5.2L and witnessed no real gain in power. Ford decided not to go larger, opting for twin independent 80-mm throttle bodies. For normal driving, it has a single 80-mm throttle body. At wide-open throttle, both 80-mm throttle bodies are engaged.

Exhaust

The Coyote's exhaust system is just as critical to power and efficiency as the rest of the package. While headers might not seem important in the big picture, they're important and were an area of focus for the development team because not enough attention has been paid to exhaust scavenging beyond the exhaust port. The Coyote had short tri-Y headers that were painstakingly thought-out and executed.

Because the Coyote's factory shorty header was unique in its approach early on, it enabled the Ti-VCT to produce 400-plus ft-lbs of torque. This approach has only improved since. Where the Coyote's exhaust system differs is between Mustang and F-150. The F-150 has a cast-iron exhaust header instead of tubular headers.

Oiling System

Because the Ti-VCT Coyote was conceived for high revs, it demanded huge oiling system refinements. The Coyote had to sustain sufficient lubrication at 7,000 rpm and beyond and under extreme driving conditions. Ford opted for an 8-quart oil pan and a suitable windage tray/pan gasket combination. Ford further solved this problem (and others) with crankcase breathing chimneys. These PCV chimneys improve drain-back and crankcase ventilation.

Cooling System

Ford engineers paid very strict attention to the Coyote's cooling system, which focused on exhaust-valve cooling along with other extremely hot areas of the engine. Ford calls this "cross-flow" cooling, which was different than the conventional cooling that the 4.6L and 5.4L Modular engines experienced.

Cross-flow cooling routes coolant upward through the block, where it enters cylinder heads at the exhaust valves for excellent heat-transfer qualities and reduced operating temperatures. Coolant runs through a long manifold cast into the cylinder head at the exhaust-valve seats. This keeps detonation issues to a minimum and durability high.

The GT350 5.2L Voodoo

Ford's 5.2L DOHC flat-plane crank V-8 was billed as the highest-revving factory V-8 in American automotive history with 526 hp and 429 ft-lbs of torque. The Voodoo can spin to 8,250 rpm but will shut down at 8,000 rpm. When listening to the 5.2L Voodoo, it is clearly different in sound from the Coyote Ti-VCT V-8 from which it spawned. With flat-plane crank technology, the Voodoo makes a snarly, raspy bark from its tailpipes.

The flat-plane crankshaft approach is nothing new, especially when it comes to exotic high-end European sports cars. However, it is surely a fresh idea for Detroit. When looking at more traditional cross-plane-crank American V-8s with 90-degree reciprocating intervals opposite the counterweights, the flat-plane approach puts pistons and rods exactly 180 degrees opposite the counterweights instead of the traditional 90 degrees. The result is a completely different sound from the traditional V-8 roar that we are used to hearing.

Flat-plane technology means better exhaust scavenging and a notable increase in power. In addition, it enables Ford to produce a lighter crankshaft, making throttle response crisp/snappy and allowing the Voodoo to top out at 7,500 rpm with peak torque roaring in at 4,750 rpm.

This is the 5.2L Voodoo engine that is available in the Shelby GT350. Although the 5.2L engine is based on the 5.0L Ti-VCT Coyote, it is not the same engine. Its flat-plane crank design is only the beginning of what makes this engine different from any other American V-8. Traditional V-8s have a cross-plane crank with huge counterweights surrounding rod journals at a 90-degree angle. (Photo Courtesy Ford Performance)

Redline (fuel shutoff) comes at 8,000 rpm.

The 5.2L flat-plane engine is a racing mill that can be enjoyed on the street because it delivers excellent fuel economy on the open road with a 3,000-rpm torque curve. Yet, it makes 526 hp at wide-open throttle. What these specifications mean for the track is peak torque coming out of turns with an incredible blast of power coming down the straights. Ford told me that torque begins to come on strong at 3,750 rpm, peaking at 4,750. To achieve 5.2 liters, Ford infused a slightly oversquare bore and stroke ratio at 94.0 mm x 92.7 mm.

Although there are positives to flat-plane technology, there are also negatives. If you're married to the traditional sound and feel from a cross-plane crank V-8 engine, the flat-plane crank "buzz" will seem foreign to you. There are also harmonics issues to some degree with flat-plane-crank engines when displacement rises above 4.5 liters. Low-end torque suffers as well with flat-plane crank engines. The 5.2L Voodoo isn't big on low-end torque. However, this isn't an engine designed or engineered for low-end torque. It is a race-bred, high-end street/track engine that does its best work at mid to high RPM.

Gen 3 Coyote: 2018–2023

The Gen 3 Coyote features a dual injection system, which consists of high-pressure direct injection and low-pressure port (shower) injection. What that means for enthusiasts is 460 hp and 420 ft-lbs of torque. The Gen 3 Coyote will easily surpass these factory numbers. The Gen 3 Coyote is good to 7,500 rpm.

The Gen 3 engine doesn't call for high-octane fuel, but it's a good idea to run the Gen 3 on 91- to 93-octane fuel. However, it can get away with 87 because electronic engine control allows for it in terms of ignition timing and fuel curve. The Gen 3 has a 12.0:1 compression ratio, which is remarkable.

Direct injection and port injection each have their advantages. Port injection costs less to develop and refine. It also keeps valve faces clean from crankcase deposits, which coke up the valve faces. With tougher emissions standards, port injection loses the battle with direct injection. Ford told me that fuel economy and emissions suffer with port injection compared to direct injection. The beauty

The Gen 3 Coyote engine appears to be much the same as the Gen 2 engine on the surface. Within the Gen 3 Coyote is an improved block, better cooling, stronger rods, vastly different and improved cylinder heads, and dual fuel injection beneath the surface. These complete crate engines are available and can be shipped right to your door. (Photo Courtesy Ford Performance)

The Gen 3 block is the best the Coyote block. It has GT350-style plasma-transfer wire arc (PTWA) cylinder walls (instead of sleeved) and larger 93-mm bores to make way for larger valves, beefier webbing, and improved cooling. The downside to the Gen 3 block (if there is a downside) is that it cannot be bored. It must be sleeved, which will make it the strongest Coyote block possible.

The passenger-side Gen 3 dual-fuel cylinder head shows the direct-injection-pump pedestal (arrow), which sits on top of a single cam lobe that works the pump in time with the exhaust cam. This approach gives the direct-injection system tremendous pressure.

The passenger-side valve cover has the direct-injection pump, which is positioned on the cam cover. Beneath this pump is a cam lobe (eccentric) that works the pump along with an electronic trigger connector signaled by the PCM, which works both port and direct injection. The direct-injection pump functions off the passenger-side exhaust cam, which sports an eccentric that works the pump.

of direct injection is that it allows fuel to be injected into the combustion chamber in a similar manner as a diesel engine under extreme pressure. This approach allows more precise control of the air/fuel volume and timing. It also helps to combine the air/fuel mixture in the combustion chamber instead of in the intake port.

Ford chose to combine these systems, creating a dual fuel system with both port and direct injection. The flexibility of this system allows both systems to function in unison.

The two systems blend on demand as you drive for reduced emissions, better fuel economy, and greater sums of power at the same time.

The Gen 3 block is similar to the Gen 1 and Gen 2 blocks, but the Gen 3 block is much stronger. The water jackets are different, and the bore size increased to 3.660 inches (93 mm), which was increased from 92.3 mm, to accommodate larger valves. On top is a revised valvetrain geometry with a more-aggressive rocker-arm ratio.

The cam profile for the Gen 3 engine is more aggressive with greater lift for improved performance. Stiffer valve springs allow the 7,500-rpm rev limit that was previously mentioned. Ford returned to the Coyote's original 12-mm head-bolt size, which seemed to work best despite changes that came in 2012.

Down below, the sinter-forged connecting rods are borrowed from the 2012–2013 Boss 302 parts shelf for incredible strength. The Coyote's forged-steel crank gets a more finite balancing process to rid the Gen 3 of destructive vibration, which has long been a Modular/Coyote dynamic. A "viscous" harmonic damper assists vibration tuning, enabling the Gen 3 to spin to 7,500 rpm. The Gen 3 employs a plastic 10-quart oil pan with improved windage and an integral pickup for a new, high-capacity Gen 2 Voodoo oil pump.

What makes the Gen 3 block even more unique is PTWA cylinder walls similar to the 5.2L Voodoo block and 93-mm cylinder bores to accommodate larger intake and exhaust valves. By contrast, the Gen 1 and Gen 2 engines have 92.2 mm bores.

Gen 3 Cylinder Heads and Valvetrain

The Gen 3 Coyote cylinder-head casting is much stronger than its predecessors to accommodate high-pressure direct fuel injection and greater compression. High-silicon cast pistons (hypereutectic) with 8.411-cc domes have deeper valve reliefs to clear larger valves (37.7-mm intake and 32-mm exhaust). Induction is refined for improved flow along with the CMCV, which was introduced on Gen 2 Coyotes in 2015. The CMCV varies induction dynamics depending upon RPM and load (short runners for high-RPM operation and long runners for low-end torque).

On the intake side, VVT with mid-lock phasers is carried over from the Gen 3 Coyote engines. Exhaust-cam phasers are oil-pressure controlled via an in-head oil-control valve for improved control at all speeds, yet modulated by a watch-spring-style return spring like Ford used in the three-valve 4.6L

and 5.4L Modular engines. Valve lift increased to 14-mm (intake and exhaust). Compression is a whopping 12.0:1, which is the quickest path to power. Gen 1 and Gen 2 are 11.0:1.

The Gen 3 Coyote heads are vastly different from Gen 1 and Gen 2. Gen 3 ports have better flow numbers that are more in line with Gen 2 5.2L Voodoo heads. Gen 3 camshafts must be used with Gen 3 timing components and phasers. Exhaust-cam journals are larger to accommodate oil seals, which prevent leakage from the exhaust phasers. Gen 3 engines use Gen 2 intake phasers and primary timing chains. Exhaust phasers are Gen 3 only and attached with a single bolt. The Gen 3 timing system is Ford part number M-6004-A501B.

The Gen 3 head gasket and cylinder heads employ bridge-cooling holes. Gen 1 and Gen 2 do not. Gen 3 cylinder heads are made of a different grade of aluminum (AS7GU) than Gen 1 and 2 (AL319). AL319, an alloy, is 6-percent silicon and 3.5-percent copper alloy with 1.0-percent iron maximum. AL319 has outstanding casting and machining characteristics. Corrosion resistance and weldability of this material are very good. The anodized color of AL319 is generally gray with a brown cast, depending on the amount and ratio of silicon and copper.

Newly developed alloys, such as AS7GU, are variants of A356, strengthened with 0.5-percent copper. As with the A356 aluminum alloy, AS7GU alloy has excellent castability while the minute addition of copper to this alloy improves creep resistance and tensile strength at intermediate temperatures. AS7GU is more user friendly. This is what makes the Gen 3 Coyote head better and stronger.

The maximum operating temperature of Coyote cylinder heads has increased from approximately 338°F to temperatures exceeding 392°F. These higher operating temperatures result in more severe high-cycle fatigue, more low-cycle fatigue, and/or fatigue damage in regions of cylinder heads that are exposed to high thermal gradients.

The most common cast-aluminum alloys are A356, 319, and AS7GU (which is A356 + 0.5-percent copper). A356 is a primary aluminum alloy with good ductility and fatigue properties at low-to-intermediate temperatures. Yet, above 392°F, creep resistance and tensile strength of this alloy are rapidly degraded. Something had to be done to improve these issues. AS7GU was the solution.

These heads are fitted with new, more-aggressive camshafts, providing greater lift but the same duration (14 mm/263 degrees on both intake and exhaust) as the Gen 2 engine. The Gen 3 cams still employ the same Ti-VCT approach as the Gen 2. However, on the exhaust side, there's a new approach to valve timing. Exhaust timing is oil-pressure controlled. Return is controlled by a watch-spring-style return spring (as with the 3V Modular engine cam phasers).

Dual Fuel-Injection Technology

The Gen 3 Coyote different because of dual fuel technology. This means that it has low-pressure port injection and high-pressure direct injection straight into the cylinders that is similar to a diesel engine. The combination of both means more power and greater efficiency. Port injection keeps the intake valve faces clean, a lesson learned with direct injection–only systems that have required extensive maintenance due to performance issues from "coked-up" valve faces. The valve faces don't carbon up, which means that there's less to fear regarding maintenance.

The Gen 3 Coyote is the ultimate evolution of the original Gen 1 that was introduced in the Mustang GT in 2011. It is the most bulletproof version of the Coyote engine family. Where the Coyote goes from here is anyone's guess. Ford is focusing more on lower displacement, hybrids, and electric vehicles, which signals a move away from V-8 power in time. Meanwhile, let us enjoy the most powerful standard production V-8 that Ford has ever produced and make the most of its potential.

The Gen 4 Coyote is fitted with a twin 80-mm throttle-body induction system. With this setup, one throttle body is used in normal driving and both throttle bodies are used at wide-open throttle. Ford Performance offers a Gen 4 Aluminator with a single 80-mm throttle body.

Gen 4 Changes

The Gen 4 engine yields obvious changes externally, including dual 80-mm throttle bodies. Yet, the Gen 4 engine is not completely a continuation of the Gen 3. Ford made significant changes to the Gen 4's cylinder head with redesigned camshaft caps and towers. The block also has a redesigned rear cover. Front and center with the Gen 4 Coyote is the Mustang Dark Horse's 500 hp. The Dark Horse Coyote gets rods from the 2020–2022 Predator engine with updated camshafts.

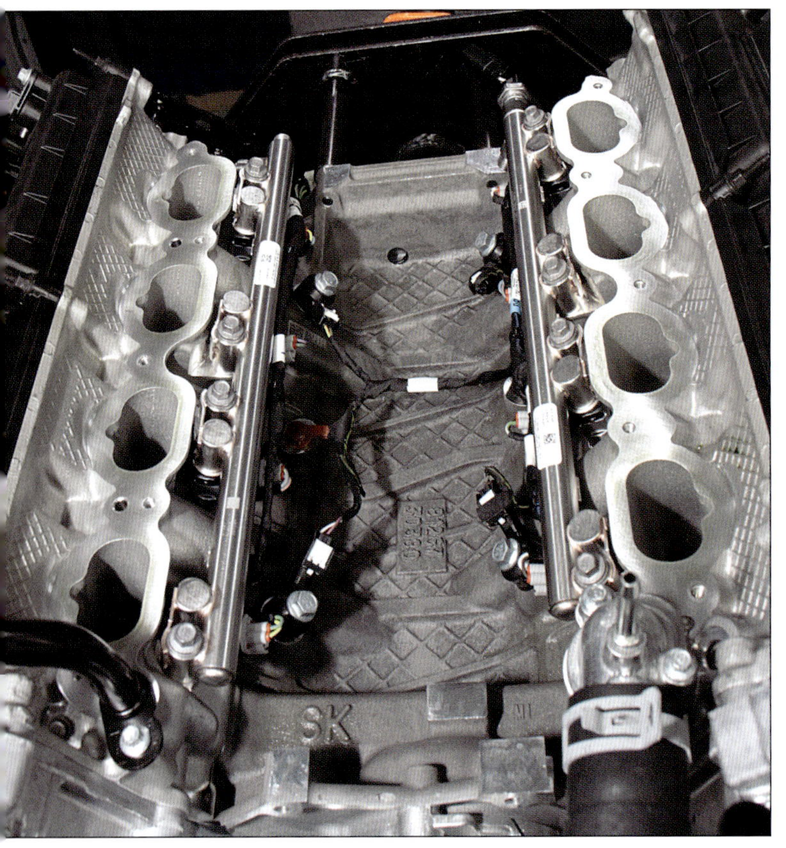

The Gen 3 and Gen 4 timing system has different oil pressure–actuated cam phasers, where the exhaust phasers are spring return.

When the intake manifold of this Gen 3 engine has been removed, the change to the hidden, high-pressure, direct-injection manifold and injectors becomes immediately apparent. This is the Gen 3 engine's most remarkable change, vastly improving efficiency and power.

Ford Coyote Evolution: 2011–2024				
	Gen 1 5.0L Coyote (2011–2014)	**Gen 2 5.0L Coyote (2015–2017)**	**Gen 3 5.0L Coyote (2018–2023)**	**Gen 4 5.0L Coyote (2024+)**
Fuel Injection	Port Fuel Injection	Port Fuel Injection	Port and Direct Injection	Port and Direct Injection
Bore Diameter	92.2 mm	92.2 mm	92.7 mm (larger to accommodate larger valves)	93 mm
Stroke	92.7 mm	92.7 mm	92.7 mm	92.7 mm
Firing Order	1-5-4-8-6-3-7-2	1-5-4-8-6-3-7-2	1-5-4-8-6-3-7-2	1-5-4-8-6-3-7-2
Compression	11.0:1	11.0:1	12.0:1	12.0:1
Peak Torque (ft-lbs)	390 at 4,250 rpm, 380 at 4,250 rpm (F-150)	400 at 4,250 rpm, 387 at 3,850 rpm (F-150)	420 at 4,250 rpm, 400 at 4,500 rpm (F-150)	415 at 4,900 rpm; 420 at 4,600 rpm (4X); 410 at 4,500 rpm (F-150)
Peak Power (hp)	420 at 6,500 rpm, 350 at 5,500 (F-150)	435 at 6,500 rpm, 385 at 5,750 rpm (F-150)	460 at 7,500 rpm, 385 at 5,750 rpm (F-150)	480 at 7,150 rpm; 460 at 7,000 rpm (4X); 400 at 5,750 rpm (F-150)
Maximum RPM	7,000	7,000	7,500	7,500 (Mustang GT)
Engine Weight (pounds)	431	431	425	431
Crankshaft	Forged Cross-Plane	Forged Cross-Plane	Forged Cross-Plane	Forged Cross-Plane
Pistons	Hypereutectic (Cast)	Hypereutectic (Cast)	Hypereutectic (Cast)	Hypereutectic (Cast)
Connecting Rod Weight (grams)	582	618	618	618
Connecting Rod Length (mm)	150.7	150.7	150.7	150.7
Cylinder Heads	AL319	AL319	AS7GU	AS7GU (Gen 4–specific castings with taller cam towers)
Valve Material	Hollow Chrome (Sodium Filled)	Hollow Chrome (Sodium Filled)	Hollow Chrome (Sodium Filled)	Hollow Chrome (Sodium Filled)
Valve Diameter (mm)	37.0 Intake, 31.0 Exhaust	37.3 Intake, 31.8 Exhaust	37.7 Intake, 32.0 Exhaust	37.0 Intake, 31.0 Exhaust
Valve Lift (mm)	12.0 Intake, 12.0 Exhaust	13.0 Intake, 13.0 Exhaust	14.0 Intake, 14.0 Exhaust	12.0 Intake, 12.0 Exhaust
Valve Spring Load (closed/open N)	265/650	300/760	293/813	265/650
Variable Cam Timing Phaser	N/A	Mid-Lock Intake	Mid-Lock Intake via Oil Control/Actuated Exhaust	Mid-Lock Intake via Oil Control/Actuated Exhaust
Intake Manifold Type	Non-CMCV	CMCV	CMCV	CMCV
Throttle Body Diameter (mm)	80	80	80	Twin 80; Single 80 (4X); Single 80 (F-150)
Oil Pan Type	Steel 8-Quart with Filter	Steel 8-Quart with Filter	Composite 10-Quart with Filter	Steel 8-Quart with Filter

Coyote Economics

During the planning of this book, I had to look at the best options available for Coyote engine builders. The focus of this book is how to *affordably* rebuild the Coyote. In cruising eBay and other online auctions, I was stunned at the outrageous sums being asked for used Coyote engine cores. Some were as low as $2,500 for a blown-up Coyote, and others were as high as $5,000 for a usable one.

How much do you invest in an expensive Coyote core? Is it generally cheaper to source a new Coyote block and related internal parts from Summit Racing Equipment and Ford Performance, where you can build an all-new Coyote from scratch? These are legitimate questions because it can often be cheaper to buy a new block, crank, rods, and pistons and have a new short-block ready to go without all the expense of machine work.

In addition, there's always the risk of a bad core with a used engine (often without a warranty), where few will accept the responsibility and refund your money. On top of that, you can buy new, completely assembled Coyote cylinder heads and have a long-block that is good to go. I will also say that with a seasoned core (used engine), you have a proven heat-treated block and heads.

Buying new components saves time because you don't have to wait for machine work. Because machine shops are becoming less common these days, the remaining shops are backlogged (sometimes for as long as a year), which takes longer than just buying new castings and building fresh. I've also seen longtime proven shops sell out to new owners, often with lackluster results. They just are not the same.

Before you spend a dime or make decisions, sit down with a calculator and the information that you have and make an educated decision. Engine rebuilding isn't what it used to be. The Coyote engine, and others like it, command extreme attention to detail. Forget shortcuts that can get you into trouble and add expense. Look to Summit Racing Equipment and Ford Performance for options that make sense. Look to their technical staffs for solutions that will help you sidestep the pitfalls.

BEFORE YOU BEGIN

Before you begin, make a plan and exercise self-discipline to follow the plan and keep changes to a minimum. It is always good to have a plan in writing. Create a written outline of what you're going to do and follow it to the letter. Focus on what you have for resources, time, and budget. Then, follow your plan.

First, what type of engine do you want to build—one for the street, street/strip, or racetrack? Determine which generation of Coyote engine you are building. The least-desirable Coyote is the 2011–2014 Gen 1 version, which doesn't have the nice refinements of the Gen 2 and Gen 3. The Gen 2 (2015–2017) has CMCV induction, which is also the quickest way to identify a Gen 2 engine (vacuum actuators at the back of the intake manifold). The Gen 3 (2018–2024) features a stronger block and heads along with dual injection, which makes the Gen 3 the most refined Coyote to date. The Gen 4 block is virtually the same as Gen 3 but with a revised rear cover. The Gen 4 is also equipped with redesigned cylinder heads.

The good news with the Ti-VCT Coyote engine is its flexibility. It is an engine that you can plan and build with a sweet combination of street and strip qualities. You can use it for the daily commute and be ready for the road-race course or drag strip on the weekend.

The most challenging part of any engine build is setting a budget: what you can afford and what you have for resources. Plans for power are always limited by budget and resources because horsepower is expensive. The cost goes up proportionately with the power planned. With power must also come durability.

Engine-building technology has made huge advances as a result of what has been learned about building techniques and making power. Cylinder-head and cam technology have come a long way. I've learned

Set yourself up with a hoist and a good vehicle support system before getting started. I always mention Harbor Freight for tools and equipment because its merchandise is affordable, and you're bound to use it multiple times, even if you loan it to friends. (Photo Courtesy Wes Duenkel)

Before starting, have a plan for the teardown and a safe, organized place for parts. The idiom "a place for everything and everything in its place" is helpful to follow.

Scan this QR code with your smartphone to buy Ford Coyote Engines: How to Build Max Performance: Revised Edition *from CarTech.*

that it is in the details that an engine build can be make or break, regardless of technology and what you have for parts. The two biggest issues I can think of are checking clearances (at least twice) while inspecting your workmanship. The best advice that I received from professional engine builders is to slow down and pay close attention to detail. Always double-check your work.

Engine projects traditionally fail due to poor planning and unrealistic expectations. The more changes that are made in the course of an engine build, the more expensive it becomes because you have to do much of it all over again. At the very least, these projects produce disappointing results because we don't amass the right combination of parts and technique to begin with. Time and money are wasted when we don't think first about what we want the engine to do. A big part of building an engine is knowing exactly what you can afford and then not giving in to ego and temptation.

Forget the belief that you can build a radical racing engine for the street and use it for the daily commute. No matter what, mixing street and race performance without conflict and disappointment at the traffic light is delusional. The options are to build a strictly street engine, a street/strip weekend bracket racing or road racing engine, or an all-out racing engine.

Street/strip race engines that are daily drivers need civilized street manners, where your teeth aren't being jarred at a traffic light but it can crack a 12-second quarter-mile elapsed time (ET) on Saturday night. Street engines need to be designed and built for good low and mid-range torque, not always horsepower. Horsepower is a high-RPM, wide-open throttle, maximum-power element.

Torque is real street power that gets a vehicle moving from a traffic light and onto the freeway. Weekend horsepower should be realistic with peak horsepower coming in somewhere around 6,500 rpm and peak torque at 4,500 rpm. Ideally, it will get a broad powerband on the street, where torque begins to come on strong around 3,000 and peaks at 4,000 to 4,500 rpm.

Arm yourself with Ford Coyote shop manuals for the Mustang or F-150 as well as CarTech's *Ford Coyote Engines: How to Build Max Performance: Revised Edition*, which provides important information regarding Coyote performance.

Horsepower and Torque

Horsepower is rooted more in advertising rhetoric than fact. It doesn't count for much unless you're going racing with the engine at high RPM most of the time. What counts on the street is torque and where in the RPM range most of it is available. Engines make torque when fuel and air are fed into combustion chambers at high velocity and squeeze the mix. Torque is what gets the vehicle going, and horsepower is the force that keeps it moving. Horsepower gets all the credit, but torque does most of the work.

Engines do their best work when they reach peak torque. Westech Performance in Southern California, which tests hundreds of engines annually, says that when an engine is below torque peak, it has more than enough time to completely fill the cylinder with air and fuel. It adds that when engine RPM rises above the torque peak, there isn't enough time to completely fill the cylinders with air and fuel.

The power that is felt from an engine's spinning crankshaft is torque multiplied by engine speed (RPM) to produce a number that provides the engine's output. This age-old theory dates back to steam engines and an inventor named James Watt. Watt invented the steam engine in the 1800s.

Watt's theory was simple. It compared the work that his steam engine could do with the same work that an equal number of horses could do. Watt determined that a single horse could pull a 180-pound load 181 feet in 1 minute. The result of multiplying 180 by 181 is 32,580 ft-lbs per minute. Watt rounded it to 33,000 ft-lbs per minute. He divided this fig-ure by 60 seconds, which worked out to 550 ft-lbs per second. This became the standard for 1 hp.

As a result of Watt's calculations more than a century ago, horsepower has become a measure of force in pounds against a distance in feet for the brief period of 1 minute. Then, this formula is applied to an engine's crankshaft at each journal throw to determine horsepower. This is based on the number 5,252.

Torque and RPM are divided by 5,252. Torque and horsepower always cross each other at 5,252 rpm (regardless of engine type). If you can solve this equation at 5,252 rpm, RPM cancels out, leaving horsepower equal to the torque figure. If you work this out on a graph, the torque, horsepower, and RPM lines should always intersect.

There are plenty of myths about making power. When it comes to seat-of-the-pants performance, there's no black magic here, just the simple physics of taking thermal expansion and turning it into rotary motion. To learn how to make power, you must understand how power is made inside an engine. How much power an engine makes depends on how much air and fuel can be pumped through the engine, plus what is done with that fuel and air mixture during the split-second that it lives and dies in the combustion chambers.

Think of an engine as an air pump. The more air and fuel that can be pumped through the cylinders, the more power will be made. This is why racers use big injectors, manifolds, cylinder heads, super-chargers, turbochargers, and nitrous oxide. Racers understand this air pump theory and practice it with reckless abandon. However, good racers also understand that there can be too much of a good thing. It can cost you a race. It can also cost you an engine.

Getting power from the Ford Coyote takes getting liberal amounts of air and fuel into the chambers, and then squeezing the mixture as

Giving Away Power

When planning power, con-sider how power gets wasted in an engine's design and assembly. Friction is the power pick-pocket that is hiding inside of our engines. Most of the friction occurs at the pistons and rings. Some of it takes place at the bearings and jour-nals. In addition, more friction occurs at piston wrist pins, lifters and bores, cam lobes, rocker-arm fulcrums, and valve stems.

The objective needs to be a compromise between having toler-ances that are too loose and too tight. Piston-to-cylinder wall clearances are critical to have good cylinder sealing—yet not too much friction where power is lost. The same is true for rod and main bearing clearances. You want liberal clearances for good oil flow and heat transfer but less friction.

On the exhaust side, you want a scavenging system that makes sense. Great breathing does not require long-tube headers. Shorty headers will do the job just as well and without the shortcomings of long-tube headers. If you go too large on header-tube size, torque is lost. Go too small, and it hurts power on the high end. This is where an exhaust system has to work hand in hand with the heads, camshaft, and induction system. ■

high as possible without engine damage. When compression is raised, it increases the power that the igniting mixture yields. It is the intense heat of compression coupled with the potent ignition-system spark that launches heat energy from the mixture. The more compression that the engine has, the greater the heat result to ignite the mixture.

When there's too much compression, the air/fuel mixture can ignite prematurely, causing preignition and detonation (pinging, or spark knock). You have to dial in the right compression ratio to get the most from the air/fuel mix. Today's street fuels won't tolerate much more than 10.0:1 compression, which is something of an exception with the Coyote thanks to improved electronic engine control. It isn't always necessary to have a higher compression ratio to get more power. Power also comes from how the cylinder is filled on the intake stroke and how much valve overlap there is once the fury is over. This means that careful thought and selection is important when it's time to choose a camshaft profile.

The thing to remember about internal combustion engines is that the air/fuel mixture does not explode in the combustion chambers. Instead, it ignites in a quick fire (reaction) just like a gas furnace or water heater. Because the mixture is compressed and ignited, it lights off more rapidly. Combustion in a piston engine is a "quick fire" that sends a flame front across the top of the piston. Under ideal circumstances, the flame front will travel smoothly across the piston dome, applying heat and pressure that act on the piston and rod uniformly to create rotary motion at the crankshaft.

Critical Inspection

Does Your Engine Need to be Rebuilt?

Before getting started, ask yourself if your Coyote needs to be rebuilt. Have you checked compression and performed a cylinder leak-down test (working compression)? What about oil consumption? Is there engine noise? Does the engine seem down on power? Consider the answers to all of these questions before jumping into a complete engine rebuild. The Coyote is a 200,000- to 300,000-mile engine when maintained properly with a steady diet of synthetic lubrication and regular cooling-system maintenance.

An engine rebuild is the process of restoring a worn-out engine to like-new condition again with machine work and replacement of critical components, such as pistons, rings, bearings, timing components, the oil pump, valves, guides, seals, and gaskets. Old-school engine ring and bearing "overhauls" won't cut it with a precision engine such as the Coyote. This is an all-or-nothing engine, where it has to be completely torn down, inspected, and fully rebuilt to factory specifications to be powerful and reliable.

Aside from known mileage, look for:

- Oil condition: Is it dirty and is there evidence of metal and sludge in the oil?
- Excessive oil consumption
- Oil pressure (you want 10 psi for every 1,000 rpm, which means you want 60 psi at 6,000 rpm)
- Overheating and potential engine damage
- Potential block and cylinder-head cracking or warping
- Evidence of coolant in the oil or bubbling in the coolant recovery tank. Also, check the odor of coolant in the tank. A blown head gasket will yield the aroma of crankcase fumes in the coolant.
- Oil and coolant leakage
- Misfire primarily on cold start, which is an indication of a blown head gasket
- Excessive noise, including the rattle of piston skirts and worn main and rod bearings as well as the chatter of rocker arms and the rattle of cam phasers
- Tailpipe emissions
- A loss of power
- Fault codes

Before beginning, visit a reputable machine shop and get an estimate of what it will cost for all of the machine work. You can save time and money by having a machine shop assemble the engine when the machine work is done. This means that the machine shop becomes responsible for the entire build and should offer a warranty. Engines that are built for racing will not come with a warranty.

There are reputable remanufacturers, such as Jasper Engines, where rebuilders can ship their engine for a complete rebuild that includes a warranty. If keeping the original Coyote engine doesn't matter, Jasper, as well as other remanufacturing operations, sell a remanufactured engine that can be shipped right to your door. Ford Performance offers all-new Coyote engine Aluminator packages if you don't want the hassle of rebuilding the engine yourself. ■

A bad "light off" that originates at two opposing points in the chamber is preignition or detonation (spark knock). Opposing flame fronts collide, creating a shock wave that hammers the piston dome, wrist pin, and rod journal. This is the pinging or spark knock (rattling) that is heard under acceleration. The objective should be a smooth quick-fire, with the flame front traveling in one smooth direction for maximum power.

The science of making power must tie in with your intended mission, and that's where most of us get it wrong all too often. In our quest for power, we forget how the vehicle is going to be used. If you are building an engine to go drag racing, the engine build should be different from the person who builds one for trailer towing or road racing.

Street engines for the daily commute need to be planned for good low and midrange torque. Drag racing engines need to make power at mid-to-high RPM ranges. Road racing engines need to be able to do it all (down low, in the midrange, and at high RPM) because they're going to be driven in all of these ranges in racing. Engines scheduled for trailer towing need plenty of low-end torque. They also need to be able to live comfortably at midrange, when we're going to be pulling a grade.

Engine Removal

Undoubtedly, the most daunting task is engine removal from the chassis. With the Mustang, you can 1) pull the engine or 2) the vehicle can be jacked up as high as possible off the floor to drop the engine/transmission and subframe as an assembly. Then, the engine and transmission can be lifted off the subframe. This approach enables you to rebuild the front end while the engine is being rebuilt.

Allow yourself a lot of room to work around the vehicle. A cluttered garage can become a huge obstacle to getting things done. The idiom "a place for everything and everything in its place" applies here.

Support the vehicle with 2- to 3-ton jack stands in six places (at the rear axle, rear frame rails, and front frame rails) in the interest of safety. Never place jack stands at the rocker panels and never support the vehicle with hydraulic jacks. Doing so can lead to the vehicle collapsing on the jack.

Engine hoists are available from Harbor Freight and Summit Racing Equipment. An engine hoist may also be rented if you rarely need one. This is true of any tool that you don't use often. Rental businesses traditionally offer a wide variety of automotive tools, such as torque wrenches, piston-ring compressors, micrometers, dial-bore gauges, and more.

As the engine is prepared for removal, take photos as you go. No matter what you believe, you're not going to remember where everything goes during reassembly. Chances are good that the engine will not be finished in a month. Take detailed photos of the engine and subframe as installed. Get underneath with good light and shoot the underpinnings to show how the engine is connected to the chassis. On top, photograph each side of the engine and take close-up, detailed images of everything that is visible. I suggest taking video footage as well.

When draining coolant and oil, have a recycling plan. Recycling is your responsibility. Most communities have engine oil and coolant recycling programs, which means that there is no excuse for pouring antifreeze down the toilet. Engine oil should never be dumped in a remote location; it should be recycled. Most auto parts stores will take used oil.

For those with F-Series trucks, removal is more involved because trucks are full-frame vehicles. The engine must be lifted out from the chassis. Be very careful disconnecting plugs and sensors. These weathertight plugs have become very brittle over time from heat and cold. Ascertain how to disconnect each plug and never force the connections.

Items such as the radiator, heater hoses, and drive belts should never be reused, unless they're in pristine condition. Replace the high-pressure fuel hoses, water pump, and harmonic damper. ATI Performance produces the best harmonic damper in the industry. Arm yourself with a complete Fel-Pro gasket set, which is OEM caliber and the best choice. Summit Racing Equipment stocks everything that you're going to need and with prompt turnaround.

Ford Performance is the best choice for parts for a Coyote build. This is not a shameless promotion. I've learned what works well and what does not. Not all aftermarket parts are OEM caliber and should be taken on a case-by-case basis. Proven names in the industry that we're all familiar with are the best choices. I've also learned Ford Performance and Motorcraft parts work best in these engines because they have the benefit of Ford's vast engineering resources.

After the engine has been removed, set it on a wooden pallet with a packing blanket to protect the oil pan. Take extra care not to impact any of the sensors and electronic components. It is a good idea to remove the intake manifold, wiring harnesses, exhaust headers, and front-dress components (the alternator, the power steering pump, etc.) before pulling the engine. Before hauling the engine to the machine shop, remove any components that won't be involved in the rebuild. There's a risk that these components can become lost at the machine shop.

Organization and a Clean Shop

It is important to begin with a clean and organized shop. If you are disassembling the engine yourself, perform the teardown where you can catalog parts and document what you have with notes and photos. Keep engine parts and fasteners in labeled containers. Take the block, heads, crankshaft, and connecting rods to a machine shop immediately upon disassembly and methodically explain to the shop what you want. This avoids any confusion and keeps your project moving. Mark each piston and rod assembly with the cylinder number that they were removed from.

Cylinder heads don't have to be torn down at home. Allow the machine shop to disassemble the heads and evaluate their condition. This gives the machine shop insight into what needs to be done with the heads.

If you cannot afford a machine shop, leave the engine assembled until you are ready. I speak from experience because too much is lost both mentally and physically once the engine is disassembled. Keep the disassembly, cleaning, machine work, and assembly as cohesive and seamless as possible.

When it is time to assemble the engine, you must have a hospital-clean shop. Even simple house dust will damage an engine's precision surfaces. Because the Coyote's tolerances are tight, it is remarkable the damage dust can do. House dust will score bearings, journals, and cylinder walls.

Whenever not working on the engine, keep it bagged and wrapped up tight. During engine assembly, thoroughly clean everything first with brake cleaner and dry components with compressed air to remove dust and debris. Avoid engine assembly on a windy day, which generates unwanted dust. Automotive bodywork will create harmful dust that will damage engine parts. Keep this kind of work away from the engine. Make sure that the engine assembly lube and oil are pure and clean. Any stray matter, no matter how small, can damage the engine.

When it is time for engine assembly, everything should be in proper order, laid out on a bench, and protected from dust. Pistons should be matched and marked to each bore. Each bore should have been measured and honed to each piston's size. Each piston should be numbered to the bore that was honed for that match (not to mention dynamic-balance issues). All piston rings should have been gapped for each bore. The engine's critical parts should be laid out on the workbench in proper order like a road map.

Take organization to extremes. Number each cylinder with a felt-tip marker at the block deck. Lay the pistons and rods out on the bench in cylinder-number order. Keep cans of brake cleaner or lacquer thinner on the workbench to handle last-minute parts cleaning during assembly. This reduces any chance of dust particles and stray matter getting where it doesn't belong. Use lint-free tack rags (static cloths) for final cleanup work. Do not use those linty shop towels, terry cloth, or paper towels for engine assembly. Keep plenty of engine oil and assembly lube nearby. Keep these items covered to keep out dust and debris.

Rarely is poor workmanship found in original factory-assembled engines, especially with today's levels of quality control. However, you will

Disassembly calls for strict discipline, which means documenting the teardown with photos and taking notes as you go. Everything must be laid out as it comes apart.

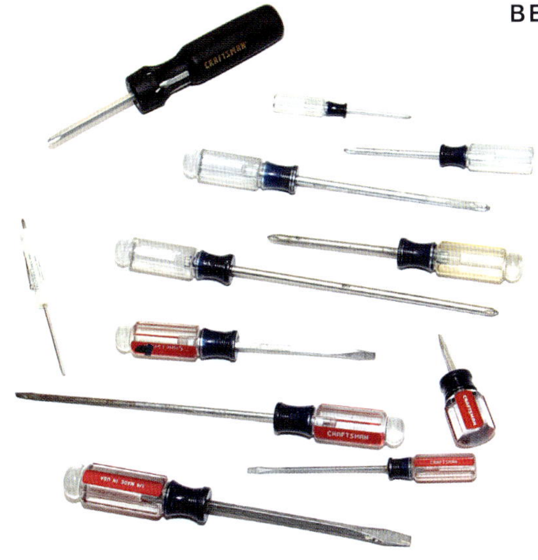

Your tool arsenal should cover the gamut of home garage hand tools, including an assortment of flathead, Phillips, and specialty screwdrivers. In addition, keep screwdrivers as small as those that are used for jewelry sizing on hand for tasks such as working with C-clips and spiral locks.

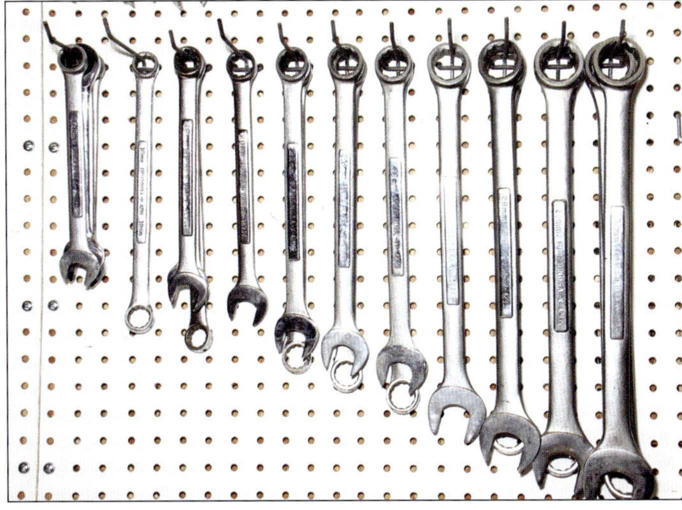

There are many approaches for garage organization. I like hanging tools (as shown) for easy access. Not everyone has the wall space for this approach. Organize your tool storage so that you know exactly where everything is.

find plenty of it in rebuilt or remanufactured Coyote engines. Incorrect parts, defective pieces reused, poor machining and assembly technique, and the absence of maintenance are all factors regarding why an engine failed. Disassembly is a forensics experience where you learn all about an engine's past. Sometimes, you have a salvageable core. Other times, you have junk.

You never know an engine's condition until you measure cylinder bores, clean castings, and do a magnetic particle inspection to check for cracks. Of course, you also need to inspect the crank, measuring journals and checking for runout. Check for irregular wear patterns too. Also check the connecting rods for abnormal wear, trueness, and journal dimensions.

The good news about remanufactured engines is that quality standards improved in this new age of strict accountable engine manufacturing. The Coyote engine is unforgiving of

Because the Coyote is a metric engine, an assortment of metric combination wrenches are needed, although most of the Coyote's fasteners can be handled with sockets.

Despite the advances in specialty tools in recent years, the humble crescent wrench in all of its sizes is the backup because it fits everything. I keep a variety of sizes on hand. A large crescent wrench makes the perfect Coyote camshaft holder.

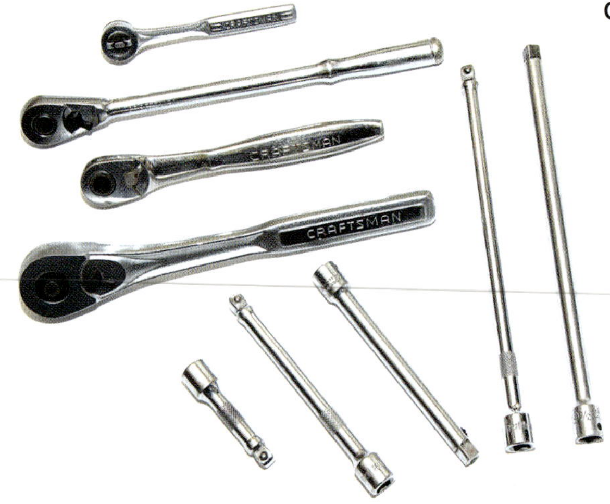

You will need 1/2-, 3/8-, and 1/4-inch-drive ratchets with an assortment of extensions in different lengths, universals, speed handles, etc. to be as efficient as possible. In my opinion, classic Craftsman ratchets with the twist adjuster are good tools. If you cruise eBay and other online auctions, a wealth of great vintage tools are out there.

Deep-well sockets (1/2, 3/8, and 1/4 inch) are a must.

sloppy work. All tolerances must be measured to exacting standards; otherwise, you can expect trouble.

For example, Performance Assembly Solutions (PAS) in Livonia, Michigan, builds new high-performance Coyote engines to Ford's exact engineering standards. There is strict accountability at every stage of teardown and assembly. Every step is documented via a computer system that will sideline any irregularity. Because the Coyote engine has been in production scarcely more than a decade, odds are slim that you will find a rebuilt core.

- Harmonic-balancer puller
- Valve-spring compressor
- Freeze-plug driver
- Seal driver
- Thread chaser
- Small grinder (if you port your own heads)
- Bolt extractors (Easy Outs) (for broken bolts in blocks and heads)
- Engine hoist
- Engine stand
- Degree wheel and pointer
- Dial indicator

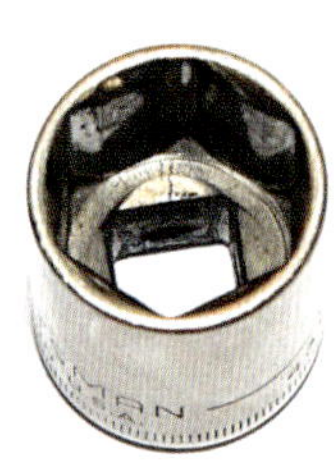

Six-point and 12-point sockets and wrenches each have their own advantages. Six-point sockets provide a good, tight wrap around a bolt head or nut. A 12-point socket provides wiggle room. It is good to have both as your budget allows.

Tools to Rent

These tools are probably going to be used only during an engine build, and you likely won't need them again until your next engine project. You can consider renting these tools on an as-needed basis.

- Torque wrench
- Torque-to-yield (torque-angle) gauge
- Piston-ring compressor

If you're on a tight budget, plenty of socket sets are available from which to choose. This 48-piece, 1/2-inch-drive Milwaukee Tool socket set is less than $250 and has several nice features, including wrenchable sockets. Smaller sizes (1/4 and 3/8 inch) are also available. Husky, Kobalt, Pittsburgh, Quinn, and a host of other brands are available from home improvement and online stores.

The swivel extension is critical for bolts that are difficult to access. GreatNeck tools can be found online or at Ace Hardware and other retailers.

Torque Wrench/Torque-Angle

Torque wrenches typically are either beam or breakaway types. I suggest the breakaway type that clicks when the specified torque is reached. Learn how to properly use a breakaway torque wrench. Two important issues apply here. Never jerk a torque wrench to reach the desired torque. When you jerk the wrench, you're not getting the correct torque. Threads must be lubricated to achieve an accurate torque reading. With dry threads, you will get an incorrect reading.

Never use a torque wrench to loosen fasteners. This will alter calibration. Secondly, never overtighten a fastener. When fasteners are tightened, this stretches the fastener. Too much torque will stress (weaken) the fastener. Torque specifications are there to ensure fastener integrity.

One other important point about torque wrenches is calibration. Have your torque wrench cleaned, lubricated, and calibrated at least once a year.

Today's engines have torque-to-yield fasteners in most applications to ensure proper fastener stretch. Cylinder heads, main caps, cam caps, rod bolts, intake manifolds, and more are fitted with torque-to-yield fasteners, which are different from the Grade 8 fasteners that are torqued once and you're finished.

The term "torque-to-yield" describes the type of fastener. The

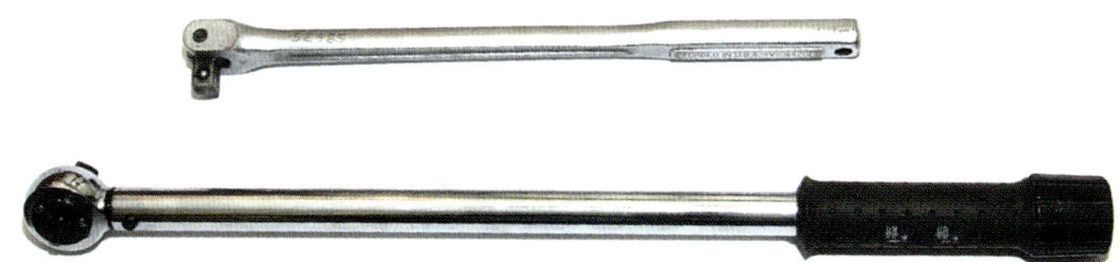

Torque wrenches should be used only to torque fasteners—never to break fasteners loose. Instead, break fasteners loose with a breaker bar. Using a torque wrench to loosen fasteners will throw the torque wrench out of calibration. Keep torque wrenches zeroed when not in use and have them calibrated once a year.

Digital torque wrenches are becoming more and more popular. They beep when the desired torque is reached. These must also be calibrated annually.

If you've never built a modern engine before, be ready for torque-to-yield fasteners and the torque-angle procedure as a means to confirm bolt stretch/tension. This is a torque-angle gauge, which works in conjunction with a torque wrench. You torque the fastener and then apply an initial number of degrees of twist, which is the torque-angle.

This torque-angle gauge is applying torque (tightening) to a torque-to-yield fastener. It is important to understand the meaning of torque-to-yield versus torque-angle. Torque-to-yield applies to the type of fastener that you are using. Torque-angle applies to the procedure or method that is used to tighten a fastener.

term "torque-angle" describes the tightening procedure. The torque-to-yield fastener is torqued per Ford specifications and then tightened a specific number of degrees further, which is what the torque-angle gauge is for. Torque-angle confirms bolt stretch.

Other Tools

Piston-ring compressors are available in different forms. The most common type available to rent is an adjustable-band type. There is also a ratcheting type that makes piston installation a snap.

Custom-size billet ring compressors are costly and not for the novice. Engine-building professionals who build a lot of engines invest in billet ring compressors because getting the job done quickly is important to these folks. Billet compressors, which are sized to the cylinder bores, make short work of piston and connecting-rod installation.

Harmonic-damper pullers are a borderline rental item. This is something you may use again and again not only for harmonic dampers but also for steering wheels and other interference-fit items. They don't cost much, which is what makes them an item to possibly purchase. Look for the multipurpose mission in any tool that you're thinking about renting. If you expect to use the tool again and again, it may be worth the investment now.

There are two basic types of valve spring compressors: 1) one used in the shop that looks like a huge C-clamp and 2) one that can be used with the head installed. For engine rebuilding, the C-clamp type is needed. These can sometimes be purchased at a discount house, such as Harbor Freight, for less than it would cost to rent one for several days. Changing valve springs with the heads installed calls for a specialized valve-spring compressor for OHC engines.

Freeze-plug and seal drivers are good investments. It is also possible to use a like-sized socket on the end of an extension as a driver. This saves money but could damage the socket. Don't be a tool abuser.

Thread chasers are a vital part of any engine build because clean threads are important. Clean threads yield an accurate torque reading when it's time to reassemble the engine. Chase every bolt hole. If

Important!

What Is Torque-to-Yield?

As you embark on your first Modular engine build, you will learn new terms, including torque-to-yield or torque-angle, to take fastener tightening to a new level. Not only do is a fastener torqued but the bolt stretch is also determined. With torque-to-yield, a fastener is torqued to a Ford specification. Then, it is tightened an additional number of degrees to achieve exacting standards.

First, always lubricate the bolt threads. Never torque fasteners dry. If a bolt bottoms out, know when to back out and use the correct fastener or check to see if there's foreign matter in the bolt hole. Never force a bolt or a nut.

When installing studs, never bottom out the stud. Run the stud down to where there is approximately 1/4 inch left. When it is time to install the nut, run the nut down flush. Then, torque to specifications. Never bottom out the stud. Again, always lubricate threads with Society of Autmotive Engineers (SAE) 30-weight engine oil. ■

A hub puller will be used to remove the harmonic damper. Use for a versatile puller with every feature imaginable. You're bound to lose bolts and washers along the way, but they are available at any hardware store.

This is a type of hub puller that has claws that grip the harmonic damper (as opposed to the type that uses bolts). Some harmonic dampers are solid and will not accommodate this type of puller. Never attach this hub puller around the outer ring.

a thread chaser is outside of your budget, use Grade-8 bolts and other fasteners with WD-40 to chase the threads. This may sound crude, but it will save you money and still do the job.

Tools should be rented only at the time that you intend to use them. Don't rent every tool mentioned here at the same time because you're not going to use all of them at the same time. For example, thread chasing should be performed when the block returns from the machine shop clean, machined, and ready for assembly. Some machine shops will have already chased the threads. Remember, thread chasing is time-consuming. Generally, machine shops don't do this unless you pay for the service. However, some machine shops view it as the cost of doing business.

Regarding the situation, it might be smart to purchase an engine stand, or it might be smart to rent one. Sometimes, renting can cost more

Through the years, I've accumulated quite an arsenal of punches and chisels. Rebuilding requires a wide variety of sizes and tips. Do not waste money on cheap chisels. Chisels can be found at swap meets and online auctions. You don't always need to buy new ones. Keep the tips free of ragged edges because they can break off and end up in your eye.

This is a nice assortment of Craftsman chisels. I suggest using chisels made from the toughest alloy that you can find. The tougher the chisel, the more you will pay, but they are worth every penny.

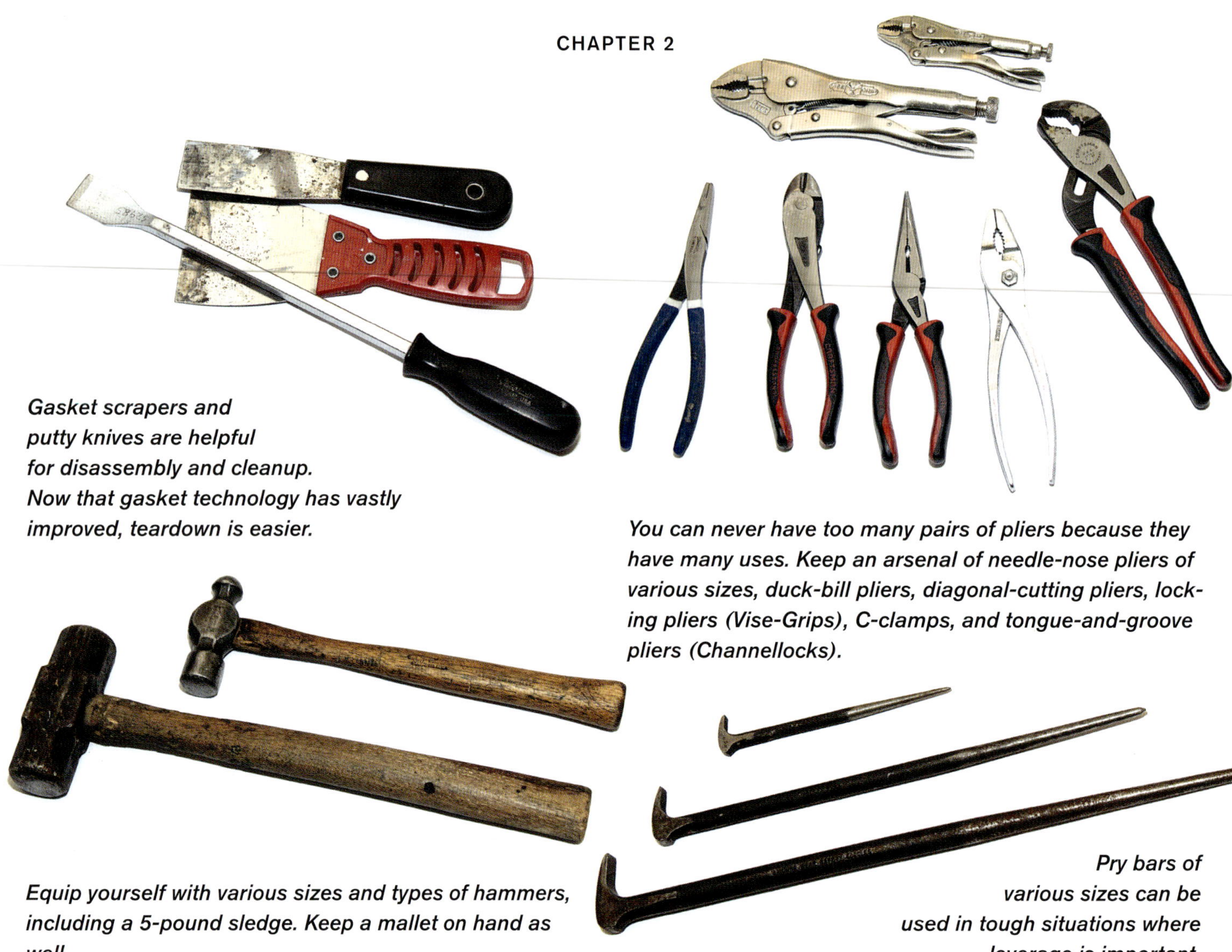

Gasket scrapers and putty knives are helpful for disassembly and cleanup. Now that gasket technology has vastly improved, teardown is easier.

You can never have too many pairs of pliers because they have many uses. Keep an arsenal of needle-nose pliers of various sizes, duck-bill pliers, diagonal-cutting pliers, locking pliers (Vise-Grips), C-clamps, and tongue-and-groove pliers (Channellocks).

Equip yourself with various sizes and types of hammers, including a 5-pound sledge. Keep a mallet on hand as well.

Pry bars of various sizes can be used in tough situations where leverage is important.

than simply buying one. In addition, engine stands can be cheap, depending on where you buy. Harbor Freight has some of the best values going at more than $100 for a stand. If you're building a heavy engine, don't cut corners here. Invest in a 1,000-pound capacity engine stand for stability and safety.

The decision to rent or buy tools boils down to how often the tool will be used and how long it is going to be needed during the engine build. Any time the tool is needed for longer than 1 to 3 days, you're better off buying it. If you have to buy, it can always be loaned to friends or sold after the engine is finished.

Don't forget about using a good engine hoist, which can also be a valuable piece of community property with your friends. Buying one seems to make the most economic sense. Did you know a good engine hoist can be picked up from Summit Racing for less than $500? If three or four people join in on the purchase of a hoist, it becomes quite affordable. These hoists fold up and roll out of the way when they're not in use. Setup time is a matter of minutes.

Jacks and jack stands are very important items. It is well documented that using inferior jacks and jack stands result in people getting hurt and killed each year. Buy only the best jack stands that are made out of angle iron and welded together with solid integrity. Make sure that the jack stands are able to support the weight of your vehicle. That doesn't mean using one jack stand to support the entire vehicle; it means using more than are necessary to have the confidence of knowing that they can support considerably more weight than they will ever have to.

Never lay under a vehicle that is being supported by a hydraulic jack or mechanical bumper jack! These jacks are not fail-safe. They can fail and do so with unspeakable consequences. Heavy-duty jack stands that are properly positioned beneath frame rails on a level surface provide the best protection.

BEFORE YOU BEGIN

I've owned a wide variety of power tools and drill bits. Never buy drill low-quality bits. Spend the money on drill bits that will last and keep a sharpener around to add life. Few things are more frustrating than a new bit that will not cut. DeWalt and Milwaukee are quality power-tool brands.

Make sure that your jacks and jack stands are always in good, serviceable condition. Keep hydraulic jacks in the "down" position whenever they aren't in use. This keeps dust and moisture off the ram. If you allow the ram to get rusty, the rust will cut the seals, rendering the jack useless. Also exercise this practice with an engine hoist by keeping the arm in the "down" position whenever the hoist isn't in use.

Use a micrometer to double-check your work. A micrometer, also known as a micrometer "screw gauge," incorporates a calibrated screw that is used for pinpoint-accurate measurements of components, such as this crank journal. Learn how to read and use it.

No tool arsenal is complete without thickness gauges. They are used here to confirm piston ring end gap. Get as many sizes as you can in a single-thickness gauge package.

Building a Coyote Stroker

A "stroker" is an engine with increased or decreased stroke. Increasing an engine's piston stroke (the distance that the piston travels in the cylinder bore) also increases displacement. By the same token, decreasing an engine's stroke reduces the distance the piston travels in the bore, which changes when and how the engine makes power. Short-stroke engines like high RPM, where they make the most torque. The focus here is more about increasing stroke to achieve greater amounts of torque along with horsepower.

Stroking an engine does more than just increase displacement. It increases torque by giving the engine more of a mechanical advantage via the stroke. When the stroke is increased, you increase the engine's crankshaft arm or lever, which makes the most of a combustion cycle. The longer the stroke, the greater the torque or twist.

Stroke comes from the length of the crankshaft's rod journal arm. Double that length to determine the engine's stroke. The length of the crankshaft's arm doubles because that arm is found in two directions: top dead center and bottom dead center. This is a simple 2:1 ratio. Take the crankshaft arm (measured from the crankshaft centerline) and double the measurement. If the arm is 1.825 inches, you have a 3.650-inch stroke.

So, how do you get more power from a stroker? Power comes from a longer crankshaft arm, but there's more. The cylinder is also filled with a greater volume of air and fuel, which yields more power all by itself. From stroke and cylinder swept volume comes torque. Torque is the truest measure of an engine's power output. When considering the crankshaft's arm, look at the distance from the crankshaft centerline to the center of the rod journal—this is where torque is born.

So, what exactly is torque? Think of the crankshaft's arm as a simple lever, like you were taught in high-school physics class. Torque equals the downward force of the stroke multiplied by the length of the lever or arm. Torque is increased when the length of the arm is increased. When the length of the arm is increased, the stroke is increased.

A stock 5.0L Coyote engine's arm is 1.825 inches. This means that the 5.0L

Use a Torque Plate

Does your machine shop use a torque plate for cylinder honing? If not, find a machine shop that does. The bolt-on torque plate simulates cylinder-head installation by getting the block dimensionally configured where it would be with heads installed and bolts torqued. You want the cylinder walls to be dimensionally where they will be when heads are installed. Without the torque plate, cylinder-wall dimensions would change after honing, which can cause serious break-in and ring-seating issues. ■

Coyote has a 3.650-inch stroke. If 0.5 inch is added to the arm, this increases the arm to 1.875 inches. Double the arm length of 1.875 inches, and the result is 3.750 inches of stroke.

Another factor with stroking is rod length. When the piston is hauled deep into the cylinder bore, you are also bringing it closer to the crankshaft counterweights, which means potential conflict. This means that a longer connecting rod is needed to get the piston down there without interference with the counterweights.

Sometimes, off-the-shelf connecting rods can be found to complete a stroker. Other times, you are forced to custom-make connecting rods. More-expensive stroker kits have custom parts, such as rods and pistons. More-affordable kits have off-the-shelf parts that have made the kit possible without expensive tooling costs. Whenever you have to custom-make connecting rods, this drives up the cost of a stroker. The same is true for custom pistons.

Stroker Power Facts

Another issue that is important to address is timing. Due to machinists retiring and shops closing, machine shops are becoming less common, so be prepared for a lengthy build process. While it used to take a week or weeks to get machining done, it now can take months. Keep this in mind before getting started.

Be very specific with a machine shop about what you want and how the engine will be used, and get a written estimate. Be prepared for surprises and steps not included in the estimate. In choosing a machine shop, take a good look at the condition of the shop and how it is maintained. Machine shops are generally not clean environments. It is a dirty business. However, observe where they assemble engines. You're going to want to see a clean room isolated from all of the teardown and machine work. Machine work generates a lot of debris, including metal shavings, dust, and dirt. It is always nice to see a well-maintained shop before committing.

Multiple methods can be used to install piston rings, including the "roll-on" approach or the use of an expander. I prefer using an expander. An expander, when used carefully, expands the ring just enough to clear the ring land without distortion.

Summit Racing Equipment offers this adjustable 4.000- to 4.090-inch piston-ring compressor, which makes light work of piston/rod installation. This is a nice compromise between a fully adjustable and a more expensive billet type.

If you build a lot of engines, billet-type ring compressors are nice to use. However, you will need several of them in various sizes in the range that you will normally use.

Since you should always degree the cam (even if you're reusing existing cams), you will need a degree wheel to ensure accurate cam timing. This large degree wheel from the Powerhouse division of Comp Cams makes light work of cam degreeing. Its large diameter makes it easier to turn the crank and read the results.

This clever little tool is used for measuring the valve-spring installed height. If you're doing your own cylinder-head work and setup, this measuring tool is needed.

If you're on a tight budget, this easy-to-read degree wheel, which is available from Summit Racing Equipment, will get the job done and do so for less money.

A dial indicator is needed to confirm true top dead center (TDC) and for cam-degreeing purposes.

Overhead-cam (OHC) engines, such as the Coyote and its Modular cousin, call for the use of a dial indicator configured like this above the finger follower (rocker arm). You need the appropriate fixture to support the dial indicator.

Proper Assembly Technique

With proper selection of parts out of the way, you can assemble an engine using tried-and-proven techniques performed by professionals. When it comes to assembly practices, engine professionals stress two main items: cleanliness and double-checking your work.

Professional engine builders stress double-checking your work because this approach saves time. If you think it's inconvenient to check your work repeatedly, consider the inconvenience involved in a teardown because there's high oil consumption or you have to collect the pieces of a blown engine because something critical was missed during the assembly process.

Engine building is an exacting exercise in physics where every detail must be covered to ensure success. There are no unimportant parts. Power comes from taking thermal energy and harnessing it above the piston during light-off. Fuel and air don't explode in a combustion chamber, as we have so often been told. Combustion is a quick-fire and the smooth application of heat energy to achieve rotary motion.

The easiest way to make power is to raise compression. However, you don't want too much compression. The compression ratio depends on your plan and the fuel octane that is available. The other quickest way to use power is less internal friction. Because the Coyote has been engineered with reduced friction, it is hard to believe that it could be reduced any further. However, there are other ways, such as more liberal clearances and lightweight components, which is a balancing act in itself because you also want durability, good oil pressure, and low oil consumption.

Even with all details already mentioned, there is no guarantee that an engine will stay together or make the power expected. It is those troublesome areas that we cannot see, including material weaknesses and defects, that can lead to failure when least expected. This means you must be attentive to everything that you have control over during the build process.

Cylinder-head stands improve access by getting the heads up and off the bench.

Valve-spring compressors can be purchased or rented. This is the tried-and-proven C-clamp-style valve-spring compressor for a home garage. It works on traditional OHV engines and will work on your overhead-cam Coyote.

Hydraulic lash adjusters can be difficult to remove. Use a pair of lifter pliers for stubborn adjusters. Most of the time, lash adjusters come out easily. Neglected Coyotes with failed finger followers can lead to seized lash adjusters. Finger followers do the same thing as rocker arms without multiplying valve lift. Lash adjusters do the same thing as hydraulic lifters.

The dial indicator serves many purposes. Here, it measures valve-stem length at the valve spring.

Regardless of what you are doing or building, a high-quality tap-and-die set is a must. Damaged threads are a part of engine-building life. Having these on hand will help you save time.

Some engine builders assemble engines on a tabletop, and that's fine for some. However, a 1,000-pound-capacity engine stand allows you to roll the block 360 degrees for easy access. Engine stands are not prohibitively expensive. Make it easy on yourself and visit Harbor Freight.

TECH TIP

Never Take New Parts for Granted

We often fall into the mistaken belief that since a part is new and right out of the box, it is a good part. Each and every part should be inspected for flaws. Although this doesn't guarantee a perfect part, you will sleep better. I have personally witnessed many moments with defective or mispackaged parts. When this happens, you can face unnecessary delays or engine failure. Examine each and every new part. ∎

Seal drivers can be used to serve several purposes, including driving freeze plugs and other block plugs.

Engine assembly lube is a must-have item for any build, although some builders choose to use engine oil. There are also assembly lubes for various purposes, including cylinder walls and piston rings. Assembly lube ensures a slippery start-up. It also stays on bearing and journal surfaces for engines that end up in storage.

Prepare a workspace surface for layout and inspection. When it is time for engine assembly, you want an exceptionally clean surface. If you live in the dusty desert or the central plains where the wind blows, keep the windows closed.

TEARDOWN AND INSPECTION

Engine teardown is a forensics exercise where you learn about an engine's past and how it has been treated. There are no unimportant parts of a teardown. Every part should be inspected and photographed to determine what to keep and what to replace. When in doubt about parts, seek the advice of a reputable machine shop before making a decision. Machine shops that have been in the business a long time have a wealth of experience and knowhow. They know what to look for and what needs to be done from experience.

When you disassemble an engine, you are the first eyewitness to the engine's condition and history. Inspect and catalog all parts in marked containers and plastic bags as the engine is disassembled. Containers, bags, and photographs are important to organization and proper assembly of the engine on the other side. You will be reminded of this when it is time to assemble the engine because you're bound to forget how it all went together. Don't be in a hurry. When you hurry, you will make mistakes and miss important details.

Inspection

Take a close look at load-bearing surfaces, such as crank and cam journals, cylinder walls, and piston skirts, as well as the overall condition of each part. Unusual wear and scoring are cause for a closer look at wear patterns. If scoring is observed, it is from metal-to-metal contact and/or damage from debris.

Look for evidence of oil starvation and metal-to-metal contact. Excessive sludge indicates neglect. Someone just didn't change the oil.

Look for evidence of coolant in the oil, which will look like gravy. When coolant gets into the oil, it is important to learn how it got there. Never write it off as just a gasket leak. Look for cracks or damage to the cylinder heads and block. A blown head

We are working with a new Coyote engine fresh from the Windsor/Essex engine plant. It is awaiting teardown at Performance Assembly Solutions (PAS) in Livonia, Michigan, which builds Ford Performance Coyote Eliminator crate engines. This is the type of organized disassembly you should follow for your home teardown. Everything should come out of the engine and be placed exactly as it was installed in a safe place.

As the engine is disassembled you should catalog, inspect, and properly store the parts.

The harmonic damper has been removed, which makes way for removing the timing cover.

gasket can be the result of over-boost or nitrous if the engine has been dogged. If coolant got into a cylinder causing a hydro-lock, it is best to confirm cylinder-wall condition with a sonic check. The first area to fail in a hydro-lock is the cylinder wall. Overheating is indicated by warped heads and the block deck, which can also be indicated by the discoloring of the aluminum castings.

Pistons, rings, and bearings should never be reused. Valves and springs, as a matter of practice, should never be reused unless you're working with a low-mileage engine with minimal wear. Camshafts, depending on journal and lobe wear, can be reused. Cam phasers, which are quite expensive, can be reused, depending on condition and mileage. Timing chains, guides, and tensioners should always be replaced, but that is also dependent upon mileage and condition.

Oil pumps should be replaced with high-volume pumps even with a stock street build. Because the Coyote's valve timing system depends upon sufficient oil pressure, and more importantly, volume, you're going to need a

Although it can be tempting to reuse today's high-tech gaskets and seals, always replace them with new ones for the best results. No one likes leakage. Silicone gasket technology makes these gaskets pliable and seemingly reusable. However, they are not always reusable.

Cam phasers and timing components should be inspected for irregular wear patterns. Shown here are the intake (right) and exhaust (left) cam phasers on the left bank (for a total of four on both banks). Exhaust cams are on the outside while intake cams are on the inside. This pair of solenoids in front direct oil pressure to the phasers to advance valve timing.

Once the harmonic damper and cam covers have been removed, this frees up the timing cover. There's quite an array of timing-cover bolts to be removed. Catalog these bolts and identify them on the packaging. Do this with every part removed. Don't kid yourself. You're never going to remember where all of these fasteners go.

Next, remove the timing cover.

high-volume pump even with the F-150. Volume ensures adequate lubrication and longevity.

The same rules that apply to a performance build apply to a stock build. The goal is durability as well as longevity for both. Replacement of parts depends on their condition. A stock F-150 Coyote with 300,000 miles on it calls for replacement of nearly everything. A 100,000-mile Coyote that has never had an oil change calls for the same thing.

Before disassembly, examine the chains and guides for smooth tracking.

Closely Inspect Crank and Cam Journals

Closely inspect the crankshaft and cam journals for wear and scoring. Excessive camshaft journal wear is cause for replacement. Minor score marks can be polished out. Crankshafts can be machined 0.010 inch and fitted with oversize bearings. Because Coyote crankshafts are plentiful and cheap, it is almost easier to replace the crank than it is to have it machined. ∎

Timing components are expensive to replace. However, they should be replaced when working with an engine with significant mileage and wear. Examine the guides, chains, and tensioners for unusual wear patterns. Chains and guides should show uniform (normal) wear. It is remarkable how durable these plastic chain guides are and how long they last.

Important!

Choose Wisely and Get a Written Estimate

Finding a machine shop that you can trust can be difficult. Every region has its trustworthy businesses as well as its notorious players. Finding a reputable machine shop and engine builder is a matter of word of mouth and social media.

Since enlisting a machine shop can be very expensive, choose a business wisely. No matter how much you may trust a machine shop, always get a written estimate where you both have a copy of the estimate and understand what's expected. Be sure that the machine shop understands that you want accountability for all of the parts that you have delivered. This means a detailed list of everything that you've provided. It is a good idea to take pictures of every part and document the part numbers. This way, you don't end up with someone else's parts.

Finally, few things are more disheartening than being presented with a higher bill than the estimate. The written estimate/agreement must include a clause stating they are to contact you prior to any work and before anything in the estimate changes. Misunderstandings can turn into thousands of dollars added to the final bill. ■

Once the inspection has been accomplished, measure the crank and cam journals with a micrometer and record the numbers. Depending on your knowledge of the subject, this is a step best performed by a machine shop before it gets to work on your engine. The machinist should measure the crank and cam journals and perform a visual inspection providing an estimate. There's little point in cleaning engine parts, which also contributes to the cost, when you're going to dispose of these components. I've seen machine shops disassemble engines, wash bad parts, charge customers for cleaning them, and then throw parts into the scrap-metal barrel.

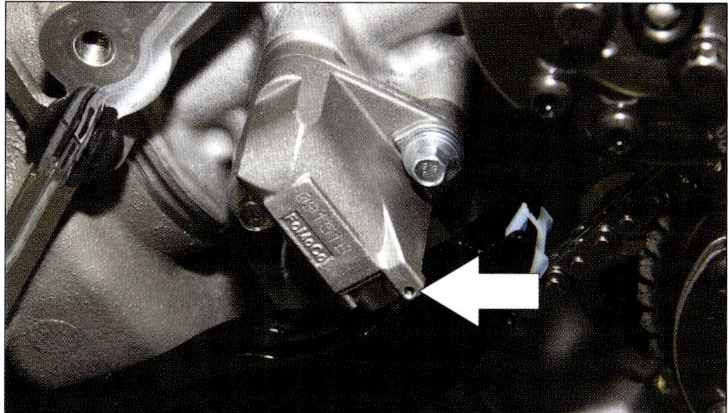

I stress using Ford Motorcraft/Ford Performance timing components, such as the chain tensioners. Do not use plastic aftermarket chain tensioners. This hole (arrow) is a provision for the installation pin, which comes with the tensioner to keep the piston compressed until you are ready to seat the guides and chains.

Timing-chain guides ride on hydraulic engine oil pressure–actuated tensioners, which apply pressure against the chain guides. To remove the tensioners, gently compress the tensioner piston with Vice-Grips (locking pliers) or Channel-locks (tongue-and-groove pliers). Then, insert an appropriately sized nail or wire into this hole to secure the piston, which takes the pressure off chains and guides for removal.

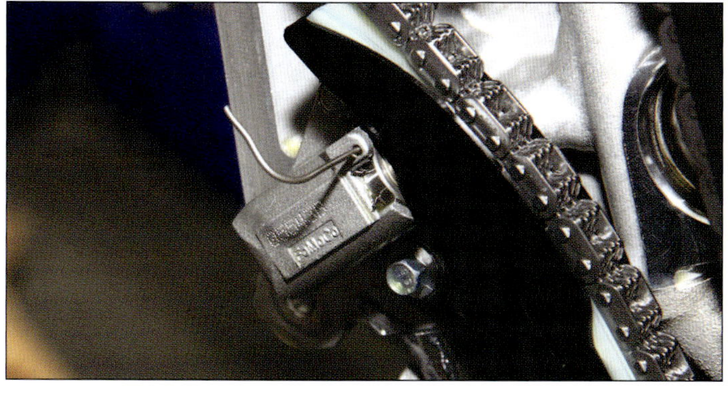

This is an example of the use of a solid-core wire to hold the tensioner piston compressed to remove the chains and guides.

This is the portion of the timing system on the driver's side, consisting of chains, guides, and tensioner.

Documentation Required

Catalog and Bag All Parts

Catalog all parts in marked plastic bags and containers in a way that the machine shop can understand, such as with each of the parts identified with a marker. This enables the machine shop to identify parts and fasteners for assembly. Strict documentation is the key to successful assembly. ∎

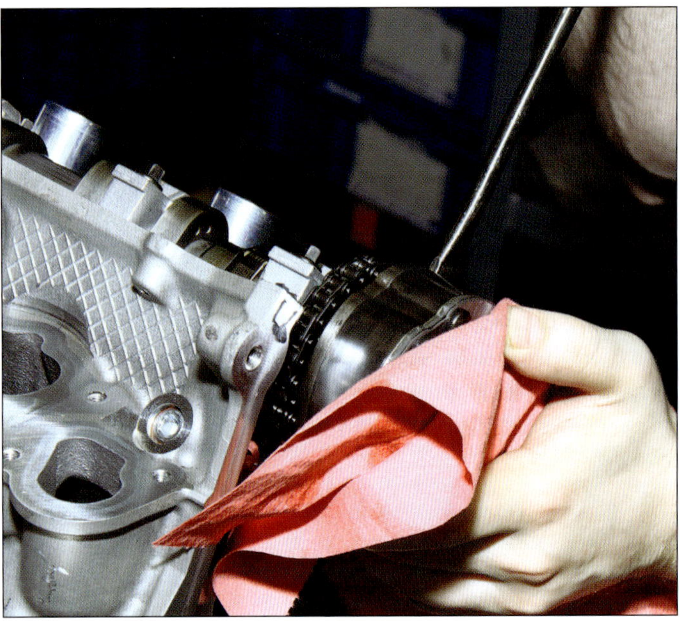

Do the same thing on the driver's side. The exhaust cam phasers are driven by the primary chains from the crankshaft.

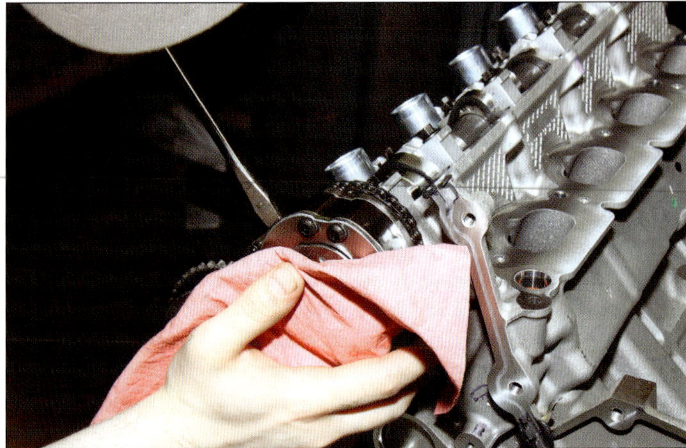

Once the phaser bolts have been removed, gently apply pressure against the back side of each phaser and hold it in your hand. This is the intake phaser, which is driven by the secondary chain.

Wear Patterns

As the engine is disassembled, inspect the rod and main bearing journals for abnormal wear patterns that might indicate irregular connecting rods and crank. "Irregular" means that the rods that are not straight or they may be twisted. Irregular connecting rods can arrive from the factory that way, or it could result from a poor machining technique during a previous rebuild.

Abnormal wear patterns appear when there's excessive wear on one side of a bearing or journal. This indicates that clearances were too tight on one side, forcing

Remove and inspect the cam phasers and filters (arrows). Inspect the filters for debris. Depending on mileage and wear, it is wise to replace the phasers, which are included in a complete Ford kit. When it comes to timing components, stick with Ford Performance parts.

This is the secondary chain tensioner and guide located at each cylinder head. Examine it for excessive wear. I strongly suggest the use of Ford Motorcraft or Ford Performance replacement parts, which have proven reliability. I've seen disturbing failure issues with aftermarket timing components. Until durability improves in the aftermarket, use Ford parts.

Choose a high-pressure Melling oil pump regardless of the performance expected. Increased volume can only be a good thing, even in a stock build.

out the oil wedge that needs to be there to prevent wear. There must be sufficient clearance between the bearing and the journal to allow proper oil flow while maintaining a healthy oil wedge.

When clearances are tight, oil-flow past the bearing and the journal becomes limited, causing higher oil temperatures, breakdown, and metal-to-metal contact. This is why all components must be "square" in their marriage with other components. A connecting rod must sit dead square on the rod journal to ensure a happy marriage with bearing and journal. The same can be said for the crankshaft. If a crank is distorted (bent or twisted),

Documentation Required

Take Photos

t is important to take photos during disassembly to keep track of how the engine went together in the first place. You will never remember how the engine went together months from now. ■

nothing will sit square, causing irregular wear, which will surely shorten engine life.

When disassembling the Coyote engine, it is easy to feel overwhelmed and intimidated by what seems very complex. However, by taking disassembly one step at a time, it becomes easier to understand. Take detailed notes and lots of photos. In addition, take photos of your Coyote while it is still in the car, paying close attention to connections, hoses, brackets, and accessories. Then, begin removal.

The Coyote's overwhelming nature comes from its Ti-VCT design. It has two primary chains from the crank to the twin overhead camshafts. The primary chains that

Closely inspect the roller finger followers and lash adjusters. A weak spot here is the roller rocker needle bearings. They can be a hidden danger, which is typically indicated by a tapping or clicking sound. Hold each of the rocker arms and spin the roller. If you feel grinding or binding, replace all of the rocker arms.

Remove the cam journal caps from the inside out. All journal caps must be removed in the proper order and marked regarding where they came off.

Lift out the cams carefully and store them standing vertically in a safe location or properly support them uniformly horizontally.

This is what a healthy camshaft should look like (modest journal and lobe wear). If lobes and journals are scored significantly, the cam is a throwaway. If wear is minor, it can be polished out. These are the sensor tangs located at the rear of each cam.

Although this lobe only exhibits minor pitting, it is risky to use. Pitting gets into the grain boundaries of the iron and will likely fail. The cam should be replaced.

These cams show normal wear with minor scoring. The journals and lobes can be polished and returned to service.

are driven by the crank drive the exhaust cams, which are located along the outside of the cylinder heads above the exhaust valves and ports. At the cylinder heads are secondary timing chains that drive both cams. The exhaust cam sprockets drive secondary chains that drive the intake cam phasers. Oil-pressure-control solenoids controlled by the PCM vector oil pressure to the cam phasers, which advances cam timing. The intake cams automatically retard to normal when timing advance isn't needed. Chain tension in both instances comes from oil pressure-actuated tensioners applying pressure on each chain.

The cylinder heads have been removed, placed on a parts cart, and properly indexed with the rest of the engine. This maintains proper visual order. This is a good practice to apply to your home garage.

As with most of today's engines, the Coyote is fitted with torque-to-yield fasteners throughout. These fasteners cannot be reused and must be replaced. Torque-angle is the process of torquing the fastener and then applying a specific number of degrees of additional torque to confirm bolt stretch.

Carefully remove the rear block cover and store it with all of its fasteners.

These rear block covers can be stubborn to remove. Gently pry around the cover's perimeter until it pops.

Important!

Harmonic Damper Inspection and Service

An engine's harmonic damper is designed to absorb or dampen the crankshaft's twist. As each cylinder hammers out a beat on the engine's crank, the crank will twist a certain amount. The harmonic damper "damps" crankshaft twist, allowing the crank to bounce back smoothly like a rotary shock absorber.

Because the harmonic damper is a steel ring that is wrapped around an iron hub and separated by rubber, it needs good rubber to get the job done. As the rubber ring dry-rots and hardens, a harmonic damper has a tough time doing its job. This is why close inspection is so important and replacement is done when necessary. ∎

I'm often asked what should be replaced during an engine rebuild. Since Ford designed and built the Coyote engine as a high-performance engine, you would be amazed at what does not need to be replaced. During the teardown, closely examine the valvetrain components—everything from camshafts, rocker arms, valve springs, keepers, retainers, cam sprockets, chains, tensioners, guides, etc.

Removal of the pistons and rods is next. Here, the technician uses a piece of conduit to carefully drive the assembly out through the deck. Pistons and rods should be placed in order and numbered as they came out of the block.

This rod journal is badly scored from a spun bearing. A damaged rod can be reconditioned, but it may save money to purchase a replacement rod. There's some risk that comes with a rod that has been overheated.

This is a good rod journal. All it needs is polishing.

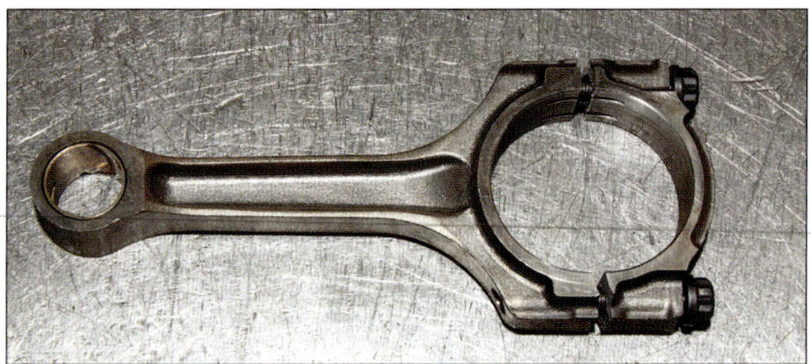

The stock powdered metal (sintered metal), forged-steel rods can be reconditioned and used again with resized (external diameter) bearings.

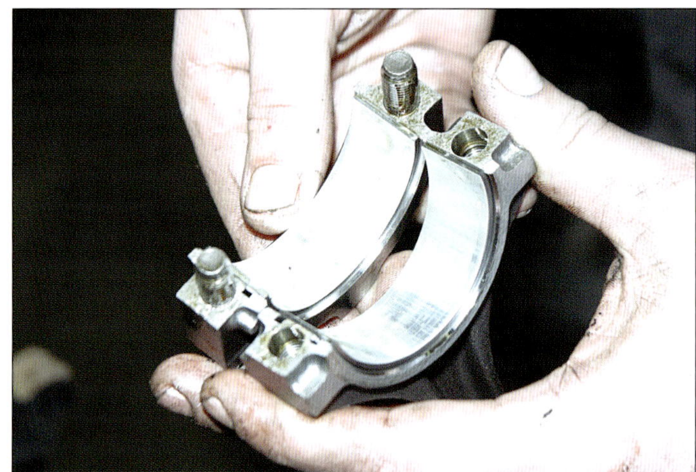

These rod bearings show normal wear. It is advisable to replace them.

Chain Tensioners

The Coyote's overhead-cam design maintains its timing by automatically adjusting timing-chain tensioners as you drive. It does this the same way that hydraulic lash adjusters maintain valve adjustment: via hydraulic pressure. Coyote engines generate hydraulic pressure via their oiling system. As the chains and sprockets wear, tensioners maintain tension against the guides and chains thanks to the engine oil pressure. It is common sense to replace both tensioners and guides.

Summit Racing Equipment offers a variety of aftermarket Coyote timing chain guides that can take severe-duty punishment. Other sources, such as Modular Mustang Racing (MMR) and Livernois, offer excellent severe-duty timing sets and the related parts for the high-revving Coyote. For the rest of us with stock Mustangs and F-150s, there is Ford Motorcraft and Ford Performance. ■

The same can be said for this main journal, yielding a perfect surface.

Remove All Block Plugs

When tearing down the block and heads, remove all of the block plugs. This means every single core plug and every oil gallery plug. All castings must be stripped to the bone. Mark each oil-gallery-plug location for proper installation of these plugs when it's time for assembly. Use a thin layer of Permatex's The Right Stuff on these plugs when it's time for installation.

Do you know why I suggest the removal of all plugs? It's because you never know what may be hiding inside, such as a stray core plug knocked inside the block by a rebuilder or the Ford factory or iron/aluminum particles trapped in oil galleries that can do engine damage. ■

I've seen chain guides in 200,000-mile engines that did not need to be replaced. I can say the same thing about tensioners, cams, and sprockets.

Unless there has been oil starvation or overheating (the PCM would never allow the latter), camshafts last virtually forever. I do suggest new chains, sprockets, guides, and tensioners for high-mileage engines. It is good to start with new compo-

nents that I am confident will last 200,000-plus miles. No matter what, always replace valve springs and seals.

When removing the oil pump, examine the pump rotor for abnormal signs of wear. I suggest this because the harmonic damper will sometimes tend to load the pump rotor. We've seen this in some teardowns, but not all. If abnormal wear patterns are visible, I suggest harmonic damper replacement or, at the very least, checking clearances at the crank snout and trigger wheel.

When cylinder heads are disassembled, inspect the valves, stems, and guides for excessive wear and damage. If the valves clean up nicely and guide wear is within the correct limits, you can get by with cleaning up the faces and seats and returning the valves to service. Measure the guides and make the decision whether or not to replace them. Valve-spring replacement depends on what you have for spring pressure. Spring pressure must fall within limits based on camshaft profile. Cylinder-head decks should be checked and at least shaved to achieve a good surface.

This piston shows normal burn and wear patterns. Coated skirts show minor scuffing. If there are tiny aluminum particles on the crown and on the spark-plug firing tip, this indicates temperature extremes from detonation or preignition.

Rings reveal a normal condition. Minor skirt scuffing is normal. Piston and ring condition are a barometer for how the engine was treated. Did it receive regular oil changes? Was the engine run hard and abused?

Never Force It

Be gentle in your execution during engine disassembly. When a part will not come loose, there's nearly always a reason why. Sometimes, it's just a sticky, stubborn gasket. Other times, it's a fastener that has been missed. Cover your bases and double-check the removal process. Never force any part. ■

This is a low-mileage Coyote with some dyno time with normal burn patterns. All it needs is fresh head gaskets and a cleaning up.

A mirror-finish cylinder wall is the norm these days, even with a new engine based on the way bores are factory-honed. I like to see a fine crosshatch pattern for good oil control and cylinder sealing. A Coyote engine with high mileage and wear will have a mirror finish. These engines are factory-equipped with hypereutectic pistons (not forged, which was common with the Modulars).

I like this crosshatch pattern in a freshly honed block. What I don't like is the score running the length of the bore, which could cause cylinder leakage and oil control issues.

This is what a blown head gasket looks like. Coolant had entered two cylinders and the engine sat for a time. Head gaskets can blow between adjacent cylinders, causing a cold misfire. Contamination from coolant only makes things worse. When coolant settles in the cylinder bore during shutdown, the toxic combination of the aluminum piston, iron rings, and the cylinder wall, and coolant causes horrific corrosion and cylinder-wall pitting wherever the piston stopped.

Critical Inspection

Inspect Cooling Passages

Water jackets and cooling passages are a quick indicator of engine health. If an engine suffers from a blown head gasket or a cracked casting, it will be apparent in water-jacket color.

Discolored water jackets indicate neglect or engine failure. A healthy water jacket will appear in its natural aluminum color. A blown head gasket or casting crack will tend to discolor cooling system passages in tan and brown. Poor cooling-system maintenance will be indicated when the gray aluminum turns a rusty brown color. ∎

Cylinder-head disassembly hasn't changed much with newer engines. Compress the valve sprints, remove the keepers, and extract the valves from the head. The valves must be kept in the proper order in which they were previously installed if you are planning to reuse them. Check the valve guides and stems for wear issues and determine whether or not to replace them.

These valves are typical of what you will find from a Coyote core. They can be media tumbled, refaced, and returned to use as long as they aren't badly burned. The stems need to be measured and polished. As long as they fall within the specifications, they are good to go.

Valves that have been tumbled look like new. Now, they only need grinding and their stems need to be measured and polished.

Engine Electronics

Exercise care working with engine electronics, vacuum hoses, and fuel lines. Sensor and fuel-injector plugs are fragile primarily due to under-hood heat and ozone, making them susceptible to breakage. When broken, they can be expensive and challenging to replace. If a harness has to be replaced, you may face availability issues (Ford's dreaded "NR" status) and/or expense.

Most sensor plugs are quick-connect and quick-disconnect without the need for special tools. Fuel-injector plugs require gentle manipulation for an easy disconnect. Protect plugs and harnesses in small plastic bags to keep out moisture and dirt. Dirt on contacts will adversely affect continuity, which can cause performance issues.

Another important element is the sensors and other engine electronic components. When rebuilding, I suggest replacing all of the engine sensors. Most important are oxygen (O_2) sensors, throttle-position sensor (TPS), mass-airflow (MAF) sensor, and manifold-absolute-pressure (MAP) sensor. Knock sensors (located in the block) should be replaced. Although coolant and air-temperature sensors tend to be secondary, they are important to proper engine electronics operation. I suggest Ford Motorcraft/Ford Performance sensors and other electronics. They deliver factory integrity and quality.

When sensors fail, they limit the powertrain control module's (PCM, also known as electronic control module) ability to control fuel mixture and spark timing. The worst case is a "no start" condition. A lean fuel mixture (short injector pulse width) can cause serious control issues and engine damage. Early spark timing can cause detonation (pinging). This comes from an electronic engine control malfunction that happens anywhere in the network. This is why an ECM should be checked during the rebuild for proper function. In addition, this is why you should begin anew with all new sensors. Since sensors are not inexpensive, it's easy to ignore replacement. However, you have to consider, what is a new

Be very careful with the engine electronic sensors that are positioned around the engine. Remove them with care and protect any wiring. The life's blood of any Coyote engine is the electronics that control this engineering marvel. Store them and mark them for identification purposes.

Remove the fuel injectors and send them to a specialty shop for cleaning and testing. Unless you are planning to make large sums of power, stock injectors can be returned to service with new O-rings. (Photo Courtesy Wes Duenkel)

engine worth to you? An engine failure costs more than replacement of all the electronics. In addition, if an engine wiring harness is in marginal condition with damaged connectors, replace the harness as well if you can find a replacement.

How does all of this stuff work? Let's begin with the throttle-position sensor (TPS). The TPS is a variable resistor similar to the volume control on a sound system. Turn it up, and it reduces resistance, allowing more power to flow. Turn it down, and it increases resistance, allowing less power through. The same can be said for an engine's MAP and MAF sensors. Both are variable resistors that provide feedback to the PCM, which controls fuel and spark curves. The PCM also controls the automatic transmission's shift points.

The coolant temperature sensor is little more than an on/off switch. When coolant temperature reaches 195°F, the coolant-temperature sensor closes, sending the PCM into closed-loop and complete- loop operation. During closed-loop operation, the PCM acknowledges all sensors, and the engine resumes normal operation. Not only does the PCM manage the engine's electronic function but it is also programed to control the fuel and spark curve based on how and where you drive. It remembers your driving habits. Disconnect the battery for an extended period of time, and the PCM has to start all over again learning these patterns and conditions.

If a malfunction is detected by the PCM via any of the sensors, including a misfire, it will trigger the check-engine light (CEL). A CEL can come from a variety of sources. Any malfunction that affects exhaust emissions will trigger it. This means any sensor or any misfiring spark plug. As the technician interfaces with the PCM, the origin of the fault can be quickly determined—right down to which cylinder misfired. This is the benefit of today's onboard diagnostics.

Another very important part of the Coyote's electrical system is also part of the fuel system: the fuel injectors. Fuel injectors only need to be replaced if they're inoperative or gummed up. They get gummed up with varnish and carbon deposits in the course of normal use. As long as they're operational, they can be

Should You Replace Fuel Injectors?

As a matter of practice, all fuel injectors should be serviced during a rebuild. Because injectors are quite expensive, consult with a fuel-injection service shop about what to do with yours. A fuel-injection service shop can clean and inspect them to determine if they need to be replaced.

As fuel injectors operate, they become contaminated with gum and carbon deposits, which causes them to lose that nice spray fan that engines like for clean, efficient combustion. When injectors get dirty, they tend to dribble, which increases hydrocarbon emissions and causes poor performance. Always replace the O-ring seals. Injectors are identified by color. ■

Coolant system neglect leads to several issues, including rust and corrosion. The lethal mix of aluminum, iron, steel, and other dissimilar metals along with an electrolyte, such as straight water, becomes a serious problem in a short time. Ethylene glycol with corrosion inhibitors prevents corrosion. Evans Coolant (used exclusively) eliminates any chance of corrosion.

Closely inspect the finger followers and lash adjustors. Spin the rollers with your fingertips and feel for any roller resistance and binding. If you're working with a high-mileage Coyote, replace all of the valvetrain components in the interest of durability.

Mileage and treatment determine whether or not to replace valve springs. If you are opting for a more aggressive cam profile, go with springs and a cam profile as a matching set. As a rule, it is best to start with new valve springs in light of the cyclic fatigue that occurs over time with valve springs.

cleaned and serviced by a fuel injection/carburetor shop. When fuel injectors become gummed and carboned up, this adversely affects the spray fan on which an engine depends. A nice, uniform spray fan is important to smooth engine operation, fuel efficiency, and power. Fuel injectors with an irregular pattern cause rough operation and poor performance.

Fuel injectors are little more than a low-voltage solenoid valve timing fired by the PCM. They malfunction when they get dirty or the electromagnet (solenoid) inside fails. Otherwise, fuel injectors are good indefinitely. Truthfully, I've seen them go beyond 200,000 miles in fleet use without service. Although this is impressive performance, I suggest regular fuel-injection service (cleaning and inspection) every 100,000 miles. Service includes ultrasonic cleaning and little else. Close inspection and test operation demonstrate whether or not they need to be replaced. Periodic cleaning and inspection costs less than replacement. A new set of fuel injectors can cost at least $800 because they cost a minimum of $100 each.

The flywheel (flexplate), the reluctor, and bolts should all be kept together as they come off the engine.

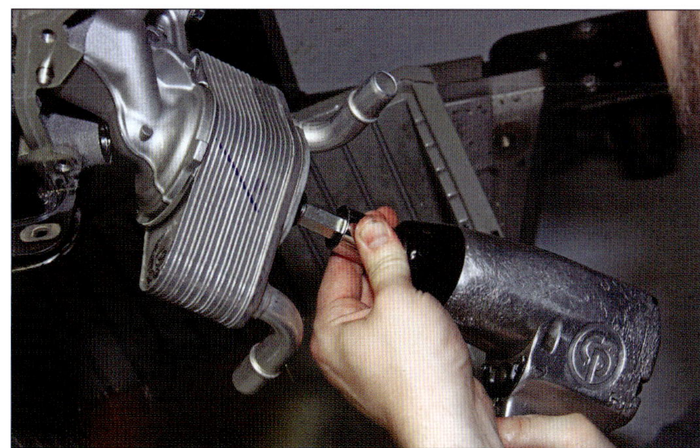

Because the oil cooler cannot be inspected internally, I suggest replacement. This eliminates any chance of debris in the oil.

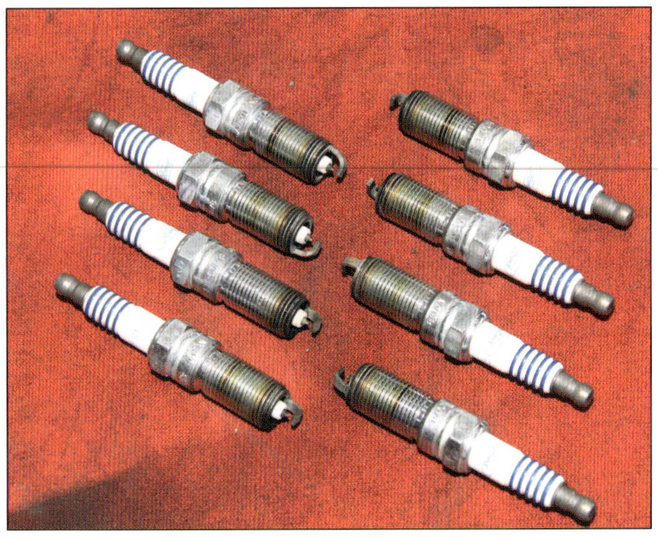

The spark plug firing tip's condition determines how the engine was treated and tuned. These plugs are normal in condition and color (white and off-white). Snow-white insulators with aluminum fragments indicate high combustion temperatures from a lean condition, boost, and ignition timing.

Some components, including the oil-to-water cooler, radiator, and hoses, should automatically be replaced. Both the cooler and radiator can be congested with debris that you won't want in a new engine. Hoses, unless they were just replaced, should be discarded. The same can be said for the serpentine belt.

Broken Fasteners

What should you do about broken fasteners? The solution is a screw extractor, which is a reverse-thread, tapered screw. Drill a hole slightly smaller into the broken fastener and use the screw extractor to twist it out. I suggest bathing the broken fastener with a penetrating lubricant like WD-40 and letting it soak for at least a day or more. Give it time to soak in.

Where it can get dicey is the risk of breaking the extractor off in the fastener. Because the extractor is harder than the fastener, this can get ugly quickly. Straight-fluted extractors typically come in a kit with the appropriate drill bits. Drill out the fastener with the appropriately sized drill bit. Carefully hammer the extractor into the hole with a brass hammer (as builders I have worked with suggest). Then, extract the fastener. If the fastener becomes impossible to remove, heat the metal with a torch around the fastener (careful . . . aluminum melts at 1,300°F) and

The Coyote features bulletproof six-bolt main caps. All main cap bolts are torque-to-yield and must be replaced.

Crank removal begins with the main cap side bolts, which are torque-to-yield and must be replaced.

Next, remove the main cap bolts, ideally from the inside out.

Collect the main cap bolts and save them in a container more for reference purposes. They cannot be reused.

Stubborn main caps get a gentle nudge with a large common screwdriver.

A machine shop that I've worked with shows how to store crankshafts. They must be stored vertically on their flanges or hung up (as shown here).

One technician showed me how to pull the main caps using the bolts themselves for the grab.

Perform crankshaft removal gingerly to avoid any damage to the journals. It is so easy to nick the journals. If necessary, get help lifting the crank out.

I like this approach to storing engine parts, where main caps and the like are stored exactly as they came out of the engine. Each item should be identified and marked as it is positioned in the engine. Main caps, for example, cannot be randomly reinstalled. They must be installed exactly where they were located.

try removing the fastener again. The heating approach is your last resort.

When all else has failed, use a punch and hammer to drive out the broken extractor. Find a high spot on the extractor and attempt to drive the extractor out in reverse of its intended direction. If that doesn't work, grind a low spot into the extractor and use that low spot to drive out the extractor. Sometimes, the heat-and-drive approach works. Above all, be patient and stay at it. Keep it bathed in WD-40.

Casting Inspection

It isn't so much what can be seen in a teardown, but what cannot be seen. Hidden flaws and cracks can stop an engine cold. It is money well spent to have a block sonic-checked to confirm cylinder-wall thickness. It is also good to have the block decks checked for imperfections that cannot be detected on the surface. Main saddles are another area of potential weakness. This same logic applies to cylinder heads and any other castings. This way, you don't waste the expense of machining flawed castings that you will have to replace later.

Remove the piston-cooling jets and inspect them for any debris or damage.

I am often asked if a Coyote block can be bored and honed. Gen 1 and Gen 2 blocks have paper-thin iron cylinder walls. Unless you are planning large sums of power, they can be honed. Gen 3 and Gen 4 blocks cannot be honed, so don't even try. They must be sleeved or replaced.

Performance Assembly Solutions uses this cart and template approach to store engine components until they are ready for assembly. You can use a similar approach at home in your shop where everything is laid out in an orderly fashion.

There are times during disassembly when fasteners are broken off in a casting. Arm yourself with a screw/bolt extractor to remove the broken fastener. These are Snap-on extractors, which are quite expensive. One type of extractor has a spiral flute structure commonly known as an EZ-Out. There are several extractor brands out there. Another type of extractor sports a straight flute structure.

A properly sized hole is drilled into the fastener to make way for the extractor. If the fastener has right-hand threads, a left-hand-thread extractor is needed, which will "bite" into the fastener. The extractor will thread into the fastener for removal.

The extractor has successfully removed the fastener. All bolt holes in the block and heads should be chased with a thread chaser or tap to ensure clean threads during assembly.

SELECTING PARTS

I have to hand it to Ford's product planners and engineers. In 2011, they came up with what is easily the greatest Ford V-8 that has ever been created. When it was introduced, the Ti-VCT Coyote V-8 seemed to be the perfect high-performance engine. It could make upward of 1,000 to 1,500 hp if your pockets were deep enough and your spine was stout enough. It has become the engine of choice for swaps as well.

Despite its birth as a high-performance engine primarily for the Mustang GT, the Coyote also became a great all-around V-8 for F-150 trucks. It will haul, tow, cruise, and make the commute. At times, searching for performance solutions, I forget that this engine is also a means to getting from Point A to Point B with efficiency. Let's talk about how to build a better one.

The Coyote was the most developed engine in modern Ford history. Yet, there is always room for improvement. When it comes to selecting parts, what do you want your Coyote to do? Will you use it for daily driving, for the street/strip, drag racing, road racing, off-road racing, rock crawling, or towing and hauling?

This is an important consideration to make before ordering parts. Once you have established what you want the engine to do, the next step is to decide the type of vehicle that it will be installed in. Is it a swap into a classic car or truck? Perhaps you're building the engine for a fleet vehicle, such as an F-150, or for a Mustang GT police pursuit vehicle? Don't laugh, local jurisdictions have Mustang pursuit vehicles. Law enforcement loves them. The bad guys hate them.

It is important to know vehicle weight, axle ratio, transmission type and gearing, and even wheel and tire sizing. Then comes the question of cost. How much are you willing to spend? The Coyote is pretty simple by design, where the cams, finger followers, lash adjusters, and the timing system are all together as a package. It is best to opt for all-new valvetrain components in the interest of durability and an engine that will go the distance unless you're working with a low-mileage core.

Selecting parts can be the most stressful part of an engine build because decisions tend to be permanent and expensive. Before getting started, resist the impulse to bench race and build more engine than

The standard Coyote block can withstand upward of 600 to 700 hp. Anything beyond 700 hp calls for a stronger block, and there are several from which to choose.

you need. When planning, always think longterm. What do you want the engine to do later on? Build additional strength into your plan, but don't go overboard.

If you are building a stocker, which many of you are, build for durability. This involves better materials that will go the distance. Fleet and work trucks call for brute durability, meaning being able to idle for hours on end in extreme heat and cold. This is where we think of high-volume oil pumps, heavy-duty chain guides, etc.

Again, I will stress the selection of Ford Motorcraft/Ford Performance parts in the interest of durability. Although I respect the aftermarket and suggest the use of aftermarket parts in performance/racing applications, Ford has the engineering resources and decades of endurance testing under its belt where parts and components have been tortured and tested to the extremes. Ford parts are a logical choice.

If your budget is limited presently, the next question is, "Will it be limited in the future? This means being realistic about parts selection and cost. A word of caution is to not overbuild and end up with more engine and expense than you need. However, know realistically what your Coyote will do later on.

Whether building a Coyote for an F-150 or the Mustang GT, the same basic rules apply to both engines. The goal is durability and longevity in each. Applying the same nuances in a Mustang GT 5.0L Coyote to an F-150 build will result in an engine planned out and built to serve you well for 200,000-plus miles. You will also have a powerful mill for work and the morning commute. With regular oil and fil-

ter changes using synthetic lubrication and high-quality oil filters from Motorcraft, Wix, or K&N every 5,000 to 7,000 miles, you can expect 300,000 miles from a Coyote.

The Block

Block selection is determined by application and your plan. If you're planning robust power increases, choose the most rugged Coyote block available. A mild street Coyote with occasional weekend racing, can get away with a Gen 2 block, especially in the F-150. For a Gen 1 Coyote application (2011–2014 Mustang GT and F-150), stay with a Gen 1 block and keep the selection simple.

Because the Gen 1 F-150 and Mustang Coyote engines do not include the engineering changes that the Gen 2 and Gen 3 have, interchangeability can be difficult because it all has to work together as a cohesive operation. The heads, block, and induction all have to be compatible, which can get tricky with the evolving Coyote line. One of the more tiresome aspects of Ford engines is the engineering changes that make compatibility tricky at best. The Gen 2 Coyote heads require some modification work to be compatible with the Gen 1 induction system because the intake port flanges have an extended lip that Gen 1 heads do not have.

If you are upgrading a Gen 1 application to the Gen 2 or Gen 3 block, the Gen 2 or Gen 3 oil filter adapter is needed due to the drainback fea-

ture added to the block. Because the newer Gen 3 Coyote blocks are affordable and still available from Ford Performance, one can be purchased for anywhere from $1,300 to $2,300 for a new block. Ford Performance also has a cast-iron Coyote block for racing extremes. The aftermarket offers sleeved Coyote blocks for racing and for fleet use, where the block can be rebuilt without concern for cylinder-wall thickness.

5.0L Gen 3 (2018) Coyote Production Cylinder Block (M-6010-M504VC)

- Original equipment engine block for the 2018–2023 Mustang GT and F-150

The discontinued Ford Performance (M-6010-M50R) Coyote race block allows you to take peak horsepower well into four-digit territory. The block deck and thicker material around the thin-wall cylinder liners give this block extraordinary strength. Cast-in cylinder supports on the intake side help hold things together. This block is no longer available from Ford. However, plenty of them are still available through online auctions and at swap meets. (Photo Courtesy Ford Performance)

- 93.0-mm bore
- Block has the plasma-transferred wire arc (PTWA) spray weld liner coating, which provides improved durability and heat transfer, reduced friction, and weight reduction compared to previous Mustang GT and F-150 aluminum blocks
- Cylinder bores are finish-honed and ready for assembly
- All blocks are finish-machined, including cylinder-head decks and crank bores (main saddles)
- Cross-bolted nodular-iron main bearing caps use 12-mm cylinder-head bolts
- Block has provisions for piston cooling jets (included)
- Includes all plugs and dowels
- Fits Mustang GT and F-150

5.2L Gen 3 Coyote Aluminum Engine Block (M-6010-M52B)

- Upgraded version of previous Ford Performance M-6010-M52 and M-6010-M52A 5.2L Coyote aluminum cylinder blocks
- Features higher-flow piston cooling jets to provide additional piston cooling
- Rod bolt path is clearance-machined in the crankcase
- Improved high-performance casting of the Coyote block with improvements to support higher-horsepower engine builds
- Utilizes longer (187-mm) cylinder-head bolts with a 12-mm thread diameter to provide greater clamping force (requires longer head-bolt kit,

This is the M-6010-504VC Gen 3 Coyote block, which is available from Summit Racing Equipment. It is the strongest Ford production block produced to date, with 93.0-mm bores and PTWA spray weld cylinder liners. Cylinder bores are finish-honed along with finish-machined decks and main saddles. This block calls for 12-mm cylinder-head bolts. It also has provisions for piston oil squirters and arrives on your doorstep with the dowels and plugs ready to go. (Photo Courtesy Ford Performance)

which is part number M-6067-M501280, or the M-6067-M52B head changing kit)

- Improved crankcase windage
- 94.0-mm bore
- Water jackets below cylinder bores have been updated to add more material for strength
- The intake side of the bore at the deck surface includes a cast-in brace to improve strength of the cylinder wall and head-gasket sealing
- Block features PTWA spray weld liner coating, which provides improved durability and heat transfer, reduced friction, and a weight savings compared to previous 5.0L Mustang GT aluminum blocks
- Cylinder-liner coating does not require unique piston rings or piston material
- Cylinder bores are finish-honed and ready to assemble
- All block features are finish-machined, including the head deck and crank bore
- Cross-bolted nodular-iron main bearing caps
- Uses 12-mm cylinder-head bolts
- Block has provisions for piston oil squirters
- Includes plugs and dowels and oil squirters
- Fits Mustang GT and F-150

Coyote Cast-Iron Race Block (M-6010-M50X)

Ford Performance produced a cast-iron version of the Coyote engine block.

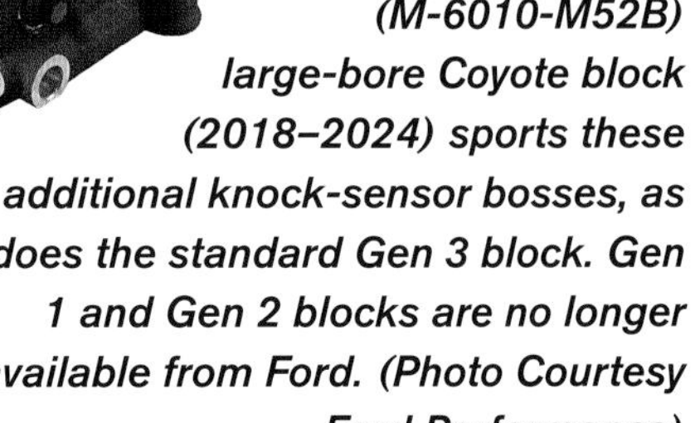

The Gen 3 5.2L (M-6010-M52B) large-bore Coyote block (2018–2024) sports these additional knock-sensor bosses, as does the standard Gen 3 block. Gen 1 and Gen 2 blocks are no longer available from Ford. (Photo Courtesy Ford Performance)

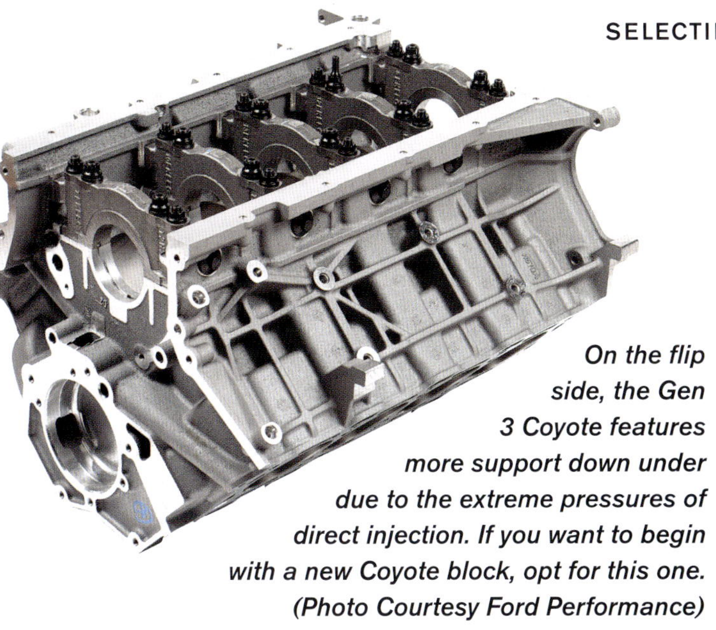

On the flip side, the Gen 3 Coyote features more support down under due to the extreme pressures of direct injection. If you want to begin with a new Coyote block, opt for this one. (Photo Courtesy Ford Performance)

Cast from a proprietary-grade, class-50 iron. Designed for extra strength for maximum-effort/boosted Coyote engine builds.

- Deck height: 227 mm (8.937 inch)
- Rough bore can be finished to the Gen 3 size (93 mm/3.661 inch)
- Maximum bore: 95.0 mm (3.740 inch)
- Maximum stroke: 99 mm (3.897 inch)
- Maximum displacement: 5.6L

With an iron-sleeved Coyote block, the sky is the limit at 1,500 to 2,000 hp.

If you're aiming for 700-plus hp, I suggest sleeving your Coyote block for enhanced durability. Because the Gen 3 Coyote block has plasma-sprayed cylinder liners, it cannot be bored, which is when sleeving becomes mandatory. Plan to spend $1,000 for the sleeves and at least another $1,000 in labor. The result will be a bulletproof Coyote block.

Plan For Power and Longevity

If the long-term plan is 600-plus hp, opt for the strongest Coyote block available, which would be a Gen 3 block. If aiming for big power, choose the M-6010-M504VC Gen 3 Coyote block, which is the strongest block to date—short of the M-6010-M50X cast-iron race block or the Gen 1 and Gen 2 race block (M-6010-M50R), the latter of which is no longer in production.

The aspect that makes the M50X block stronger isn't so much bottom end, which is the same as the stock block, according to Ford Performance. Instead, it is the block deck and thicker material around the thin-wall cylinder liners that give this discontinued race block extraordinary strength. The M50X is a good value if you can find one.

Because the M-6010-M50R has been discontinued, you are better off looking at Ford Performance's current lineup of new Coyote blocks. They make more economic sense than extensive machine work on an existing block. Since the Gen 3 block is the strongest production block, this is a good place to start. The downside to the Gen 3 block is the paper-thin plasma-sprayed cylinder liners, which cannot be bored. Your only option is to sleeve the Gen 3 block, which can cost upward of $1,000-plus in labor and another $1,000 for a set of eight sleeves. ∎

For 2015–2024 (Gen 2 and Gen 3), this arrow indicates the additional oil return passage for the revised oil-filter adapter. Both the Gen 2 and Gen 3 blocks and oil-filter adapter must match.

The early 2011–2014 Coyote block (Gen 1) does not have the oil return hole that was just mentioned. Note the difference at the oil-filter adapter, which doesn't have the return passage that is found on the updated 2015–2023 block. The 2011–2014 block has a different oil filter adapter than the 2015–2017 block. They do not interchange.

- Standard Coyote 100-mm bore spacing
- Lengthened bores for added strength
- Revised deck design for added strength around the water jackets
- Designed for 12-mm ARP head stud kit 456-4303
- Head bolt holes are not machined for the production-length head bolts
- Material available to drill and tap for production-length head bolts
- Billet-steel six-bolt main caps with ARP hardware
- Accepts Gen 1 and Gen 2 Coyote 5.0L cylinder heads
- Accepts Gen 1, Gen 2, and Gen 3 GT350 5.2L cylinder heads

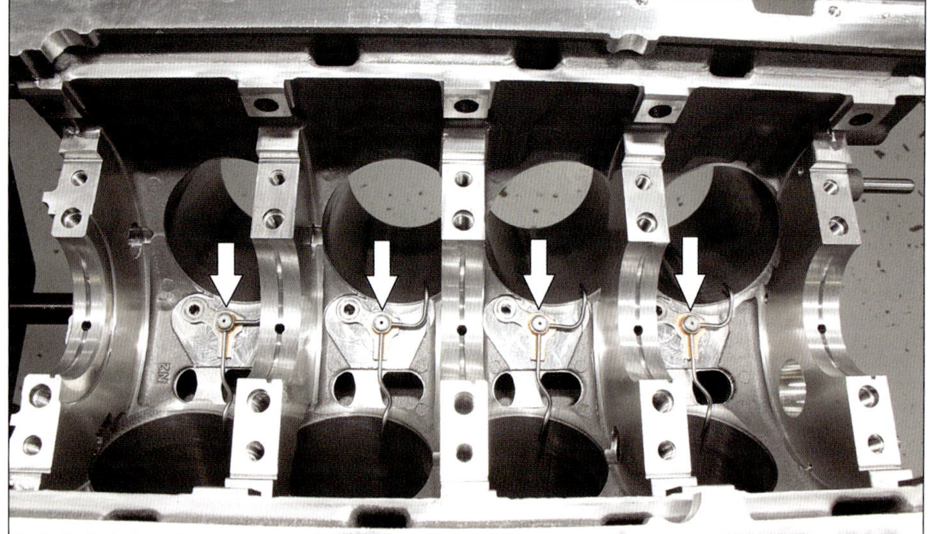

There is some confusion regarding these piston cooling jets, which provide oil cooling via direct-contact cooling between the oil and piston. Coyote blocks from 2011–2013 had them. Then, Ford dropped these cooling jets for a short time. During 2015–2017 production, piston cooling jets returned. Expect to see some blocks with this provision and some without.

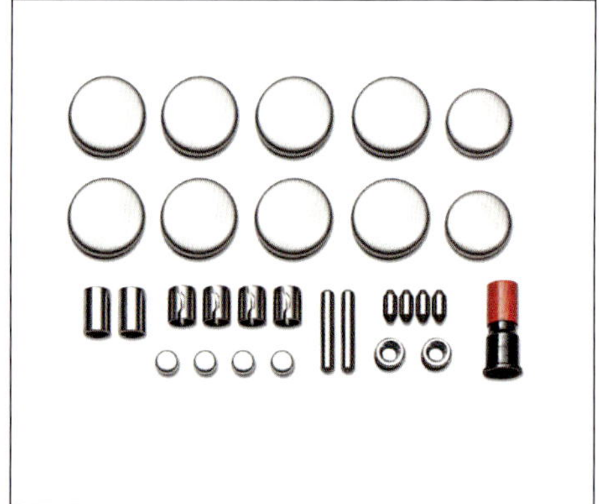

This is the M-6026-BOSS50 block plug and dowel kit for the 2012–2013 Boss 5.0L block. Each kit contains 2 threaded drain plugs, 14 freeze plugs, 4 cylinder-head dowels, 2 bellhousing dowel pins, 4 front/rear-cover dowels, and 1 water-heater tube. (Photo Courtesy Ford Performance)

- Requires head gasket to match cylinder head
- Weight: 203 pounds when finished to a 94-mm bore
- Recommended forged-steel M-6303-M52B or M-6303-M52P crankshaft
- Fits Mustang GT and F-150

It makes more economic sense to begin with a fresh block when considering the cost of machine work and the Coyote's paper-thin cylinder walls. Because the Coyote's cylinder walls are so thin, the most that you can do with an existing Gen 1 or Gen 2 block is a mild honing. The Gen 3 and Voodoo blocks both have plasma-sprayed cylinder walls, which means that they cannot be bored. They must be sleeved. It can also be safely said that all Coyote blocks should be sleeved if you intend to make a lot of power.

The Gen 3 head studs/bolts (12 mm) will fit through the Gen 2 head-bolt holes (Gen 2 blocks get 11-mm bolts/studs), which allows the use of studs/bolts to clamp the heads and block together. Engine builders with whom I have spoken with suggest the Gen 2 head gasket with Gen 2 heads on a Gen 3 block.

Although many people tend to focus on the Mustang GT and performance goals, you can build a powerful Coyote for the F-150 as well. An F-150 Coyote can be planned out for improved low-to-midrange torque with a hotter cam and improved induction to provide more power for the freeway. Just be mindful of fitment and hood clearance issues with the F-150 when you're planning the induction package. When building a stock Coyote for an F-150, all of the same rules for the Mustang GT apply to the F-150. The more durability

that you weave into an F-150, the better your investment.

Sleeves Equal Endurance

Because Coyote engines sport paper-thin cylinder walls (Gen 1 and Gen 2), they don't have the durability of iron- or steel-sleeved aluminum blocks. The Gen 3 blocks have plasma-lined cylinder bores and cannot be bored and honed. They must be sleeved for extraordinary strength.

Thin cylinder walls and plasma-lined cylinders are prone to failure with high-horsepower engines. L&M Engines has the fix for this problem with its exclusive cylinder sleeving service. All blocks are sleeved with L&M's in-house, custom-designed, flanged, double-thick sleeves and installed with a proprietary nitrogen shrink-fit process to ensure proper contact between the engine block and cylinder sleeves. This process allows for optimal heat transfer to the engine water jackets. All L&M blocks come with machined decks with proprietary finish and all bores are semifinished to allow a standard bore size. L&M representatives told me that the company has installed more than 4,000 sleeves without a single failure.

Livernois Motorsports & Engineering is another terrific option to get you into a sleeved Coyote block with premium ductile-iron sleeves with a secure, hatted design to properly index and strengthen the block for Coyote builds exceeding 800 hp. Livernois representatives said that each component is engineered and assembled to work seamlessly as a package.

These Livernois block sleeves can be purchased and get in-house CNC machining and sleeve installation in

your provided block. You must provide a clean and structurally sound (no damage) Coyote block. For more information, contact Livernois (livernoismotorsports.com).

Rotating Assembly

The Coyote's bottom end can withstand 600 hp safely with the stock sintered-metal connecting rods, which are 5.933 inches center to center (the same as the 4.6L SOHC/DOHC Modular engines). Although the size is the same, the Coyote and the 4.6L do not share the same connecting rod.

As I have said before, when planning your Coyote's bottom end, first decide what the engine is ultimately going to be. Planning a street stocker is easy. Planning for greater sums of power in the future takes more extensive thought because it needs a foundation on which it can grow, even though the budget may not currently permit it.

The Coyote's stock crank can withstand in excess of 1,000-plus hp. Some racers have told me it can take up to 1,500 hp. The optional Ford Performance Boss 302 crank (M-6303-M50B) is a cut above the Coyote's standard steel crank. It is money well spent if you're expecting huge performance gains. What makes this crank "race ready" is machining and balancing with chamfered oil holes and polished journals. It is good to go right out of the box, although it is suggested that you measure and inspect it.

The Coyote's sintered-metal rod is similar to the tried-and-proven 4.6L Modular rod, but it will not interchange. The term "powdered metal," is an often misunderstood. Powdered metal actually refers to a

The Coyote's induction-hardened, forged-steel, eight-bolt crankshaft is fully counterweighted and can handle 400 to 1,500 hp. Some engine builders have told me that it can handle 2,000 hp, but I would suggest caution. It has the same dimensions as the 4.6L Modular crank, with 2.652-inch main journals and 2.086-inch rod journals. However, they are not interchangeable with each other. (Photo Courtesy Ford Performance)

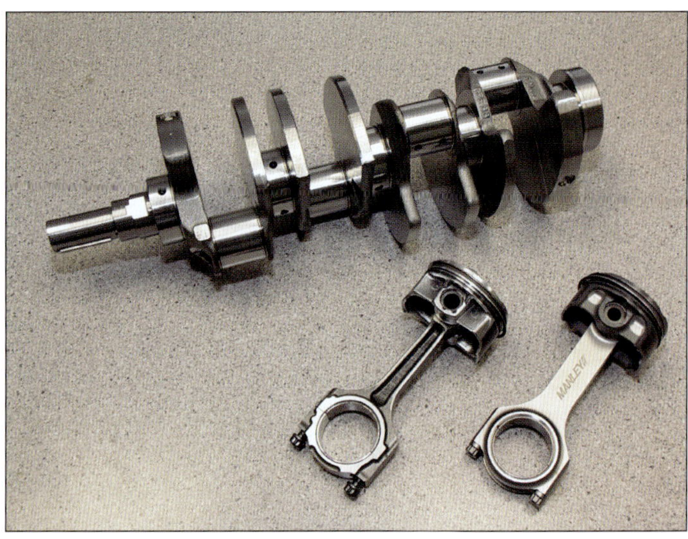

If you expect to go over 600 to 700 hp, opt for aftermarket I-beam or H-beam rods from Manley or Eagle. Forged and coated pistons are a must above 600 to 700 hp.

high-tech forging process, which is stronger than classic I-beam forged connecting rods. The 2012–2013 Boss 302 connecting rod is also a cracked, sintered-metal rod with more metal at the big end, although it is very similar to the standard rod.

You don't always have to opt for the Boss rod when the aftermarket offers a wealth of heavy-duty I-beam and H-beam connecting rods for the Coyote. Scat, Eagle, and Manley offer a generous lineup of rods for Coyote applications. Boosted and nitrous applications must be fitted with heavy-duty I- or H-beam rods.

Manley coated and forged pistons come in a variety of positive and negative dish configurations. D.S.S. is another terrific option for a broad selection of pistons from Summit Racing Equipment. If you're going to boost or use nitrous, consult with your engine builder to determine the safest compression ratio for your application. Expect to see 9.0, 9.5, 10.0, 10.5, 11.0, or 11.5:1 (and higher if need be). Custom configurations are available, depending upon budget.

If you're going to push your Coyote to more than 1,000 hp, Ford Performance's Boss steel crank (M-6303-M50B) is good life insurance.

This dished piston reduces the compression ratio by increasing chamber volume (positive volume) in cc's for boosted and nitrous applications. Acceptable compression ratios for boosted and nitrous applications are anywhere from 8.0:1 to 9.0:1. Summit Racing Equipment offers an enormous array of aftermarket performance pistons from Manley, Mahle, JE Pistons, and D.S.S. Summit Racing Equipment offers hundreds of D.S.S. piston choices in various specifications that can be special ordered.

By contrast, a domed piston (negative volume) raises compression by reducing chamber volume. Coated pistons (right) keep destructive heat away from the piston.

Piston-ring selection is undoubtedly the most challenging because choice depends on how you intend to use the engine. You want ductile iron on top and cast iron in the middle. Extreme performance applications call for steel on top to handle the heat.

Summit Racing Equipment offers Race Series rod bearing sets for the Ford Coyote (SUM-1442HXS). These tri-metal copper lead alloy bearing sets provide a low-friction pivot point between the connecting rod and the crank. This means durability and longevity over stock aluminum bearings under the toughest conditions. Street applications can live happily with stock aluminum bearings.

Summit Racing Equipment's Race Series main bearings (SUM-5655HXS) offer the same benefits as the Race Series rod bearings. They are comprised of the same super-tough tri-metal copper lead alloy, which offers unequaled durability. Aluminum bearings work well in street/strip applications.

Manley forged and coated high-compression pistons are available in two different configurations. There are low-friction slugs with a 1.2-mm, 1.2-mm, and 3.0-mm ring pack. There are basically three Manley forged pistons (at the time that this book was written) for the Coyote in 9.5, 10.0, and 11.0:1 dishes/compression ratios. Coated Manley/MMR pistons can withstand the extremes of heat and pressure. The colorful red coatings protect the piston from the extreme temperatures associated with boost and nitrous.

The Coyote's tight dimensions make it virtually impossible to increase stroke, although it can be stroked. Livernois Motorsports enables you to make the most of the Coyote's displacement with balanced, ready-to-build bottom-end kits for the Ti-VCT. These include custom-dome forged and coated 10.0:1 or 11.0:1 pistons with increased top and second ring-land thicknesses (0.300+ for the top ring, 0.200+ for the second ring), standard 1.5-mm, 1.5-mm, and 3.0-mm ring-package stacks (with a steel top ring), 4340 Livernois/Manley H-beam rods, coated rod bearings (mains additional), and Ford's virtually indestructible forged-steel crankshaft. This is a nice option if you desire the simplicity of a kit.

Piston-Ring Selection

The humble piston ring dates back to 1854, when John Ramsbottom demonstrated the friction-reducing and sealing value of piston rings along with cooling benefits. In those days, it was more about steam engines and less about internal combustion. That quickly changed as internal combustion became more widespread in the late 1800s.

The most significant ring is the top compression ring, which is the first line of defense in cylinder sealing. The top ring faces extremes of heat and pressure. This is true whether you're building a stocker or chasing horsepower. Because the top ring faces extremes of heat and pressure, material and ring face coating are crucial. Are you going racing or facing the grueling demeanor of city traffic? Will your Coyote be operating in dusty conditions? What about short trips and idle time? Idle time in hot conditions will take a toll on engine life.

Piston rings provide cylinder and combustion chamber sealing, which keeps critical heat energy contained where it belongs above the piston, where it becomes propulsion. Any heat energy that escapes past the piston rings is lost power. You will never recover that heat, which was lost to the atmosphere. Did you know that 75 percent of an engine's heat energy is lost and never recovered?

Heat energy contained above the piston becomes power at the crankshaft. Aside from cylinder sealing, piston rings also carry destructive heat away from the piston to the water jacket via the cylinder wall. This controls heat and prevents piston meltdown.

What we want most from piston rings is cylinder sealing along with tension low enough to achieve less friction yet good cylinder sealing. In Detroit's quest for efficiency and lower emissions, we live in an age of skinny, low-tension compression rings that are sometimes as narrow as 0.023 inch (0.6 mm). This works if you have perfectly honed cylinder walls and a low-friction surface. Without that, rings tend to distort and will lose optimum cylinder sealing.

Proper ring selection comes from understanding ring function, material, piston design, and bore dynamics. It's a mouthful, but it's important to understand. Pistons, rings, and cylinder bores must have a perfect marriage to function properly and keep heat energy where it belongs— above the piston.

It begins with ring selection and proper engine break-in, which are critical to endurance and reliable ring function. The type of piston ring that you choose depends on how you intend to use your Coyote. Mild street performance engines, as we see in the F-150, call for a more vanilla ring package than supercharged, turbocharged, or nitrous-fed extreme racing engines. Racing engines demand a much stouter ring package, where rings must be able to withstand the extremes of heat and pressure. The ring that is chosen boils down to how much power you want to make. If the engine is bone stock as delivered from the factory and needs freshening up, all it is going to need are iron or ductile-iron rings.

If you're planning nitrous or forced induction, a top compression ring that is capable of withstanding the heat and pressure associated with these dynamics is needed. This calls for high-end materials, according to Total Seal. Total Seal suggests using its AP stainless-steel top ring with physical vapor deposition (PVD) for forced-induction (boost) and nitrous applications.

Total Seal's high-performance piston ring sets include an AP steel top ring that has been coated using PVD-applied C-33 chromium nitride antifriction coating for not only greater efficiency but also for durability. Total Seal's C-33 coating is easy on cylinder walls, while the steel top ring handles extreme pressures. Napier secondary rings and three-piece stainless oil control rings are standard with the AP stainless-steel ring set.

Pistons and rings are generally sold in sets unless you're reusing old pistons or are choosing a different type of ring. Manufacturers, such as Speed Pro, sell pistons and rings as sets for your convenience. This

This heat-treated, billet-steel timing gear (left, part number 467891) from Modular Motorsports Racing (MMR) is a direct replacement for 2011–2014 Coyote's stock crankshaft gears. This hardened-steel gear is proven to 3,000-plus hp and 10,000 rpm, according to MMR. This particular gear will not fit 2015–2024 Coyote engines. Order MMR part number 467892 for anything after 2014.

makes piston and ring selection easy for engine builders. Look at what the manufacturer suggests for the type of driving that you intend to do and make a decision.

It is important to how well the piston rings mate to the hone of the bore. Your machine shop should have a part average test (PAT) gauge to accurately measure the final hone's surface roughness. Total Seal said that typical values (measured in microinches) for general performance applications should be around RPK 8-12, RK 20-30, and RVK 30-50. Is your machine shop capable of this type of work? Not all of them are. If a machine shop can finish late-model engines with their thin rings to maintain original emissions compliance and factory tolerances, the answer is affirmative.

There have been great recent advancements in piston-ring technology. Ring materials, coatings, edge profiles, and even ring thickness have all seen vast improvements in oil-control, sealing, and wear. However, it only works when executed properly.

Most of you reading this book are building street and occasional weekend strip engines. You want power for the freeway and traffic light. I am often asked what the best ring is to use. The choice depends on how you intend to use the engine. What is the power expected, compression ratio, fuel use expected, and power adder that you might be thinking about?

What you want most in a ring package is cylinder sealing, durability, minimal friction and blowby, and longevity. Piston-ring types include cast iron, ductile iron, and steel. Steel is best for extremes. Chromoly has toughness and internal lubrication in its molybdenum content. It endures.

Today's pistons offer the best technology that has ever been incorporated into a power-making slug. As a result, a lot of thought has gone into their design. Each piston employs three types of rings: a top compression ring, a secondary ring, and an oil-control ring. Each ring package performs a specific duty. The top ring is exposed to the heat extremes of combustion while maintaining cylinder sealing.

Although many of us identify the secondary ring as a "compression" ring, that is not what it does. It is a popular misconception. The secondary ring provides cylinder sealing and it controls oil. It carries oil up the cylinder wall for lubrication purposes while carrying oil back down the cylinder wall to the sump. The secondary ring is also made of a different material than the top ring while assisting in heat transfer to the water jackets. At the bottom of the ring package is the oil-control ring, which carries oil to the cylinder wall.

Each ring is comprised of different materials. With a stocker, there is a ductile-iron top ring, cast-iron secondary ring, and the composite two-piece oil-control ring package. The one-piece oil-control ring that was used many years ago is not common today. The two-piece oil-control ring consists of a coil spring of sorts to provide tension to hold the ring against the cylinder wall. Three-piece oil-control rings are most common today, consisting of two rings and an expander in between for tension to hold the rings against the cylinder

Most Coyote builds can get along fine with a stock harmonic damper. Unless you're going racing, you do not need an SFI-rated damper.

The aftermarket offers a wealth of harmonic dampers with different approaches to design and function. I prefer the ATI Super Damper, which appears to make the most sense for form and function. In addition, the Super Damper is rebuildable and easy to service.

Choose an SFI-rated Harmonic Damper

If you're going racing or building a street/strip Coyote, use a race-proven harmonic damper. The aftermarket offers a nice variety of harmonic dampers for the Coyote. The ATI Super Damper is optimal for Coyote applications and is the most widely trusted. The Super Damper is engineered to dampen crank twist, and it exceeds SFI 18.1 specifications. Although the stock Coyote harmonic damper does an excellent job, it is suggested that you opt for an SFI-rated damper if power is going to be pushed above 800 hp. ■

No matter how much power is planned for a Coyote, spend the money on oiling-system improvements, such as a high-pressure oil pump with a hardened-steel rotor. This particular pump in red is from MMR with hardened-steel internals. Melling also offers a high-pressure oil pump with billet-steel internals for the Coyote.

It isn't even necessary to buy a steel-billet-rotor oil pump. The pump can be upgraded with a hardened-steel oil-pump-rotor package, which is available from several sources, and it will fit the factory oil pump. This steel billet rotor kit is available from Boundary Racing Pumps, which creates a lot of Coyote perfor-

mance products. These brute Black gears feature a unique ported design that is treated with MartenWear and a cold-finish surface finish. (Photo Courtesy Wes Duenkel)

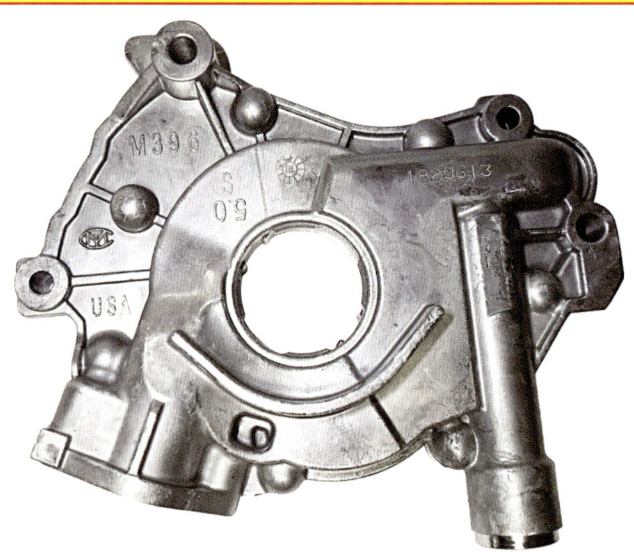

The Coyote oil pump already delivers plenty of volume. What is needed most in a pump is the pressure that will be had from the Moroso 22203 Racing Oil Pump. This is a nice piece, whether you're building a stocker or going racing. I like this pump for what it delivers for less than $300.

Oil filters are not all created equal. Ford Motorcraft and Ford Performance oil filters are among the best filters. They employ synthetic-polymer/cellulose-fiber blend media, a heavy-gauge base and canister for higher burst strength and impulse fatigue resistance, a high-quality silicone anti-drainback valve, non-stick sealing gasket for ease of installation and removal, and long life with synthetic motor oils. They also offer up to 50-percent more filtering capacity than standard oil filters. The same can be said for Wix and K&N filters.

walls to wipe oil down and off the walls.

Ductile iron is a form of cast iron that is known for impact and fatigue resistance, elongation resistance, and wear resistance as a result of spherical (round) graphite structures in its metallurgy. This makes ductile iron an excellent material for the top ring. Ductile iron is also known as ductile cast iron, spheroidal graphite cast iron, or nodular cast iron.

Another element that is known as "ring profile" is important to know during ring selection. Ring profile is the outer edge of a ring that maintains the seal against both the cylinder wall and the combustion chamber. Ring manufacturers employ different faces or profiles for cylinder sealing, oil control, and assorted other purposes. When you're examining piston rings, it is not always possible to see—let alone understand—these profiles. They will use a dot or the word "top" on the ring face to properly orient the ring installation in the piston because you don't want to install rings upside down.

A square-face piston ring is known for positive sealing, but it eventually wears into a barrel shape. This is common with the top compression ring, which takes a beating. A barrel-shaped piston ring as a top ring yields better wear qualities. Secondary rings are typically taper-faced, not for compression sealing but for wiping oil down the cylinder wall. Another style is the Napier type, which is also located in the second ring groove to help wipe oil down the cylinder wall.

There has long been a discussion addressing ring thickness. For many years, piston-ring sizing has been in fractional SAE measurements (5/64-, 1/16-, 3/16-, and 0.043-inch sizes). Today, ring thickness is metric and all about reduced friction. The Coyote is certainly a metric engine, with ring thicknesses of 1.2 mm for the top and secondary rings and 3.0 mm thicknesses. With reduced internal friction, greater sums of power have been achieved.

Lubrication

The Coyote's oiling system is one of the best that Ford has ever created because it was born to be a high-performance engine. Choose a high-volume pump with hardened-steel internals even with a stock F-150/Mustang GT application. The existing pump can be upgraded with hardened-steel internals. There are a few pan and pickup options to complement the pump.

Pan selection depends upon the kind of driving that is intended for the vehicle. Stock applications in the F-150 and Mustang GT are easy picks. For greater capacity for fleet use or long, hot idle conditions, opt for a deeper pan with greater

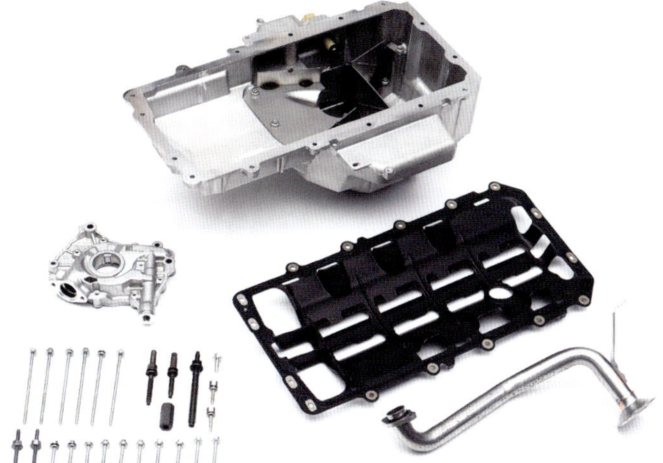

The M-6675-M52S oil pan kit from Ford Performance is a good way to cover the entire oiling system in one purchase. It fits all 5.2L and 5.0L Coyote engines and includes the production 2020 GT500 high-output oil pump, pickup tube, oil pan, windage tray/gasket and all of the installation hardware. I like the cast/machined aluminum oil pan, which employs the FP350S race car–inspired baffle system to keep the pickup submerged during cornering, braking, and acceleration. (Photo Courtesy Ford Performance)

This is the Ford Performance GT350 5.2L oil pan and pump kit (M-6675-M52) for all 5.2L and 5.0L Coyote engines. This kit includes the production GT350 high-output oil pump, oil pan, high-pressure sending unit, and all of the hardware. This race-ready composite oil pan includes integral windage and slosh baffles with the oil pickup integrated into the pan sump. (Photo Courtesy Ford Performance)

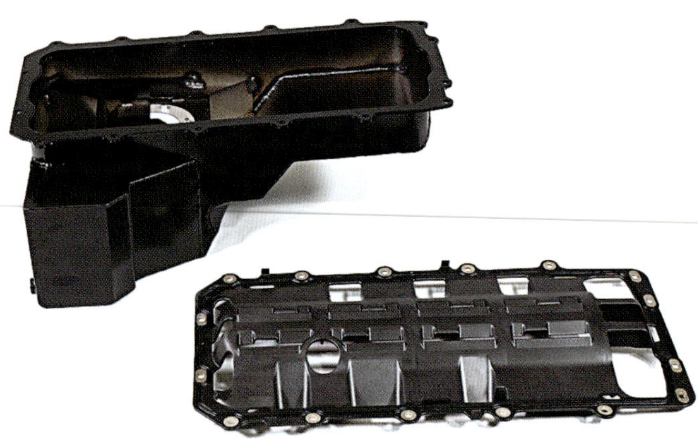

This is the M-6675-M52RR 5.0L/5.2L Road Race Pan that is used on the Shelby FP350S race car. It is fitted with an internal baffle and trap-door system that is designed for road race applications to keep oil around the pickup during hard cornering. It holds 12 quarts. This is a nice piece with black powder coating and a pipe-plug fitting for the oil-temperature gauge. It does not include the pickup. For 2011–2017 5.0L Gen 1 and Gen 2 Coyotes, order the M-6622-M50RR pickup tube. For 2018–2021 Gen 3 5.0L applications, order the M-6622-M52RR pickup tube. For the more robust 5.2L engine, order the M-6622-M52RR pickup tube. (Photo Courtesy Ford Performance)

The 5.2L Coyote GT350 oil pan and pump kit (M-6675-M52) is a nice piece for a Coyote project. It will fit all 5.2L and 5.0L Coyote engines. It includes the production GT350 high-output oil pump, pan, and a high-pressure oil-pressure sending unit and related hardware. I like this unique composite oil pan, as it features windage and slosh baffles with the oil pickup integrated into the floor of the pan for easy service and installation. This pan is used on the Ford Performance M-6007-A52XS crate engine. (Photo Courtesy Ford Performance)

The Ford Performance engine oil-to-water cooler (M-6642-MB) was original equipment on the 2012–2013 Boss 302 Mustang and fits all 2011–2014 Gen 1 Coyote engines. This is an easy modification to make if you have a Gen 1 engine. (Photo Courtesy Ford Performance)

If you intend to run an external oil cooler, plan on the M-6881-M50A oil line adapter for 2015–2024 Coyote engines. This is a nice billet piece for Gen 2 and Gen 3 engines. It will not fit Gen 1 2011–2014 Coyote blocks. (Photo Courtesy Ford Performance)

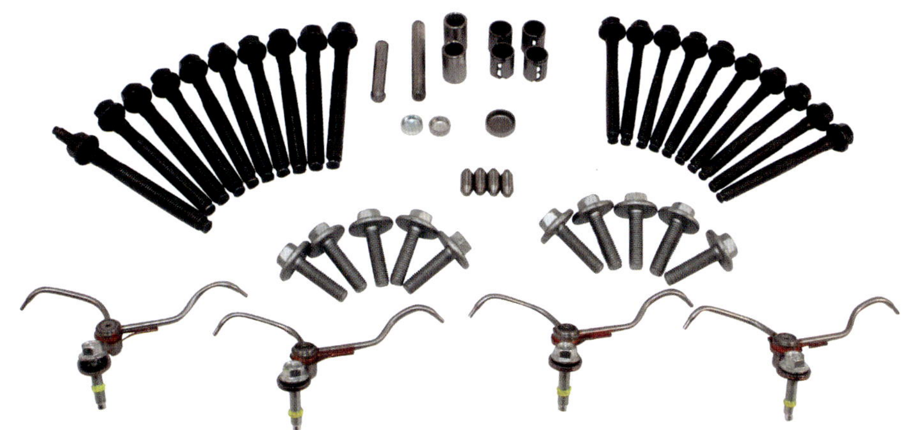

The 2011–2017 5.0L Coyote block hardware kit (M-6026-A50A) has virtually everything needed to complete a 2011–2017 5.0L Coyote engine build. This kit includes outer main cap bolts, inner main cap bolts, side main cap bolts, the oil pickup stud, piston cooling jets and hardware, the 19-mm main oil gallery cup plug, 14-mm main oil gallery cup plug, 3/4-inch water-jacket pipe plug, transmission dowels, front/rear cover dowels, cylinder-head dowels, and timing-chain-guide dowels. (Photo Courtesy Ford Performance)

capacity to ensure that the Coyote engine always has a generous supply of oil. The deeper pan provides capacity, and it serves as a heat sink to shed excess heat. For road racing, opt for a pan designed with baffling for hard corners and straights. Drag racing calls for a deep-sump pan, where oil stays where it belongs under hard acceleration.

Cylinder-Head Selection

The Coyote cylinder head was an innovative design when this engine was introduced in 2011. It was a well-thought-out casting with an abundance of engineering knowledge going in. At the time, the aftermarket considered offering a Coyote head but soon realized that it couldn't improve on Ford's factory casting. The good news is that the aftermarket offers excellent CNC-ported and massaged Coyote cylinder heads.

The Coyote head has only improved over time with a wealth of options for the engine builder. It is important to know that Coyote heads are left-side (driver-side) and right-side (passenger-side) specific regardless of generation and marked with an "L" or "R" to indicate the

The Gen 2 Coyote head (M-6049-M50A) features the extended intake flange for the CMCV intake manifold. This revision creates interference issues with the 2011–2012 intake manifold due to its extensive ribbing.

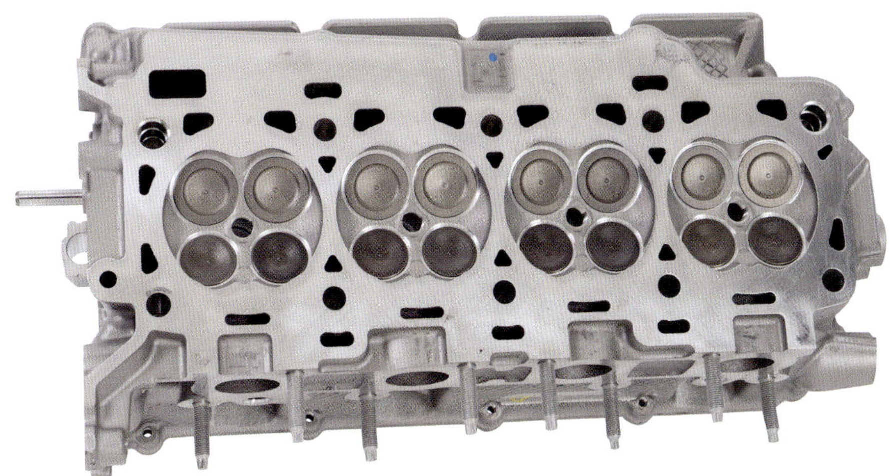

The revised 2015–2017 57-cc chamber yields larger 1.485-inch (37.7-mm) intake valves and 1.248-inch (31.7-mm) exhaust valves.

side. The 2011–2014 57-cc Coyote combustion chamber offered the best characteristics ever in a Ford chamber when it was introduced. Spark plugs were centered in the middle of the chamber amid two 1.460-inch (37.0-mm) intake and two 1.220-inch (31.0-mm) exhaust valves. Ford managed to go one better with head refinements to follow.

Gen 2 2015–2017

The revised 2015–2017 Coyote cylinder head with high-flow intake ports (196-cc volume) offers stiffer valve springs, larger 1.485-inch (37.7-mm) intake and 1.248-inch (31.7-mm) exhaust valves, a 57-cc chamber, and a wider intake port flange to accommodate the CMCV induction system introduced that year. The Gen 2 head casting delivers improved intake-port flow and is undoubtedly the best baseline head produced to date.

Gen 3 2018–2023

The most current Coyote head is the Gen 3 dual-injection cylinder head that was designed for direct injection (M-6049-M50B [right] and M-6050-M50B [left]). This is surely a different Coyote head with provisions for both direct injection and port injection. The Gen 3 Coyote's proven valvetrain remains but with stiffer springs for a higher 7,500-rpm redline. This head makes a whole lot of power.

The Gen 3 combustion chamber has been revised to accommodate high-pressure direct injection along with larger valves and improved airflow that is on a par with the legendary GT350 CNC-ported Voodoo

Total Engine Airflow (TEA) is one option for getting CNC-ported Coyote heads that have Ferrea stainless-steel valves. These are nice, hand-crafted pieces that can bolt onto a Coyote. Make sure that the valve springs match your cam profile. TEA is one of several sources for CNC-ported heads.

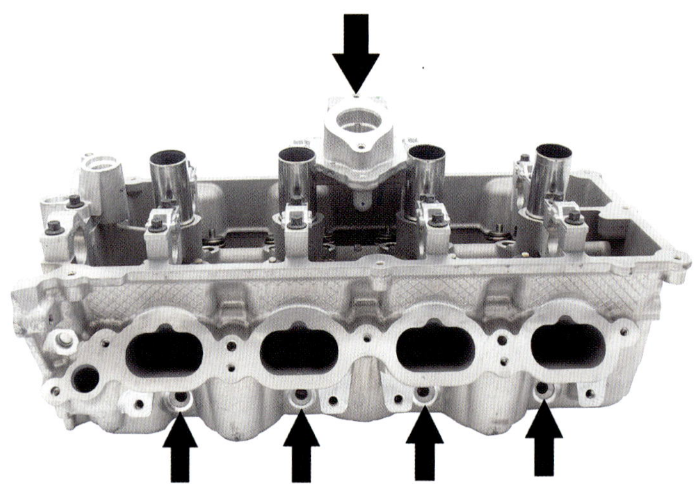

The most dramatic cylinder-head change to date has been the dual-injection Gen 3 Coyote head that was introduced in 2018. It was replaced for 2024 with the improved Gen 4 cylinder head with taller cam towers and cam seals. The most obvious difference is the passenger-side Gen 3 and Gen 4 head with the direct-injection pump boss. Along the surface are the direct-injector ports.

TEA intake ports are not just CNC machined, they are also hand-ported to achieve a buttery-smooth finish. This removes all lines and ridges that can cause turbulence.

The driver-side (left-hand) Gen 3 cylinder head lacks the pump boss that is on the passenger's side. However, it does have the four direct-injector ports along the intake side (the exhaust side is shown).

The Gen 3 chamber is similar to the Gen 1 and Gen 2. However, it has the direct-injector port alongside both intake valves (arrow). The Gen 3 also has port injection, which is what the engine operates on most of the time. Direct injection steps in when additional power is required. If you examine earlier Gen 1 and Gen 2 head chambers, there is a provision for the direct injector in each chamber.

heads. Combustion-chamber volume is 55.9 cc, which is less than the Gen 1 and Gen 2's 57 cc, to increase compression to 12.0:1.

Gen 3 intake valve sizing is 1.485-inch (37.7-mm), which makes it 4 mm larger than the Gen 2. The intake-port volume has been increased to 205 cc. Exhaust valves are 1.259 inches (32 mm), which is 22 mm larger than the Gen 2.

The driver-side Gen 3 head is a completely different casting compared with the Gen 1 and Gen 2. Exhaust cam number-1 journals are larger with the Gen 3. The exhaust-cam phaser solenoid has been relocated to the cylinder head. The Gen 3 cylinder will not fit the Gen 1 or Gen 2 block. You must use the Gen 3 block.

Gen 4 2024–2025

If you think that Ford couldn't improve on the Gen 3 (2015–2023) Coyote head, Ford's engineering brain trust took this high-flow cylinder head casting a step further for 2024. The casting gained revised cam towers and caps, camshaft seals, and other nice refinements. Aside from these cylinder-head refinements, there is little else.

Shelby GT350 Voodoo Heads

There's also the Shelby GT350 Voodoo 5.2L head from Ford Performance, which means even greater power from a Coyote engine. It is important to understand what makes the Voodoo head different. It is an entirely different casting with its own valvetrain geometry, which means that these parts do not interchange with other Coyote valvetrain components.

The GT350 Voodoo has precision CNC porting right out of the box, which contributes significantly to airflow and power. It is bolt-on ready. You can expect to see more than 320-cfm intake flow and 220-cfm exhaust flow using these heads. Although you can bolt these heads onto the 5.0L Coyote block, consider building a 5.2L short-block (larger bores) to go with these heads to avoid valve shrouding issues. These heads have smaller CNC-machined chambers and more generous valve sizing than the standard Coyote.

The GT350 head (M-6049-M52 and M-6050-M52) comes semifinished. It has larger 38.3-mm intake valves and 32.5-mm exhaust valves. It also calls for GT350-specific camshafts, rocker arms, and hydraulic lash adjusters, which are not interchangeable with other Coyote heads. These heads come from Ford Performance without camshafts (M-6550-M52), rocker arms, and lash adjusters (M-6564-M52). All must be ordered separately.

Boss 302 Head

The 2012–2013 Boss 302 cylinder-head casting (M-6049-M50 [right] and M-6050-M50 [left]) is a different head casting made of an improved 356 aluminum alloy (versus 319 for the base Coyote heads) with CNC-machined ports and chambers. According to Ford Performance, there's a measure of copper in the 356 alloy, which improves heat transfer under extreme conditions.

In addition, the Boss 302 head casting employs a thicker deck for exceptional strength around the 57-cc chambers. The result is one of the best Coyote head castings that was originally available from Ford Performance. It is no longer available from Ford, but these heads can be found in inventories, at swap meets, and in online auctions. Also note that this is a Gen 1 Coyote head casting void of the Gen 2's extended intake-port flanges. It will not work with the Gen 2 CMCV induction system.

Gen 3 5.2L GT500 Head

This is the upgraded version of the Ford Performance (M-6049-M52A [right] and M-6050-M52A [left]) 5.2L cylinder head, which is also the production 2021–2024 GT500. It is the improved high-performance 5.2L head casting, which provides added strength and increased size of the central cooling passages to support high-power engine builds.

You can expect CNC fully ported intake and exhaust ports as well as combustion chambers. In addition, it has larger port sizing than the standard 5.0L Coyote cylinder heads, with larger 1.504-inch (38.2-mm) intake and 1.386-inch (32.5-mm) exhaust valves. The improved valvetrain geometry allows for higher valve lift in these castings. They also come with lightweight, hollow-stem intake valves and sodium-filled exhaust valves for extreme duty along with stiffer exhaust springs, improved valve guides, and upgraded exhaust-valve seats.

These heads arrive loaded except for camshafts, rocker arms, and lash adjusters. When building a 5.0L Coyote, a unique camshaft (M-6550-M52 or M-6550-M52A) is needed due to valvetrain geometry differences. It is also going to need 5.2L rocker arms and lash adjusters (M-6564-M52). Finally, it is critical to check piston-to-valve clearances with these heads.

Camshaft and Valvetrain

Camshaft selection seems like wild/weird science. However, there is a motive to the madness of cam profile and function. Camshaft selection has a direct effect on an engine's personality. Personality is all about valve timing events (lift, duration, overlap, and lobe separation angle) and how they relate to the timing of the combustion cycle (suck, squeeze, bang, and blow).

Lift is lobe lift and valve lift in a conventional pushrod OHV engine. Lobe lift is the amount of lift at the cam lobe. Valve lift is the enhanced lift that comes with rocker-arm ratio, where lift is multiplied in a pushrod engine. However, this is not the case with the Coyote. Since the Coyote is an overhead-cam engine, finger followers (not rocker arms) open the valves the same amount as lobe lift. Finger followers do not multiply valve lift.

Duration is how long the valves are off their seats and how that is

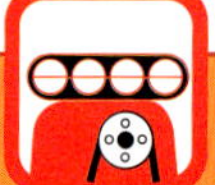

Ported Coyote Heads

You can purchase CNC/hand-ported Coyote cylinder heads from Livernois Motorsports, Frankenstein Engine Dynamics, CHI, JPC Racing, Mustang 6G, L&M Engines, Total Engine Airflow (TEA), and more. TEA makes a nice CNC-ported Coyote head with Ferrea stainless-steel valves.

L&R Engines in Los Angeles opted for a pair of TEA CNC-ported heads for a build in Southern California. These are nice hand-crafted pieces that you can bolt onto a Coyote. Airflow improvements are in the 4- to 5-percent range. The TEA intake ports are not only CNC machined but they are also hand-worked to remove all lines and ridges that can cause turbulence. ■

Camshaft selection requires homework and consultation with cam manufacturer helplines. Remember that tech-help people are also salespeople. Look to seasoned Coyote builders and racers for experienced advice. Street/strip Coyotes call for a modest cam profile (even stock) where low-to-midrange torque is paramount. Drag racing calls for a horsepower-focused cam, where peak horsepower and torque arrive at the same RPM range. Road-racing engines call for both torque and horsepower. You want torque coming out of the turns and horsepower for the straights. Choose wisely. (Photo Courtesy Comp Cams)

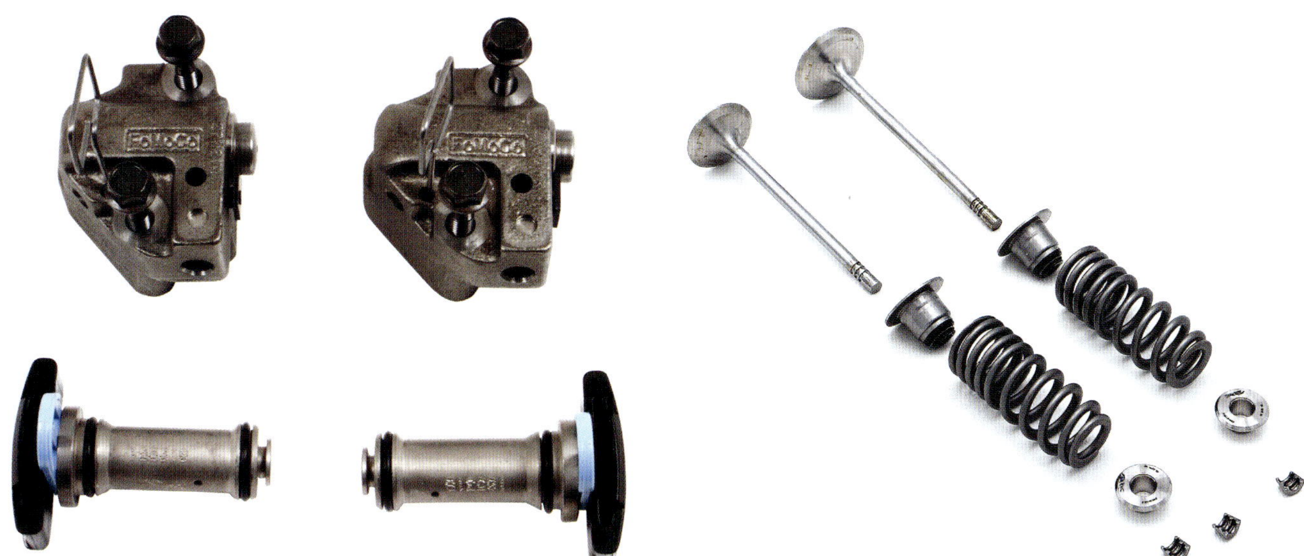

Timing components (chains, guides, tensioners, and phasers) can be purchased as a complete set (including phasers) or individually as needed. I will stress again the use of Ford Motorcraft and Ford Performance timing components because they offer durability and proper fitment. (Photo Courtesy Ford Performance)

Unless you've opted for new heads, expect to replace all valves and valvetrain components in the interest of durability. Much depends on the overall condition of the heads and components. Springs should be compatible with the cam profile that you have chosen. (Photo Courtesy Ford Performance)

timed with piston travel. Overlap is the moment when both valves are off their seats at the same time in that transition between the exhaust and intake strokes. Valve overlap allows the fresh air/fuel charge entering the chamber to scavenge (move) hot exhaust gasses out of the chamber. At the same time that exhaust gasses are exiting, they also draw in fresh air and fuel.

Lobe separation angle is the distance in degrees between the centerlines of both cam lobes. A high lobe separation angle (wider) gives better idle quality and an improved intake manifold vacuum. However, a high lobe separation angle with excessive duration can hurt horsepower and torque numbers.

So, what does any of this have to do with cam selection? Plenty. Cam selection comes from understanding what camshafts do and how they affect valve timing events, drivability, and power. You need to under-

Beehive valve springs are the best for any Coyote build because they can stand the high revs, even with a stocker. In addition, they're quite stable at high RPM. (Photo Courtesy Ford Performance)

stand all of this while selecting a cam profile and be willing to take good professional advice from an engine builder with a lot of experience.

Cam manufacturers such as Comp Cams, Crane, Isky, Steeda, Ford Performance, Livernois Motorsports, Roush, and Modular Motorsports Racing all have technical support staff ready to help you select the right cam profile. The main thing to remember about technical support is that they are also sales staff, and that can affect the information you receive. They are paid to sell camshaft kits and parts. How-

ever, they're not always going to give the right advice. Seek advice from a variety of sources to learn what will work best for your application.

There are suitable off-the-shelf grinds from which to choose, ranging from mild street to all-out racing because Coyote engines serve many purposes in both trucks and cars in factory applications and vehicle swaps. Good drivability is desired for the daily commute and weekend getaways, while enjoying the benefits of a burst of power when it is needed most on the freeway and Saturday-night bracket racing.

The biggest mistake that Coyote enthusiasts make when planning a build is ordering too much cam for

The Coyote calls for M-6571-A50 valve seals from Ford Performance. Valve seals are also available from a variety of sources, such as Summit Racing Equipment. (Photo Courtesy Ford Performance)

Extend your reach with the Ford Performance M-6010-M52A 12-mm long head-bolt kit for the 5.0L and 5.2L Coyote engines. These extra-long torque-to-yield head bolts come in a package of 20 that fits 2018–2024 Gen 3 and 4 Coyote engines. They provide greater clamping power than previous 5.0L and 5.2L bolts. For a complete head changing kit for 5.2L applications, order the M-6067-M52B kit. This will not fit the 2015–2018 5.2L or Ford Performance M-6010-M52 blocks.

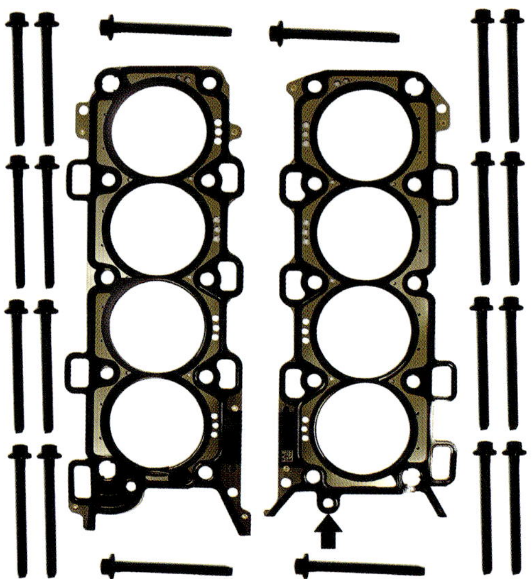

The gasket set that is chosen depends on the generation. This is the head change kit (M-6067-M50) from Ford Performance for 2015–2017 Gen 2 Coyotes. Gen 1 has a (2011–2014) a standalone kit, as does Gen 3 (2018–2024) with dual injection. You're going to want all of the gaskets necessary for a complete Coyote build. (Photo Courtesy Ford Performance)

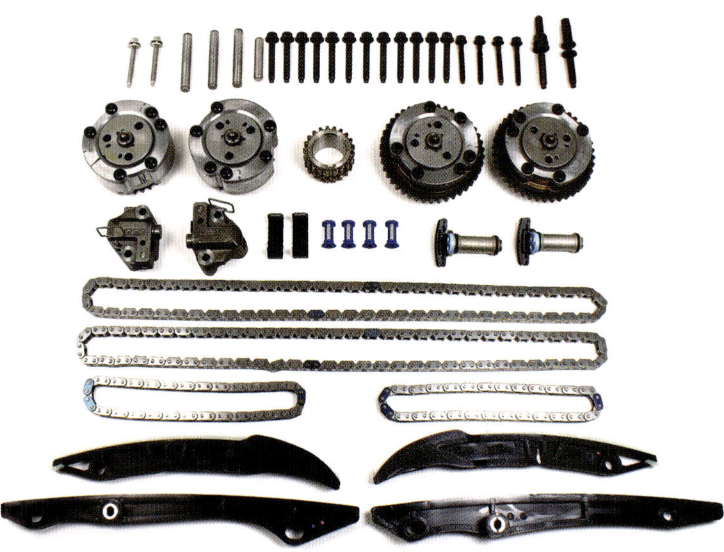

Start fresh with new timing components unless you're working with a low-mileage core. When building a Gen 1 Coyote, use M-6004-A504 (2011–2014), M-6004-A5015 (2014–2017) for the Gen 2 Coyote, or M-6004-A5018 (2018–2024) for the Gen 3 and 4 Coyotes. Ford Performance also offers the M-6004-A5015B high-performance kit for the Gen 2. These are complete kits with everything that is needed. (Photo Courtesy Ford Performance)

the kind of driving expected. Then, they end in traffic frustrated with engine smoothness. Forget bench racing and big numbers to impress your friends. You want civilized street performance with a smooth idle in stopped traffic. This is why stock Ford cam grinds work exceedingly well. You don't have to get crazy with lift, duration, and lobe separation.

In truth, most Coyote builds never rev beyond 5,000 rpm and spend most of their time between idle and 2,500 rpm. The beauty of the Coyote is its rugged demeanor and raw ability to make power when it is needed as it came from the factory. Factory cam grinds deliver plentiful street power without resorting to a cam swap.

The aftermarket offers a broad range of cam profiles for the Coyote. For example, Comp Cams offers the new CR-series line, which was designed to improve stock Gen 2 Coyote performance without modifications to cylinder heads or cam phasers. You can expect a broader torque curve with the CR series. The CR-series cams feature faster ramps with more lift along with more area under the lift curve. In addition, the Comp CR-series camshafts can be installed with stock Gen 2 valve springs along with the Ford Gen 2 mid-lock phaser system without limiters or any modifications. Comp said that three profiles are available for naturally aspirated engines, and an additional two grinds are available specifically for blower applications. For greater valve-spring pressure and higher RPM, Comp offers two spring kits (26113 and 26125) designed to withstand high revs.

Comp offers its Thumpr- and Mutha Thumpr-series cam kits for serious racers who will operate their Coyote at high RPM, where peak horsepower comes in around 6,500 to 7,500 rpm. They will be running boost and/or nitrous, where greater amounts of lift, duration, and wide lobe separation angle will be needed. This is not the grind wanted for an F-150 work truck. Plan for where an engine lives most of the time. Street and weekend racing calls for a cam profile that you can live with in both environments.

Ford Performance Boss Cam

The 2012–2013 Boss 302 camshaft kit (M-6550-M50EXT and M-6550-M50BINT) offers more lift and duration for improved performance without having to use cam phaser locks. Not only were these cams used in the 2012–2013 Boss 302 Coyote but they were also used in the Cobra Jet. They are good cams for the money with few modifications required.

With the Coyote, you should get used to new terms. Your planning should include finger followers and lash adjusters. Finger followers are rocker arms, but they do not multiply lift. Lash adjusters are hydraulic lifters, but they work differently than lifters. Cam lobes ride the roller "finger" followers, which push down on the valve and spring.

I suggest the replacement of valvetrain components, such as hydraulic lash adjustors, where wear issues aren't always as apparent. (Photo Courtesy Ford Performance)

An area to watch closely is the finger followers (rocker arms), which employ rollers supported by needle bearings inside. When these followers get a lot of miles on them, the needle bearings can wear out and stop supporting the rollers. When this happens, the roller gives out, and the follower falls into the cam lobe. (Photo Courtesy Ford Performance)

Cam phasers can be reused, depending upon wear and condition. It is good insurance to replace them during an engine build. As a rule, Gen 1 and Gen 2 phasers don't exhibit a failure pattern.

Chains and Guides

The 5.0L Ti-VCT Coyote has a series of timing chains and guides similar to the 4.6L/5.4L Modular engine. Chain tensioners are oil-pressure actuated, just like the 4.6L and 5.4L Modular engines. Chains travel through

Boss 302 Camshaft Specifications	
Intake	Exhaust
Lift: 12 mm (0.472 inch)	Lift: 13 mm (0.512 inch)
Duration: 260 degrees	Duration: 263 degrees

The Gen 3 Coyote phasers have both oil-pressure and return-spring operation (like the 3V Modular) where the exhaust cam phaser return spring can fail from cyclic fatigue. I haven't seen a failure pattern yet with Gen 3 phasers, but you can bet that it is coming. (Photo Courtesy Ford Performance)

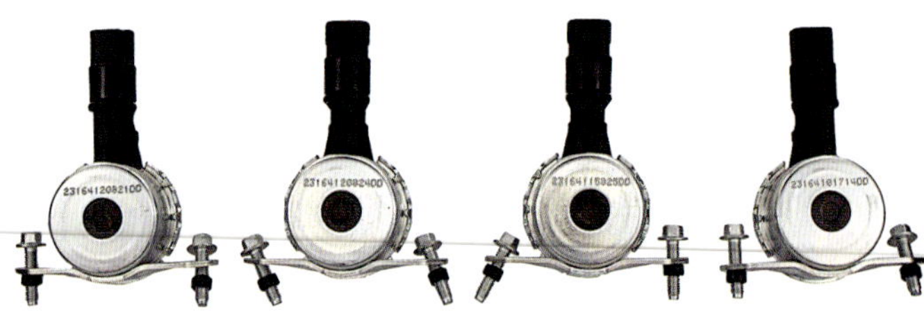

Opt for a set of 5.0L Coyote high-strength variable-cam-timing (VCT) solenoids (M-6297-M50A). They are stronger than the stock solenoids. These VCT solenoids have stronger mounts and can handle the punishment of racing. They fit 2013–2017 5.0L engines (both F-150 and Mustang GT) and the 2015–2018 GT350 5.2L engines.

plastic guides between the crank and the camshaft sprockets. Installation and proper timing of these chains and sprockets is simple if you take your time and pay close attention to what you're doing.

It can be said with confidence that the stock Ford chain guides will take tremendous amounts of abuse in excess of 1,000 to 1,500 hp. They are "life of the engine" pieces that are engineered to last 100,000 to 200,000 miles in normal use. However, if you don't stay on top of oil and filter changes and use synthetic engine oil as a matter of routine, they will not last.

Modular Mustang Racing (MMR) has billet chain guides for Coyote projects for those looking for more durability than the factory pieces. The MMR pieces can be found in a lot of drag racing and road racing Coyotes. For street only, it is possible to get by with the original Ford parts M-6004-A504 complete chain drive kit.

When opting for an aftermarket high-performance camshaft,

Depending on the generation of the build and the vehicle, you may need to invest in a complete Ford Performance timing and cam cover kit to get it compatible with both the vehicle and the engine.

some kits call for the installation of cam phaser locks to keep timing consistent and to eliminate the risk of valve-to-piston contact. Comp Cams has an adjustable cam-phaser-lock system that enables one to lock in cam timing. In addition, the lock system can be fine-tuned for individual requirements.

Cam selection is quite simple when you understand what you want the engine to do. Street cams should have a good measure of low-end torque. Peak torque should roll in at around 2,500 to 3,000 rpm, with peak horsepower at 6,000 to 6,500 rpm. Road-race cams need peak torque for coming out of the turns (3,500 to 4,500 rpm) and

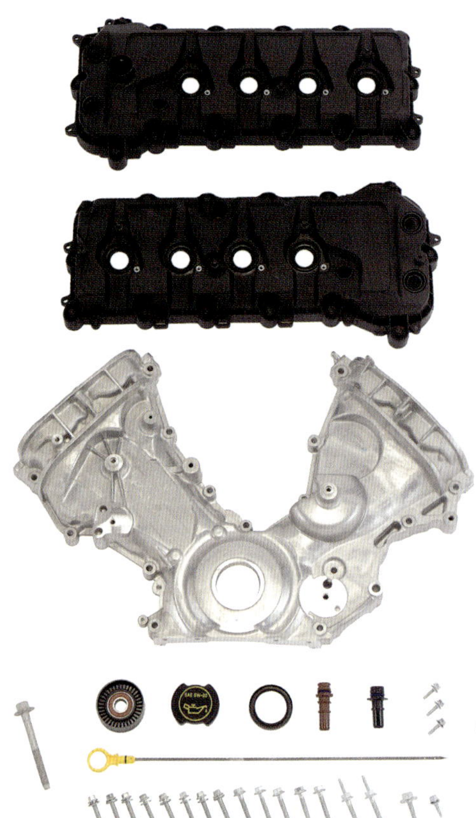

peak horsepower for the straights (6,500 to 7,500 rpm). Drag-racing cam profiles witness peak horsepower and torque at the same RPM range: 6,500 to 7,500 rpm. Of course, results vary from engine to engine.

Phaser limiters and adjustable phaser locks allow independent control over intake and exhaust centerlines and eliminate piston-to-valve clearance issues that can occur with larger aftermarket camshafts. Comp Cams phaser limiters for the Coyote engines physically limit maximum cam phasing to 20 crank degrees (10 cam degrees). These locks allow you to take full advantage of VVT without needing to install custom pistons. (Photo Courtesy Comp Cams)

MMR timing chain guides are constructed of billet aluminum instead of plastic, which eliminates timing variations during high-RPM operation. They work with all other factory and aftermarket components, and you get a lifetime warranty against breakage. If you expect to go over 600 to 700 hp, you need them.

MMR phaser locks allow you to make full adjustment and lock out for stock or race applications to stabilize valvetrain events. This kit completely deletes factory phaser internals and saves 3 pounds of rotating weight. MMR suggests this kit for all applications over 600 hp.

Ford Performance introduced cast-aluminum cam covers for the 2011–2017 Coyote engine. These aluminum camshaft covers allow much greater heat dissipation and protection from exhaust-manifold heat. In addition, they can be powder coated. Because they are cast aluminum, they hide any valvetrain noise. (Photo Courtesy Ford Performance)

Cooling System

The Coyote's factory cooling system is undoubtedly the best that Ford has ever put together because there's nothing to worry about. The infrastructure throughout the engine makes sure that every area of the engine gets good heat transfer. This has only improved with Gen 2, Gen 3, and Gen 4 Coyotes. The only things that you need to do are replace the water pump and all related plumbing along with the thermostat. Because the Coyote's quick-connect hoses and fittings are problematic (they leak), opt for new O-rings, as they tend to be the source of leaks.

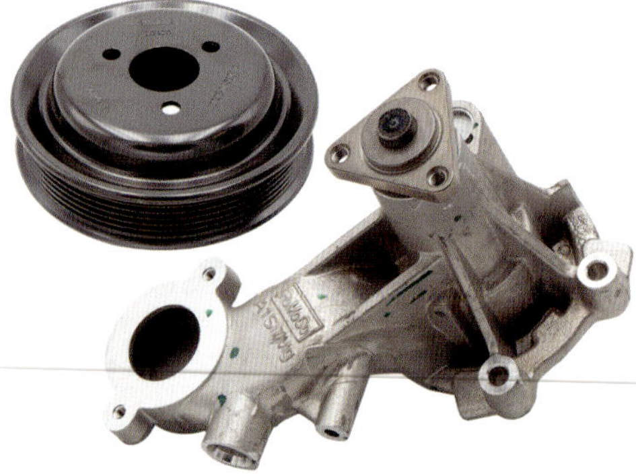

Ford Performance water pumps and related parts (hoses, the thermostat neck, etc.) are available for all Coyote generations and applications. You just need know the generation and vehicle application. (Photo Courtesy Ford Performance)

Even when not replacing the water pump, use a new O-ring seal.

Always replace the two-stage thermostat.

The thermostat is located here, where it controls coolant flow in an unconventional manner from the radiator into the block through the thermostat and prioritizes the hottest parts of the engine at the heads.

Never leave any part of the cooling system to chance. All hoses and necks should be replaced. Pay close attention to connectors and O-rings, which are problematic on Coyote engines.

You may not be thinking about it now, but you're going to want a good infrastructure to support a fresh Coyote engine. The aftermarket offers an array of high-capacity radiators for late-model (F-150 and Mustang) and vintage swap applications.

When planning a build, cooling fans are the furthest thing from your mind. However, they are an important part of the infrastructure when it's time to fire. They need to function properly.

Induction

The Coyote's factory induction system is a keeper when seeking mild street/strip performance. You can warm up a Coyote with hotter cams and heads and still get by with the factory induction. It is that good.

The automotive aftermarket offers a wealth of induction systems for the F-150 and Mustang GT Coyote engine family. Look to Edelbrock, Ford Performance, Holley, and Summit Racing Equipment for induction systems. Ford Performance offers the greatest selection of Coyote induction packages, including the Boss 302, Cobra Jet, and GT350 Voodoo. Before stepping into aftermarket induction, check underhood measures and clearances before buying.

Ford Performance points out that the Gen 1 (2011–2014) Boss 302 intake is functional only with a manual transmission. It is not compatible with automatics. The best option is the Boss 302 intake manifold installation kit (M-9444-M50B), which includes all of the necessary components to complete the

Pay close attention to induction when shopping for engines and intake manifolds. Gen 1 Coyotes (2011– 2014) have a very different intake manifold than the Gen 2 (2015–2017), which has the CMCV system that the Gen 1 does not have. The Gen 1 intake manifold lacks the Gen 2's CMCV system, which makes it look quite bare.

The Gen 2 Coyote (2015–2017) received a new induction system for a new Mustang platform (2015) known as CMCV. CMCV's purpose is to increase tumble and swirl in the Gen 2's combustion chambers, resulting in a faster burn, more power, and decreased emissions. Both the F-150 and Mustang were equipped with the CMCV system.

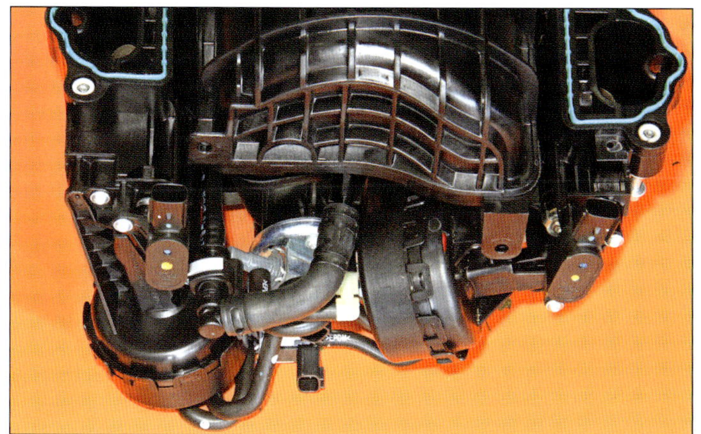

The CMCV actuators work the flappers (valves), modulating runner length and function. They're actuated by intake manifold vacuum and controlled electronically by the PCM. CMCVs cannot be adapted to a Gen 1 Coyote. If you're building a Gen 1 Coyote, the Gen 2 intake manifold will not fit.

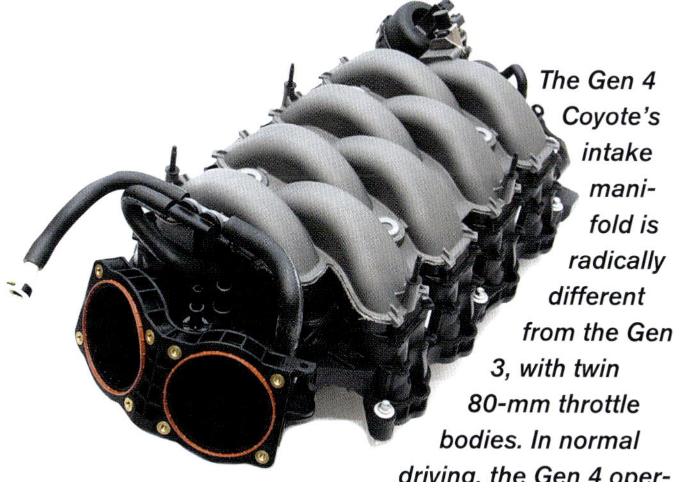

The Gen 4 Coyote's intake manifold is radically different from the Gen 3, with twin 80-mm throttle bodies. In normal driving, the Gen 4 operates on one 80-mm throttle body. Put the pedal to the floor, and you are using both throttle bodies. This means that the Gen 4 also features all-new electronics that are not compatible with the Gen 3.

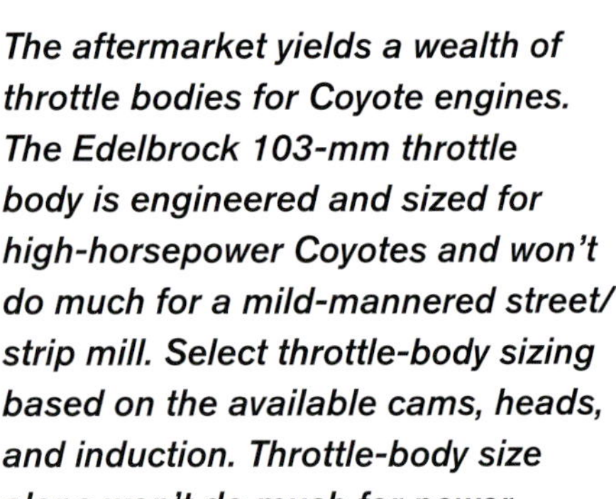

The Boss 302 intake manifold (2012–2013) from Ford Performance is Gen 1 only, meaning that it cannot be adapted to Gen 2, Gen 3, or Gen 4 engines. The good news for Gen 1 builders is that this is a terrific intake manifold for a sweet combination of midrange torque and high-RPM horsepower.

The aftermarket yields a wealth of throttle bodies for Coyote engines. The Edelbrock 103-mm throttle body is engineered and sized for high-horsepower Coyotes and won't do much for a mild-mannered street/strip mill. Select throttle-body sizing based on the available cams, heads, and induction. Throttle-body size alone won't do much for power.

installation. Expect minor wiring harness modifications for installation. When installing the Boss 302 intake, have the Mustang or F-Series truck dyno tuned and calibrated. Otherwise, you risk engine damage.

The Boss manifold provides a nice balance of high-end power and midrange torque for road racing. This makes the Boss 302 manifold a terrific street manifold because it offers both driving elements.

You will have to order the Ford Performance M-9926-CJ65 or M-9926-MSVT throttle body along with the M-9444-M50B installation kit. Expect to order the Ford Performance M-9603-M50CJ Cobra Jet cold-air kit or an equivalent to

mate to the oval throttle body. Expect some issues with original equipment and/or Ford Performance strut-tower braces.

Finally, there's the GT350 Shelby Voodoo intake manifold, which offers a more subtle appearance (M-9424-M52) for only 2015–2024 (Gen 3 and Gen 4) engines with CMCV induction. This swap is going to need the 87-mm M-9926-M52 throttle body. This manifold offers the same kind of power as the Boss 302 manifold. It is more a street-race/road-race manifold that is good for 7,500 rpm with good midrange torque and high-RPM power.

One other Ford Performance option is the M-9424-M50D twin-throttle-body intake, which is standard equipment on the 2024 Mustang GT and the exotic Dark Horse Mustang. It employs twin 80-mm throttle bodies (JL3Z-9E926) and includes intake-to-cylinder head gaskets. The twin throttle body JL3Z manifold is not compatible with Gen 1 and Gen 2 electronics.

Other induction options are available, depending on what you want the engine to do. For street and weekend racing, look for the sweet combination of low-to-midrange torque more than high-end power. This means using long intake runners to get the velocity necessary to make torque.

Throttle Body

If building a stock Coyote, stepping up to a larger throttle body will not make any real difference in power alone. Throttle bodies need to match the expected demand, which means that you need to be thinking about packaging that includes

cams, cylinder heads, and the complete induction system.

Selecting a throttle body boils down to design and flow rates. Check specifications and seek proof of how a throttle body has performed in dyno and real open-road testing. The Coyote's throttle body regulates airflow depending upon demand. The more power is needed, the more the throttle body opens and contributes airflow.

The Coyote's throttle body is fitted with a throttle-position sensor (TPS), which is a variable resistor that provides feedback to the PCM to control fuel-injector pulse width and fuel flow. Coyote engines have never been controlled with a throttle cable. Instead, they use a throttle-control motor drive that is modulated by the PCM. What you are concerned with most here is the size and design. Throttle-body size is measured in millimeters. What the throttle body does is determined by the bore shape and throttle-blade thickness.

The larger the throttle bore, the greater the airflow. We also know

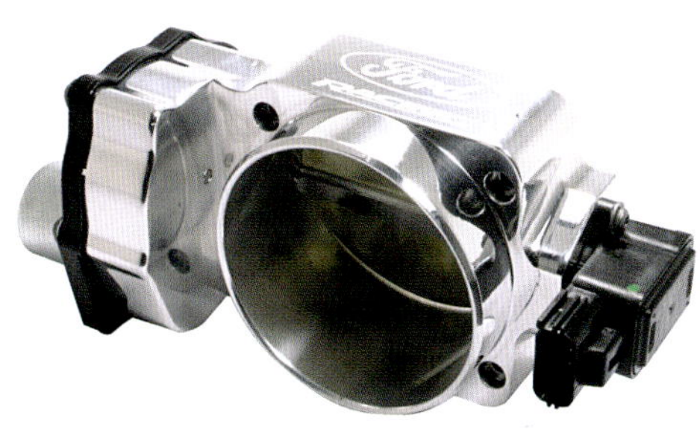

The FAST 87-mm "Big Mouth" throttle body enables builders to go larger without going overboard. This is a nice compromise for 2011–2021 Coyotes, as it is an affordable throttle body that will improve airflow without being too imposing. It can be bolted onto a stock Coyote intake in an F-150 or a Mustang.

This is the Ford Performance 90-mm throttle body (M-9926-M5090) for 2011–2014 Mustang 5.0L and F-150 Coyote engines. It offers increased airflow over the stock 80-mm throttle body. Choose a throttle body based on what dyno testing tells you. The 90-mm size calls for the use of a 4.000-inch-inner-diameter silicone hose adapter or reducer. You will need a 4.000-inch inlet tube to enjoy the full benefit of this throttle body.

Fuel injector choice depends upon the power expected. Because fuel injectors are expensive, you don't want to make a bad decision. Fuel-injector size is rated in pounds per hour (lb/hr) flow. When building a mild street/strip Coyote, do not waste your money on larger injectors, thinking that you will make more power. Larger injectors alone will not mean more power, but instead they will mean more fuel.

a poorly designed 90-mm throttle body isn't always going to flow better than a well-designed, smaller 80-mm unit. Throttle-body size and design can affect low-end torque as well as high-RPM power. What will it do at part throttle versus full throttle? Does a single, large throttle body make more or less power than a twin-bore throttle body?

I've been told that a larger throttle body will typically outflow a smaller one, presuming both are of an equal design. I've also learned that a dual 55-mm throttle body will flow

While you're focused on fuel delivery, think about aesthetics as well as function. I like this lightweight Summit Racing Equipment fuel-rail kit (SUM-227154) for the Ford Coyote. These 3/4-inch fuel rails are precision CNC-machined from high-strength aluminum with a nice black anodized finish. These fuel-rail kits include fittings with Viton O-rings, mounting brackets, and stainless-steel hardware.

The Ford Performance Cobra Jet cold-air kit (M-9603-M50CJ) is a nice finishing touch to a high-power Coyote build. It fits 2011–2014 Mustang GTs and 2012–2013 Boss 302s with the Cobra Jet dual-throttle-body 5.0L intake manifold (M-9424-M50CJB). You will need the M-9926-MSVT, M-9926-CJ65, or M-9926-SCJ manifold and dual throttle body. Professional calibration (not included) is necessary to prevent engine damage.

The Ford Performance M-9603-M8B 2018–2021 Mustang GT calibration with cold-air intake and throttle-body kit has a built-in Pro Cal 4 calibration. It features enhanced throttle response via Ford's proprietary software and engineering for both automatics and manuals. It allows axle-ratio changes and gear-ratio changes up to 4.09:1. Expect to see a torque increase of 42 ft-lbs at 2,000 rpm, 18-plus ft-lbs at 4,500 rpm, and 19 more hp at 6,500 rpm. Premium fuel (91 octane or higher) is required.

890 cfm. Since 1 hp calls for 1.5 cfm through a throttle body, a dual throttle body could, in theory, make 593 hp. Where it gets tricky is accounting for manifold and cylinder-head design along with the cam profile.

A popular Coyote modification has been using the Boss 302 intake with Boss heads, which offer a pleasant balance of midrange torque and high-RPM power. This is the real beauty of the Boss top-end package. The Boss intake manifold's intake runners deliver a good compromise of horsepower and torque. The Coyote has been media-tested in more ways than I could ever cover here. To begin with, there are two different intake-manifold throttle-body adapters, depending upon which intake manifold you happen to be using. The M-9474-M50 is designed for the 2011–2014 GT intake manifold.

What will an additional 10-mm of throttle body gain in terms of power? It will provide about 219 cfm (without the adapter) of maximum airflow capacity. Looking at the numbers, the factory throttle-body flows 913 cfm and 1,101 cfm with the 90

mm when paired with the adapter, and 1,132 cfm without it. Airflow numbers have been validated on Ford Performance's in-house SuperFlow SF-1020 flow bench at 28 inches.

The electronics tied to the larger throttle body are the same that are found on the GT500 throttle body, which are also used with the race-bred Cobra Jet intake manifold. However, it becomes complicated because you will need to unpin the factory throttle-body connectors and transfer them to the new plugs. Swap these plugs in one at a time to avoid any confusion. In addition, like the Cobra Jet throttle body, the Ford Performance 90-mm throttle body will require a professional dyno tune to function properly and safely.

BBK Performance offers a nice variety of throttle bodies for the Coyote. The 85-mm throttle body (part number 1851) is a nice pick that will gain quicker throttle response and some high-end horsepower increases. Much depends on what you have for cams, heads, and induction. Remember, throttle-body selection depends on the entire engine package.

Throttle-body selection alone offers little gain without the corresponding cam, head, and intake.

Injectors

Fuel-injector sizing and selection can be challenging. However, this is an easy decision to make when you are armed with the correct information. Let's start with the basics of Coyote injection. All Coyote engines are fitted with Bosch USCAR EV14 injectors. They are the third generation in a family of Bosch fuel injectors. It gets confusing trying to understand each type and what it does.

The only injector that is used on the Coyote is the EV14, which is the most current generation of Bosch injector. It is narrower than the classic fat and stubby EV1 and shorter than the EV6. The EV14 is skinny compared to the EV1 and EV6, although at times, it is easy to get the EV14 mixed up with the EV6.

The EV6 and EV14 are high-impedance fuel injectors that have the latest injection technology. Impedance is resistance to the flow of electricity. The EV14 has a higher flow rate and can handle a whopping 2,000 hp. If you're reading this book, you're probably not up for 2,000 hp. The EV14 uses a USCAR connector instead of the older Jetronic/Minitimer connectors.

Let's talk about impedance and why it is important to injector selection. There are low-impedance and high-impedance injectors. A low-impedance injector is coiled in such a way that it reduces resistance to electricity flow. By contrast, high-impedance injectors resist the flow of electricity, which calls for increased current from the PCM. It is important to know whether your injector is compatible with the PCM in terms of impedance.

Stock Coyote Fuel-Injector Sizes

Year	Model	Injector Size
2011–2017	Mustang GT 5.0L	34 lbs/hr
2018–2020	Mustang GT/Mach 1 5.0L	28 lbs/hr
2020–2022	GT500	55 lbs/hr
2011–2012	GT500	47 lbs/hr
2013–2014	GT500	52 lbs/hr
2016–2020	GT350	34 lbs/hr

The amount of fuel that can be delivered from injectors over a specific period is listed in pounds per hour (lbs/hr). A right-sized fuel injector will provide sufficient fuel under a full load at an 80-percent duty cycle. The duty cycle is rated in percentages. If a fuel injector is rated at 80-percent duty cycle at wide-open throttle, it means that it is closed 20 percent of that time, while at 80 percent of the duty cycle, it is open. To accurately calculate a Coyote's required fuel flow rate, use the following formula courtesy of Summit Racing Equipment.

Begin your calculations with this equation:

$$\frac{\text{Horsepower} \times \text{Brake Specific Fuel Consumption [BSFC]}}{\text{Number of Injectors} \times \text{Injector Duty Cycle}}$$

A naturally aspirated, 300-hp V-8 engine (BSFC at 0.5) with eight fuel injectors will require 23.4 lbs/hr of fuel per injector at an 80-percent (0.8) duty cycle.

$$(300 \times 0.5) \div (8 \times 0.8) = 23.4 \text{ lbs/hr}$$

You're not going to find a fuel injector specific to your calculated needs. However, you can fine-tune the flow rate by adjusting fuel pressure. As fuel pressure increases, so does the amount of fuel that can pass through an open injector. Getting the right amount of fuel could be as simple as making a fuel-pressure-regulator adjustment.

Most fuel injectors are flow-rated at 43.5 psi. Ford Motorcraft rates its fuel injectors at 39.15 psi. Suffice it to say, Ford's fuel pressure is typically right around 40 psi. To calculate the flow rate at a given pressure, use this formula:

$$[\text{Advertised Flow Rate}] \times [\text{the Square Root of (Your Pressure} \div \text{Rated Pressure)}]$$

For example, what happens to the output of a 24 lbs/hr injector rated at 43.5 psi if you run it at 50 psi?

$$50 \div 43.5 = 1.149$$
$$\sqrt{1.149} = 1.072$$
$$24 \times 1.072 = 25.73 \text{ lbs/hr}$$

This quick-reference table from Summit Racing Equipment serves as a baseline for sizing injectors. Of course, your results will vary.

Injector Flow Rate (lbs/hr)	Horsepower (Naturally Aspirated Engine)	Horsepower (Engine with Power Adders)
19	225–290	185–240
24	280–360	240–300
36	350–450	350–450
42	425–540	410–525
46	540–690	450–575
52	610–775	510–650
60	710–900	590–750

NOTE: This chart lists some general guidelines for gasoline engines with eight injectors.

Ignition

There's no magic to ignition-coil selection. Based on my own experience, Ford Motorcraft and Ford Performance coils yield durability and longevity. They will last the life of an engine and be ready for the next one. Aftermarket high-performance ignition coils feature a more potent spark on average, which is important in boosted applications. In my opinion, MSD remains the best choice for coil-on-plug ignition parts for high-performance applications. In all fairness, the same can be said for Accel, Granatelli, FAST, E3, Ford Performance, and a host of other high-performance coils.

Ford Motorcraft spark plugs are an excellent choice for street and weekend strip applications for the same reason that the coils are: they last. Your main concern should be the heat range. The standard Coyote spark plug for naturally aspirated (not boosted) applications is the Motorcraft SP519K platinum-tip spark plug, which is original equipment in these engines. It is the standard heat range for naturally aspirated Coyotes engines. This means that it is optimal for 2011–2023 5.0L and 5.2L Coyote engines.

The lower-heat-range Coyote spark plug is the M-12405-M50A cold plug. It is recommended for use with the 2011–2014 Mustang GT 5.0L Coyote supercharger kits (M-6066-MGT525D and M-6066-MGT624D) and for use with any 2011–2021 Mustang GT running an aftermarket supercharger. This Motorcraft plug is one heat range colder than the stock 2011–2023 Mustang GT 5.0L 4V Ti-VCT spark plugs. It is also suitable for use on the 2018 Cobra Jet engine (M-6007-SCJ50). The colder plug is strongly suggested

Summit Racing Equipment offers a variety of ignition systems for the Coyote, including its own "Summit" brand of ignition parts that offer quality and longevity.

MSD ignition components are a given with any race-ready Coyote build. If you're opting for boost and high-RPM operation, raise the benchmark with a powerful high-energy ignition.

When considering spark plugs, keep the heat range in mind. There are standard platinum-tip spark plugs for the Coyote and "cold" spark plugs for boosted applications, where you would run a colder plug.

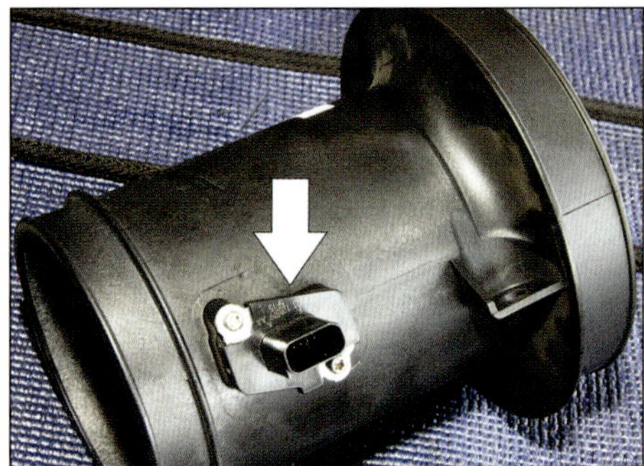

When making a list and checking it twice, keep engine electronics in mind. I've never seen a mass airflow (MAF) sensor fail, but it can get dirty and then can fail. Inspect the MAF sensor for any debris and have it checked by an engine-tuning professional who can test it with a multimeter and visually inspect it for damage and debris.

for extreme-duty applications. Ford wants you to employ a 0.035-inch gap. Supercharged applications call for a periodic plug reading to make sure that the Coyote is safe from destructive detonation.

The aftermarket offers a variety of spark plugs for the Coyote. Stick with the recommended heat ranges for naturally aspirated and supercharged applications—similar to what you should do with the Motorcraft spark plugs. Based on what I've learned from seasoned engine builders and tuners, stick with NGK and Bosch platinum-tip spark plugs if Motorcraft isn't working for you. Brisk is another brand that I hear mentioned favorably in Coyote circles.

Parker Performance (ppflco.com), which has a lot of Coyote experience, states, "Typically, for less than 1,000 rear-wheel hp, we suggest NGK Iridium (6510s), which is a heat range of 7 (one step colder than stock heat range).

"Brisk RR14S work as well, but they don't seem to last as long as the NGK units do. One thing that we like about the Brisks over the NGKs is that they have a non-projected tip (sunken tip), which seems to be better for all-out racing applications. We do check the gap a little more frequently on the NGK 6510s as we increase power (and tighter on gap)."

Engine Electronics

I cannot stress enough the importance of the Coyote's electronic engine control and its effect on performance and durability. The powertrain control module (PCM) is a Coyote's nerve center. It takes feedback from various sensors and controls engine function based on feedback. It is important to understand the difference between a PCM and an engine control module (ECM), which focuses primarily on engine function. The ECM takes data input gathered from the various engine sensors and goes to work controlling fuel and spark curves, ignition timing, the air/fuel mixture, fuel-injection timing, etc.

The PCM controls both engine and transmission programming. It controls shift points in automatic transmissions while handling all of the duties of an ECM. Bringing engine and transmission functions together as a team improves efficiency and power management.

What makes this all so important is cohesive function via properly working sensors and connections. All sensors need to be in proper working order. Not all sensors have to be replaced, especially if they appear to be in good physical condition. If your Coyote suffered from engine failure, examine the PCM and all sensors to ascertain if electronics caused engine failure.

To determine if the PCM is in proper working order, it has to be

There's little to go wrong with a crank sensor, which is located at the flywheel/flexplate at the end of the crankshaft. The crank sensor provides feedback to the PCM with signals (a pulse at the speed of the crank).

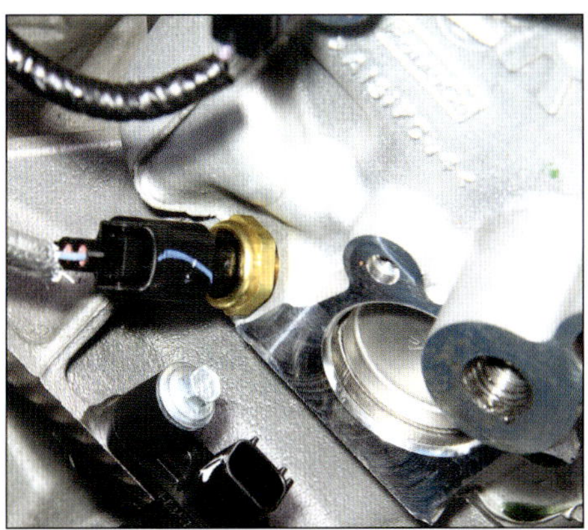

Confirm proper sensor and sender continuity prior to installation. Senders are for instruments, and sensors are for PCM feedback and function.

If you're going racing, order an SFI-rated flywheel, which has a line of flywheels for F-150 and Mustang Coyote applications.

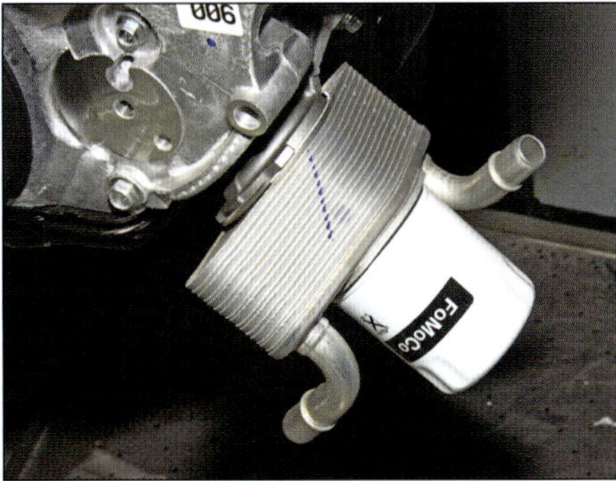

evaluated by professionals who can look inside of it to confirm function. Most of the time, all the PCM needs is a reflash and you're back in business. Checking fault codes will typically find malfunctioning sensors, bad ignition coils, etc.

More Details

Right when you think that all of your bases are covered, there's always more in store—all of those loose ends that you haven't thought of. Once the base Coyote engine assembly is covered, there are pesky items, including fasteners, block plugs, miscellaneous hardware, brackets, hoses, lines, accessories, fittings, and more to source and install. These are the important items to consider during the planning stages

Replace the factory oil cooler because it is virtually impossible to know its condition, and you don't want contaminants in the oil.

so that you're not waiting for FedEx when you're ready to fire the engine.

If you pulled your Coyote and inventoried all related parts before the teardown, then you have little to be concerned about. It is all still there. All of these parts normally need clean-up and placement on the shelf until you're ready for installation. If you're building a Coyote for a swap, there is a lot to consider, such as the infrastructure necessary to install and fire the engine. A swap involves the entire fuel system and the electronics necessary to make the engine run. Then, there's the exhaust system, cooling system, and a host of other considerations.

Some items, including the high-pressure direct-injection fuel lines on Gen 3 or Gen 4 Coyotes, must be replaced. Engine mounts should be serviceable and ready for reuse. Did you remember to replace any torque-angle fasteners? The list is lengthy, and it is up to you to fulfill the need.

Gen 3 Coyotes are equipped with this direct-injection pump, which is actuated by a cam lobe located beneath the pump.

MACHINE SHOP

Now that you've disassembled the engine and have cleaned and cataloged all of the parts, it is time to deliver your stuff to a trusted machine shop. Never opt for the lowest bid for the purpose of saving money. Choose the best machine shop in your area and be willing to pay for it.

Avoid general-purpose machine shops that turns brake drums and rotors and do routine machine work. The Coyote commands the best state-of-the-art equipment, technique, and experience. Check around, read reviews, and consult with locals about the best machine shops that have experience with Coyote engines.

Select a user-friendly machine shop with an experienced proprietor who is willing to listen and respectfully answer any questions. Invite them to show their work and provide references. Be prepared that not all shops will do this. I stress this because few things are worse than an uncooperative shop where you are at the mercy of a combative machinist. Seek a legitimate written estimate. There will always be unexpected issues that drive the cost up. Ask for a phone call or a text message regarding any price increases before any further work is done.

Since crate engines are becoming more popular, the number of machine shops from coast to coast is dwindling as old timers retire, and young people become less interested in professional trades, it has become challenging to find a reputable, experienced machine shop. It may take longer for you to get machine work accomplished and an engine com-pleted, so be ready for delays that can sometimes last for months.

When consulting with a machinist, ask questions and be the devil's advocate for your build project. Since these engines have thin iron cylinder liners, anything beyond 0.010-inch oversize is unacceptable. If the bores have more than 0.011-inch taper from top to bottom, the block must be sleeved or replaced. Sleeving can run upward of $1,000 in labor with

Cylinder-bore dimensions are checked with a bore checker before performing machine work. Then, a dial-bore gauge is applied at four locations for 360 degrees at the top, middle, and bottom of the bores.

Gen 1 and Gen 2 blocks can be bored and honed a total of 0.005 to 0.010 inch. The boring process is nothing more than a light shave (if that). If you're anticipating big power gains, it is worth the investment to have the block sleeved.

A torque plate must always be used on the Coyote block for the honing process. Sharp eyes will notice that this is a Modular block, but the principle is the same.

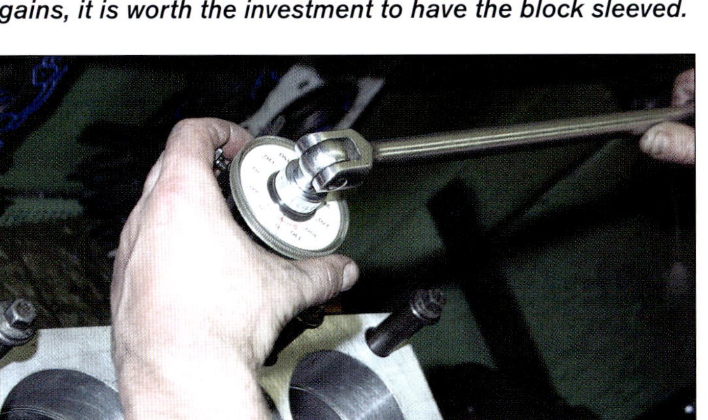

Torque the torque plate just like the cylinder heads. Do the initial torque in proper order and then use a torque-angle gauge to complete the torque before honing. Keep in mind that Coyote blocks with plasma-sprayed cylinder walls cannot be bored or honed because the cylinder walls are too thin.

Coyote blocks don't normally require boring. Instead, finish honing to get a crosshatch finish is needed for good ring seating and cylinder sealing.

most machine shops. While the Gen 1 and Gen 2 Coyote blocks can be bored and honed, the Gen 3 block (with its plasma-sprayed cylinder liners) cannot be bored/honed. The Gen 3 must be sleeved.

Economics dictate what to do with a Coyote block. Because new Coyote blocks are plentiful and affordable, you're often better off starting with a new block. Compare machining quotes with the cost of a new block, and the decision comes easily. If having a matching-number block means a lot to you, go the machine-shop route and keep your Mustang or F-150's original block.

Due to the strict tolerances of the Coyote engine, it is advisable to have a machine shop perform the valve job instead of doing it yourself. If you desire port and bowl work, seek the expertise of a knowledgeable head-porting shop and check out their work or opt for off-the-shelf CNC or custom-ported heads. Anyone can hang up a shingle and promote themselves as a head-porting specialist. Talk with racers and locals and learn who does the best port work. Be willing to ship the heads hundreds of miles away to get the best work.

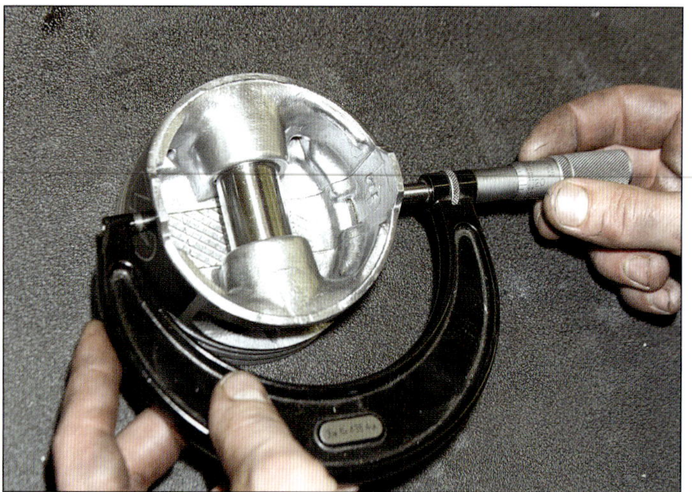

Cylinder bores are match-honed to each piston size. The pistons are measured and then each bore is honed to that individual piston size. Each piston should be identified with the cylinder number.

Block decks are milled in the minimum amount necessary to get them perfected. Some builders I've worked with suggest a "rough cut" for better head-gasket sealing. This is an approach that the factory has been using on new Coyote block decks to improve sealing.

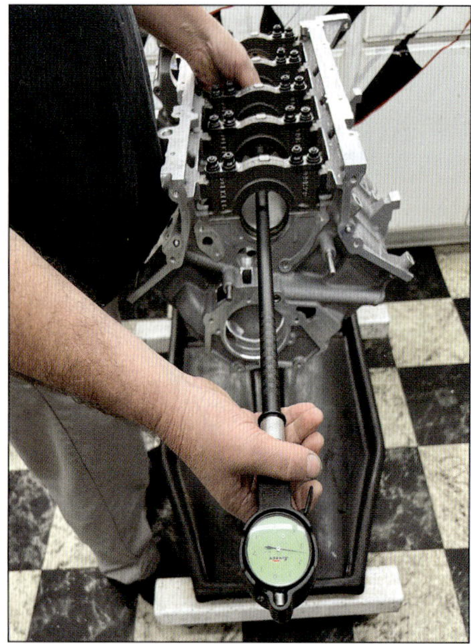

The main bore sizing is checked with a dial-bore gauge and then align-honed.

I align-hone the main saddles to improve bearing security and accuracy.

Important!

Get a Written Estimate

When you're in negotiations with a machine shop, get it all down in writing with an ironclad written estimate so that everyone understands what's expected. Vague verbal agreements are not enforceable, no matter how nice and agreeable the proprietor may seem. When things go wrong (and they can), shops tend to have memory lapses that can lead to big misunderstandings. Get that written agreement. ■

This block has been align-honed with a crosshatch pattern in each bearing saddle. This ensures bearing security. A popular misconception is that the bearing tangs secure the bearing. This has never been true. Bearing tangs are there for reference purposes (alignment)—not bearing security.

It is also best to have a machine shop do the assembly work. Having the shop do the assembly is good for peace of mind. It doesn't always guarantee success, but it improves the odds. It also holds the shop responsible for any failure from proven negligence. Racing engines virtually never come with a warranty, so don't expect one. If they do, they're going to look at why the engine failed.

Finding a Reputable Machine Shop

Because the Coyote has been around for more than a decade, most seasoned machine shops should have some experience with this engine. If not, find a shop that does. Old-school machine shops may or may not have the necessary equipment and tooling to work with the Coyote. The more progressive shops will welcome your business. Quarter Mile Performance in Los Angeles, California, is a state-of-the-art shop with all of the latest technology. It specializes in late-model power, including the Ford Modular engine, the Coyote, GM's LS and LT engines, and Chrysler's Hemi.

QMP has the latest CNC technology. It uses Cam Doctor, Cam Tunnel, CK-10 hone, a climate-controlled clean room for assembly, diamond hone, SF-600 flow bench, DCB-2000 balancing technology, and a wealth of basic state-of-the-art machining equipment for blocks and heads. This is the caliber of machine shop that you want for your Coyote project.

Brian Roche Racing Engines in Baltimore, Maryland, is another terrific, state-of-the-art shop of the same caliber with the latest technology and extensive experience. It specializes in late-model engines such as the Coyote as well as the more conven-

tional iron pushrod engines of the past. QMP and Roche are only two examples on opposite coasts.

There's also L&R Engines just south of Los Angeles in Santa Fe Springs, California. Derek and his people have extensive experience with both the Modular and Coyote engines. Moreover, these guys are passionate about their work, offering the best user-friendly service.

Precision Engine Machine Co. in Maryland has nearly six decades of experience. Precision Engine Machine was founded in 1967 by Billy Ford and Dick Burgess. Jan Norris, a longtime friend of mine, started his machinist apprenticeship in the 1970s. After completing his apprenticeship, Jan took over the machine shop at B&J Automotive. Sometime later, he joined Precision Engine Machine Co. and ultimately took over the business. Jan, his son Michael, and his grandson Branden continue the tradition and do incredible work.

Finding exceptional talent and state-of-the-art facilities in your area requires a lot of research and word of mouth. Every region of the country has its best talent. Canvass the area and chat with a lot of people. It is good to get feedback from reputable auto repair shops. Repair shops cannot afford to pull failed engines and go through the rebuild process again. They want positive results the first time.

Be Prepared

Before heading to the machine shop, make sure that you're ready for the delivery. Have everything cataloged and protected so that you can hand the shop an organized package that it can store with ease.

Be Organized

Before heading to the machine shop, have everything cataloged and organized. Have you taken photos of everything before disassembly? Have you taken notes?

If you have disassembled the engine, all loose parts should be in marked containers and boxes. Make an inventory list of all parts. Make this effort a part of your agreement. Some engine builders prefer for you to deliver the engine assembled, allowing them to tear it down so that they can examine everything. ■

Torque-to-yield fasteners can be kept at home because they cannot be reused. Gaskets and the like should be thrown away. When the disassembled engine is delivered, get a timeline for completion and, as I've said before, get it all in writing with a written estimate and agreement.

Machine Work

Machine work on an engine block and cylinder heads is an effort to get these castings back to serviceable condition. Here's what needs to be done.

Engine Block

- Bore and finish-hone the cylinders. The Coyote's paper-thin cylinder walls cannot always be bored and honed. If dimensions are beyond allowable tolerances, sleeve or replace the block. Gen 1 and Gen 2 blocks can be honed, but there are limits. Gen 3 blocks cannot be bored or honed and must be sleeved.

- Taper each cylinder at the block deck for ease of assembly.
- Mill block decks.
- Align-hone main bearing bores for good bearing security.
- Chase bolt holes.
- Chase and clean oil galleries and cooling passages.
- Tap and remove any broken bolts.
- Notch cylinder skirts as necessary for stroker clearance.

Moving Parts
- Inspect and machine crankshaft (grinding or polishing journals).
- Recondition connecting rods.
- Polish camshaft journals.

Cylinder Heads
- Check and mill head decks (watch chamber size).
- Check and replace valve guides as necessary.
- Recondition or replace valves.
- Inspect and reface or replace valve seats as necessary.
- Chase and clean bolt holes and spark-plug holes.

Rod cap bolts get a dab of moly lube and are then secured and torqued to secure the bolts. Then, they are reconditioned to get the large end square. You may also opt for ARP rod bolts, which don't require torque-angle treatment.

The small end of the stock Coyote rod is bushed is shown. Reconditioning should include new bushings.

Since Coyote blocks require a lot of forethought, know which generation you have. The Gen 1 (2011–2014) and Gen 2 (2015–2017) Coyote blocks can be bored and honed. However, there is very little room for boring and honing. The Gen 3 and Gen 4 (2018–2024) blocks have plasma moly-sprayed cylinder walls (like the Shelby GT350 Voodoo block) and are not serviceable. They can only be sleeved. If the expense of installing cylinder liners is too much, consider the purchase of a new Gen 3 block. It ends up costing more to sleeve than to replace the block.

Milling the block decks makes these surfaces true for a nice marriage with the cylinder-head deck surfaces. I like to see block decks "rough cut" for good cylinder-head sealing. This is especially important when

The Coyote's stock, cracked powdered-metal connecting rods can be reconditioned and fitted with oversize (external diameter) rod bearings and reused. Powdered metal is a phrase that makes enthusiasts nervous. However, powdered metal, or sintered metal, is a sophisticated forging process that makes these rods stronger forgings.

This rod-bearing bore gets a good finish honing for improved bearing security. It is important to note that you can reuse the Coyote's powdered metal rods without consequence.

running boost, nitrous, or a lot of compression. Once boring/honing is out of the way along with decking, cylinders should be tapered at the deck for piston installation and minimum risk to piston rings.

I like to see machine shops perform good housekeeping in the wake of machine work. Oil galleries and cooling passages should be thoroughly chased and washed to remove debris and metal fragments that could cause engine damage. Bolt holes should be chased with a thread chaser or tap to ensure accurate torque readings. All block contact surfaces should be as smooth as the decks.

Coyote cylinder heads require a minimum of machine work. They have steel seats and state-of-the-art valve-guide technology. I suggest starting with new valves and guides as the need and your budget dictate. Because the aftermarket offers an abundance of ported Coyote cylinder heads, it usually makes economic sense to buy ported heads.

Dynamic Balancing

Dynamic balancing is the process of getting rotating and reciprocating parts in perfect balance (weight-wise) for smoothness. Vibration is a destructive dynamic because it can cause wear and tear to an engine and driveline. It is the shaky nature of vibration that does the damage. What you want is smoothness for durability.

Vibration is the most befuddling thing because an engine may run smoothly at 1,500 rpm and have quite a shake at 3,500 rpm. The Modular engine family (4.6L and 5.4L) has always been plagued with harmonics in the 2,000- to 2,500-rpm

It is mandatory to have the Coyote's rotating mass dynamic balanced for smoothness and durability. A connecting rod is weighed to determine bobweight. No two rods will weigh the same. Everything is weighted to the lightest reciprocating mass of the eight piston/rod assemblies.

This is a bobweight balancing machine that simulates the total weight of the piston, rings, connecting rod, and bearing. Some precision balancers even include oil weight.

range. Ford engineers managed to eliminate this frustrating dynamic with the Coyote.

According to Fluidampr, engine vibration occurs in three forms: unbalanced vibration, axial vibration, and torsional vibration. These are unique forms of engine vibration, and there are three different ways to control them. This becomes the monkey motion of physics and dynamic balance. Vibration is what

These bobweights simulate the reciprocating weight on each rod journal. The balancer spins the crank to determine reciprocating weights and indicates where metal must be removed or added to each crankshaft counterweight. This works like a tire-balancing machine, where weight is added or subtracted to get it in proper dynamic balance.

The crank is spun on the balancer much like spin balancing a tire and wheel.

This screen indicates where weight needs to be added or subtracted.

Some weight is removed from this counterweight to make it equal to the corresponding reciprocating mass. Weight can also be added by drilling (as shown) and filling the counterweight with Mallory metal (tungsten).

Important!

Internal versus External Balance

The subject of internal versus external balance does not apply to the Coyote because the Coyote is an internally balanced engine.

However, it is important to address what this means. If there isn't enough space inside an engine block to locate all of the crankshaft counterweights (such as the 289/302-ci small-blocks and some FE-Series big-blocks), engineers will add this offset weight to the harmonic damper and the flywheel/flexplate. This is known as external balancing, where weight has to be added to each end of the crank. ■

makes engines come apart at high RPM. Unbalanced vibration is controlled via dynamic balancing. The Coyote's bottom end consists of the crankshaft, connecting rods, pistons, rings, a flexplate or flywheel, and the harmonic damper.

These components in rotary and reciprocating motion create all kinds of potential for vibration. Fluidampr representatives said that these masses in motion have stiffness and inertia properties, which directly affect dynamic balance. How much does the component flex, twist, and move, and at what velocity and force? What do heat and force do to these components?

There are incredible forces imposed on the crankshaft. Eight pistons and rods exert force on the crank in eight separate events. The combustion pressure spike from each piston acts on the crank in its own way. As RPM increases along with the forces acting on each journal, it gets crazier.

Fluidampr adds that torsional vibration has a frequency measured in hertz or cycles per second. It gets complicated where the frequency is RPM times order divided by 60 hertz (cycles per second), which is how often a vibration event that occurs during one revolution of the crankshaft.

In a four-stroke Coyote engine, the primary order is half the number of cylinders because only half of the cylinders fire during one complete crankshaft revolution. All eight bores will have fired in two crank revolutions. Other orders are deviations from vibration oscillating through the crankshaft. As RPM increases, the frequency of each order increases.

Axial vibration comes from crankshaft endplay. This is why getting crankshaft endplay just right is so important. As the crank oscillates back and forth, this affects vibration and smoothness.

Dynamic balancing gets reciprocating and rotary parts on the same page so that the piston and rod dance happily around the counterweighted crankshaft. The counterweights must weigh the same as the corresponding piston-and-rod assembly. This is a very time-consuming task for the balancer because there are no unimportant parts. Every part matters.

To make this easier to understand, let's talk about dynamic balancing and how it is achieved during a rebuild. Dynamic balancing is where we get rotational balance weight (crank and counterweights) in synch with reciprocating weight (pistons and rods). Dynamic balancing is mandatory for all engine builds.

Ted Eaton of Eaton Balancing in Lorena, Texas, explained that dynamic balance deals with the physics of achieving a rotating mass that is the most conducive to transmitting as much potential power as possible to an engine's flywheel, rather than having it wasted within the confines of the engine.

Eaton is world-renowned for his powerful vintage Ford Y-Block V-8s. He stressed that by eliminating the power-robbing vibration that can be caused by a state of imbalance, power that would normally be dissipated through an engine's main bearings and into the block can instead be redirected to the flange end of the crankshaft proportionally by the degree to which the rotating mass is balanced. In short, he said that the better the balance, the more the potential power will be seen at the flywheel. Behind the wheel with a balanced engine, it becomes a smoother engine with improved acceleration. In addition, you get more power from a good balancing job.

"The physics of balancing can be broken down into two types of imbalance: static and dynamic," Eaton said. "Static imbalance will manifest itself as a maximum amount of out-of-balance in a single area or plane along the outermost surface of a rotating axis. On the other hand, a rotating part can be in a perfect state of static balance but can be off significantly when examining its dynamic balance.

"If a vibration is observed, static imbalance is the force most likely being felt, but dynamic out-of-balance can also be present, depending upon the rotating mass's length. Even when physical vibration is not being felt, the dynamic imbalance can be present in severe enough levels to be quite destructive or power-robbing, although no shake or vibration is physically evident.

"Static out-of-balance can be found in any rotating part regardless of the length along its rotating axis but dynamic out-of-balance becomes more significant as rotating pieces increase in length along its rotating axis," Eaton continued. "Very narrow rotating parts, such as flywheels, will not exhibit much in the way of dynamic out-of-balance but can be good examples of static imbalance. A longer item like a crankshaft may not show evidence of being out of balance statically but can be off significantly when looking at its dynamic aspects."

Engine balancing begins with static balancing, where pistons, rings, rods, bearings, and even oil are weighed on a scale one at a time to ascertain weight. Each is weighed to the lightest reciprocating assembly.

"To precision-balance an engine, all pieces of the rotating assembly must be considered," Eaton said. "A list of these parts include the crankshaft, harmonic damper or front hub, flywheel, clutch disc, and pressure plate (manual transmission), connecting rods, pistons with their pins and respective locks, compression and oil rings, rod bearings, and the lower timing gear."

Eaton said everything that moves or rotates as part of the engine assembly short of the camshaft and its sprocket should be a part of the balancing operation. Also worth considering are the belt pulleys and their retaining bolts. All machine work or modifications, including rod reconditioning, piston dome or valve relief machining, and general deburring or polishing of any of the internal engine parts must have been already performed before having the assembly balanced. Doing so after the fact will only nullify the effects of having the rotating assembly precision balanced.

"When taking all the necessary parts to your favorite shop for balancing, it's important to note that the connecting rods or the piston rings must not yet be installed on the pistons," Eaton said. "Likewise, the rod bearings do not need to be installed in the rods or the rods installed on the crankshaft. Because the rods must be balanced end for end separately, they are required to be independent or apart from the pistons. Although the rings could technically be on the pistons during the balancing procedure, they also need to remain uninstalled to ensure that no machining chips are caught in the ring lands during any of the weight-reduction operations being performed."

Dynamic balancing performed by your machine shop is conducted in two operations: weighing and/or match weighing the various components followed by spin balancing the crankshaft itself. A V-8 engine requires a bobweight installed on each crank journal for balancing purposes that employs 100 percent of the rotating mass but only a fraction or a percentage of the reciprocating mass for each piston/rod assembly.

The Coyote requires a bobweight to be installed on each crank rod journal during dynamic balancing that represents not only 100 percent of the rotating mass but also a standard value of 50 percent that represents the reciprocating mass, according to Eaton. Even this standard reciprocating factor is subject to change for a 90-degree V-8 engine in special circumstances.

The Details

I've covered the basics of machine shop protocol. Now, onward to the pesky details. Most machine shops cover the basics of machine work, but they don't always sweat out the finite details.

Close attention to detail includes how the block, heads, and cylinder decks are machined. The Coyote block and head decks should be milled as the factory milled them to begin with something of a "rough cut," with ridges that bite into the head

Block sleeving enables you to have a stronger version of the Coyote block. You may purchase a sleeved Coyote block from a variety of sources, or you can have your block sleeved.

Beginning with the GT350 Voodoo Coyote engine, Ford took a new approach to cylinder walls, which featured PTWA spray weld liner-coated cylinder walls. This approach continued with the Gen 3 (2018–2024) Coyote block (shown here). This coating provides improved durability and heat transfer, reduced friction, and weight savings when compared to Gen 1 and Gen 2 Coyote aluminum blocks.

gaskets for improved sealing. The top of each cylinder should receive a taper cut, which eases piston installation without the risk of ring damage. Bolt holes should always be chased with a tap or thread chaser to clean up threads and remove machining debris. Use engine assembly lube or SAE 30-weight engine oil in very light amounts in the bolt holes for accurate torque readings. Too much oil and assembly lube in the bolt holes can cause "hydraulic-ing," where you can crack the block by applying

After the cylinders have been honed, they are each double-checked with a dial-bore gauge to confirm the original findings.

This close-up of the Gen 3 Coyote cylinder liner demonstrates just how thin these cylinder walls are. Note the block deck "rough cut" for better cylinder sealing.

Lay out and measure the pistons to ascertain piston-to-cylinder wall clearances.

too much torque. Keep thread lubricant to a minimum.

Clear the oil galleries and cooling passages of debris. This is especially important with oil galleries, where metal shavings can be trapped and cause engine damage later on. Oil passages can be chased with soap and water with a tube brush, and they you can use WD-40 to flush them. Remember, cleanliness is everything to longevity. Stray metal can hibernate in oil galleries and cooling passages for thousands of miles and then become dislodged to circulate through the engine, doing extensive damage.

Another item that machine shops tend to miss is debris left inside of the water jackets. I've seen new Ford blocks and crate engines with freeze plugs left inside the water jackets, which is a word to the wise before getting started. In the rush of manufacturing and production quotas, mistakes are made.

New and remanufactured blocks must have all block plugs removed for inspection and cleaning. Never trust a new or remanufactured block or head casting. Remove all plugs and then flush thoroughly before assembly begins. Stray freeze plugs that are left in the block will cause overheating issues by restricting coolant flow.

Coyote cylinder heads need very little attention because they were so well-engineered to begin with. Rarely do valve seats need replacement. The most they need is refacing along with new valves. Guides may call for replacement or bronze bushings

Double-check the connecting-rod journal clearances with the bearings installed.

Check the crank rod journals to determine bearing clearances.

Unless crank journals have been badly damaged via engine failure, all that the journals need is polishing.

Valve springs must be compatible with the cam profile that you selected.

Depending upon their condition, the valves can be refaced, especially for stock rebuilds.

The Coyote's efficiency and durability are evident in its cylinder heads. Because these heads are fitted with hardened valve seats, the most you can expect to do is reface the valve seats and faces. Rarely is there the need to replace them. Your machine shop should check valve stem-to-guide clearances. Excessive clearances call for guide replacement or bronze inserts.

Valve stems are measured and resurfaced, then pressed back into service. Valve stem-to-guide clearances are confirmed. The valve guides can be replaced.

Viton valve-stem seals offer the greatest durability. They offer oil control around the seal lip to where just the right amount of oil reaches the guide and stem.

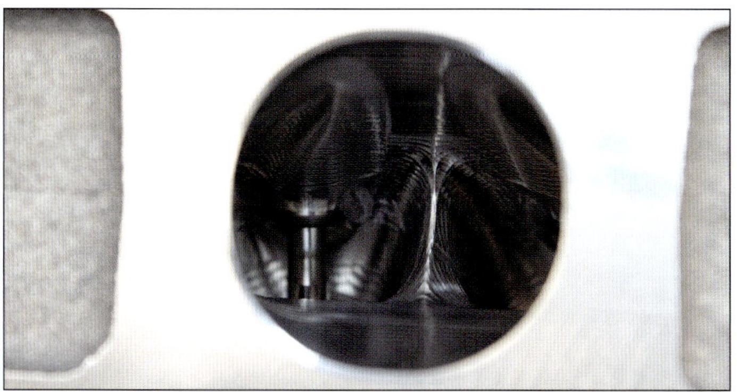

Custom port work is expensive. You can have this done or look to a variety of aftermarket sources, such as Livernois and Total Engine Airflow, for ready-to-race CNC-ported heads. Ford Performance is also an excellent source for CNC-ported heads. This is the Coyote exhaust port.

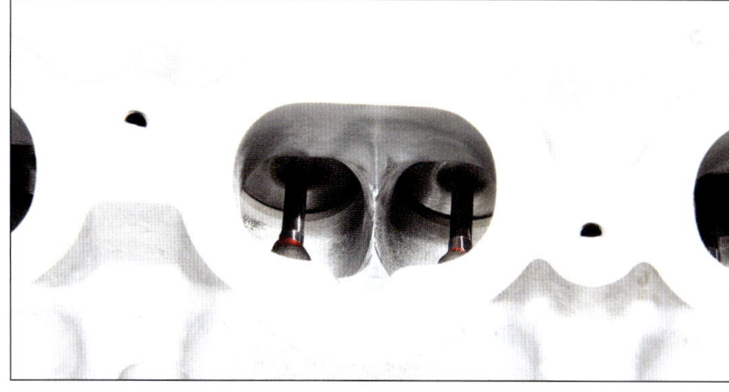

This is a CNC-ported intake port with defined machining lines in the aluminum. These may also be hand-finished for smoothness. It can be endlessly debated whether a smooth surface is better than CNC-ported lines. The latter can keep fuel droplets in suspension.

to get clearances back where they should be. Coyote heads were engineered as high-performance pieces, which means that they are generally in good condition even after 100,000 miles. They were developed for extremes of abuse and longevity, and under normal conditions and routine maintenance, they will last 200,000-plus miles.

CNC-porting offers consistency because all heads receive the same treatment. It is also more cost-effective. When you get into custom hand porting (shown here), it gets expensive.

Head Bolt/Stud Conversion

I've learned from L&M Engines in Pennsylvania that the 11-mm to 12-mm head-bolt conversion is causing a common problem with Coyote builds. The issue is block cracking, which leads to coolant leakage into the oil pan. Other issues include cracks at the base of the knock-sensor bosses, which is where the 11-mm head bolt terminates. This is caused by the high pressures that are caused by high power, which applies great stress to the 11-mm threads ending at the coolant jacket, cracking the block.

The 12-mm head bolt, as used in 2011 model year (Gen 1) blocks, extends past the coolant jacket and ends in the main web, where the stress originates at the crank and mains. The 2011 model year Gen 1 12-mm blocks are not prone to cracks because the stud terminates at the main web, according to Michael Rouscher of L&M Engines. This is also recommended by Ford Performance for high-horsepower and twin-turbo Coyote applications

"The combustion force is always trying to lift the head, and these forces are transmitted to the cylinder-head bolt," Rouscher said. "As we increase pressure (torque), we increase the stress to the bolt at the local area, eventually exceeding the tensile strength of the block material and forming cracks.

"All of these forces originate at the crankshaft, and the reactive force is at the bolt. If we tie the bolt to the crankshaft area, we transmit that force back to the crank instead of through the aluminum coolant jacket or knock-sensor-boss area, which is thin and nonstructural.

"The remedy is to convert to 12-mm head bolts, which tie the head forces to the crankshaft via the main web," Rouscher continued. "The challenge in conversion is to obtain a 90-degree head stud to the deck. The reason for this challenge is that it is very difficult to move an existing hole center and to drill off-center, which creates an angled (cockeyed) hole. The existing holes in blocks do not always meet the Ford blueprint after measuring hundreds of head-bolt holes, which results in always drilling off-center to the existing hole, creating a cockeyed hole (not 90 degrees to the deck)."

FINAL ASSEMBLY

Final assembly is performed when all of the components that have been meticulously cleaned up and machined come together as a complete engine that is ready for use. I cannot stress enough the importance of close attention to detail in assembly. Since today's high-tech, finitely machined engines employ tight tolerances, they are intolerant of sloppy assembly work and dust and debris. The best advice that I can offer is to not be in a hurry. Take your time and methodically assemble the engine.

The assembly area must be dust- and clutter-free. If you live in a dusty environment, such as the desert or dry plains, everything must be protected from the elements. Something as finite as house dust must be avoided. As the engine is assembled, all parts must be cleaned with a high-evaporative solvent, such as brake cleaner, to eliminate any dust. When you're not working on assembly, keep the engine bagged and protected from the elements.

Lay out everything in its proper order, with the pistons and connecting rods coordinated with the crankshaft and numbered to the bore with which they are matched. This ensures that proper dynamic balance and bore fitment are maintained. This is important for dynamic balance, where pistons, rods, and journals are matched to the crank journals. It is also important to match the pistons to the bores that they were machined to.

In this chapter, we are working with two generations of Coyote engines (Gen 2 and Gen 3), which will reveal some obvious differences. This was done to demonstrate the best approach possible for each step and to show variations in these engines. In this chapter, we're working with L&R Engines and QMP Racing Engines in Los Angeles as well as Tommy's Auto Machine & Parts in Springfield, Tennessee, under the watchful eye of seasoned technical writer Wes Duenkel.

Aside from machine work, final assembly is the most critical phase of an engine build. You are the last line of defense in an engine build because you are the inspector and the assembler. Take your time and pay close attention to detail.

A good, solid engine stand is needed for assembly. Harbor Freight offers a great selection of suitable engine stands. Renting an engine stand can get expensive if it's sitting in your garage for months, so a purchase makes more economic sense. Opt for a minimum weight capacity of 1,000 pounds.

This Ford Performance Gen 3 Coyote block has been professionally cleaned and machined by QMP Racing Engines in Chatsworth, California, which employs the latest state-of-the-art CNC equipment. It is ready for assembly.

With the block inverted, closely inspect all areas that have been machined. Do a final washdown and blast all oil galleries and cooling passages with soapy water and a high-evaporative solvent along with compressed air to remove any debris.

Lay out all short-block components in an orderly fashion. This is a good template to follow for your Coyote's assembly.

These main bearing saddles have been align-honed to get a nice crosshatch pattern for bearing security. Oil cooling jets have been installed. Not all Coyote blocks have the cooling jets.

These piston-cooling jets help cool pistons as they reach the bottom of the bore. Ford decided not to use the piston cooling jets for a short time with early Gen 2 blocks.

Before Beginning Assembly

Important! 

Organization and cleanliness are the most important elements of assembly. How clean and neat is your shop? Even the most minute amounts of house dust can result in engine damage. This is why the working environment must be as clean as a hospital.

Before each phase of assembly, spray parts with brake cleaner or lacquer thinner. The high evaporation nature of these solvents gets the parts clean and evaporates without a trace. Then, lubricate these parts as necessary while your attention is on that specific part of the engine. ■

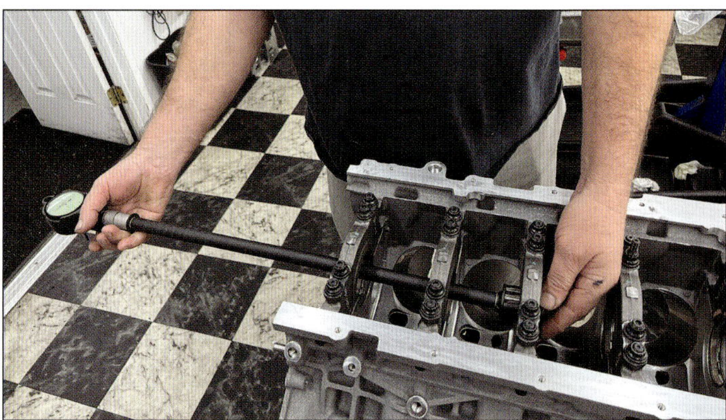

Your machine shop should have already checked main saddle dimensions in the wake of the align honing of the main saddles. As a measure of caution, check the saddles with a dial-bore gauge before assembly begins.

Getting Started

With the block mounted on a safe and stable engine stand, which can be purchased from Harbor Freight or rented locally, you're ready to get started.

The bearings and crankshaft are the first components installed along with block plugs and inserts. Measure the crank journals and installed main bearings at least twice and record those measurements to ensure proper clearances. Check dimensions with a dial-bore gauge and micrometer. Never apply engine assembly lube between the bearing and main saddle, which can adversely affect bearing security. The saddle and bearing must be kept dry. Engine assembly lube should be liberally applied to the bearing surfaces before installing the crank to ensure a slippery start-up.

Shims at the number-5 main thrust are installed with the crank and main cap. With the mains adequately lubed, torque them to the specification found in the appendix while checking for freedom of crank rotation with each bolt tightened. They must be tightened per Ford specifications in proper order. Upon completion, check the crank for freedom of rotation. You should be able to turn the crank with one index finger. If it becomes difficult to turn, clearances are too tight and must be checked.

Also, check crankshaft endplay, which should never be any more than 0.011 inch or any less than

Check all crank-journal dimensions. Compare journal and installed bearing dimensions to confirm bearing clearances.

Never touch the main and rod bearing surfaces during installation. Acids in skin oil will contaminate bearing surfaces. The main saddle and bearing back surfaces must be clean, which also means no oil or assembly lube. I've seen engine builders use lube or engine oil between the bearings and block. This is unnecessary. Clean contact surfaces provide the best bearing security. Seat the bearings as shown at the edges.

Apply engine assembly lube to the main bearings. Check the oil gallery hole's alignment.

Use engine assembly lube, such as Amsoil Assembly Lube for Engine Builders, which has staying power for engines that could end up in storage. It also ensures a wet start-up.

0.006 inch. Before checking endplay, whack each end of the crank with a mallet to "seat" the thrust and center the crank. Then, check endplay. Endplay must fall in between these numbers. If endplay is too tight,

the crank journal will wipe out the thrust (shims and journal), resulting in major engine damage.

What makes the Coyote different from any engine you may have previously built is the torque-angle (torque-to-yield) one-time-use fasteners. The fasteners are torqued in phases and then they receive a specific number of degrees tighter to ascertain bolt stretch. This is a more accurate system of tightening fasteners.

The Coyote's main caps and cylinder heads, as two examples, are

torque-to-yield to ensure accurate fastener torque application. If you opt for aftermarket ARP fasteners, refer to ARP's torque specifications with studs and with bolts. Never assume. Always check and confirm with ARP.

Main cap vertical bolts/studs are torqued first (in order) per Ford's specifications. Then, the side bolts are torqued once the vertical fasteners are tight. Side bolts must have Permatex's The Right Stuff between the heads and block to prevent oil leaks. Use moly lube on the threads

The Coyote's forged-steel crank is seated in the block and gently rotated to distribute assembly lube.

Next, install the number-5 main journal thrust shims (two).

With the two thrust shims installed, seat the number-5 main cap first.

Apply moly lube to fastener threads and bolt-head contact surfaces to achieve an accurate torque assessment. Never use moly lube on bearings and journals.

Final Inspection

Before each assembly phase, take a close look at every part again. This is your last line of defense before assembly. Inspect every part closely when it arrives from the supplier because this gives you the freedom to return anything that is faulty. Inspecting parts just before assembly is simply double-checking your work. Never take for granted that a new part is acceptable for service just because it's new. Defective and mispackaged parts get shipped all the time. It is a good idea to have all of these parts on hand long before you begin assembly. ■

and bolt heads for smooth and accurate torque readings. Never jerk a torque wrench. Instead, apply smooth, even pressure.

Reciprocating Parts

Installing pistons and rods is where the rubber meets the road in power production. This is where we take the thermal energy of a light-up and turn it into

A breakaway torque wrench is used here for tightening main cap bolts. I cannot stress enough the importance of following Ford's recommended torque sequence for tightening these bolts. Tighten the fasteners in two values. Then, apply torque-angle. (Photo Courtesy Wes Duenkel)

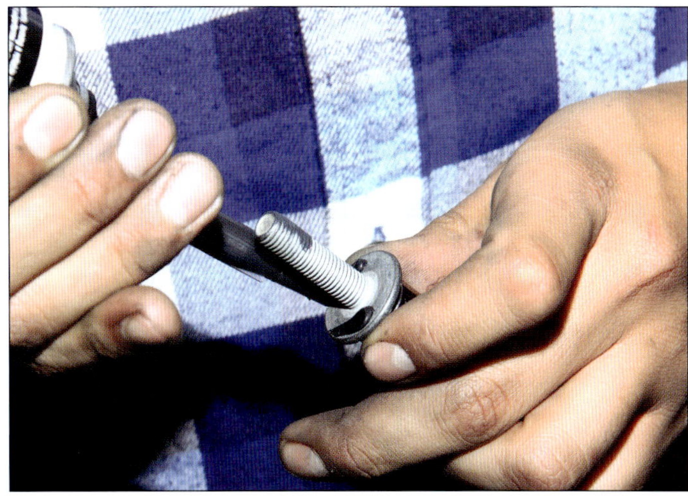

Use a modest amount of The Right Stuff RTV sealer on side bolt main cap flanges. This seals this joint and keeps oil inside the engine. Use moly lube on the bolt threads.

Use a Tack Rag

Important! 

Never use a shop towel to wipe out cylinder walls and apply engine oil or assembly lube to cylinder walls. Instead, always use an electrostatic tack rag with solvent and then engine oil to wipe out the bores. Use automatic transmission fluid as a cleaning agent and a short-term lubricant for cylinder walls. You will be amazed at the contaminants that automatic transmission fluid catches off the cylinder walls. Once the cylinder walls are clean, use SAE 30-weight engine oil or the appropriate assembly lubricant to coat the cylinder walls.

Never use shop towels during engine assembly because they yield unacceptable amounts of lint and trapped dirt, which can adversely affect surfaces between moving parts even though there's an oil wedge. It is remarkable just how much debris you will find in the break-in oil when it is time for that first oil change. I've seen engines come off of dynos with lint and dirt trapped in the filter medium. It's a good idea to cut a filter open after a dyno pull or break-in to see what's inside. ■

Apply 30-weight engine oil or assembly lube that specific for cylinder walls for proper ring seating. This is important to the ring-to-cylinder wall relationship during the all-important break-in.

Shop towels contain lint and other debris, which can cause engine damage. Do not use them.

Use only lint-free tack rags to wipe down each cylinder bore. Automatic transmission fluid, which is a detergent, captures any dirt and debris while coating the cylinder wall. Examine the towel after wipedown and observe the dirt captured. (Photo Courtesy Wes Duenkel)

Torque the side bolts in Ford's specified order and then apply an additional 60 degrees of torque-angle.

Check the crankshaft endplay after a couple of whacks at each end of the crank with a mallet to get it all centered. The endplay should not exceed 0.006 to 0.011 inch.

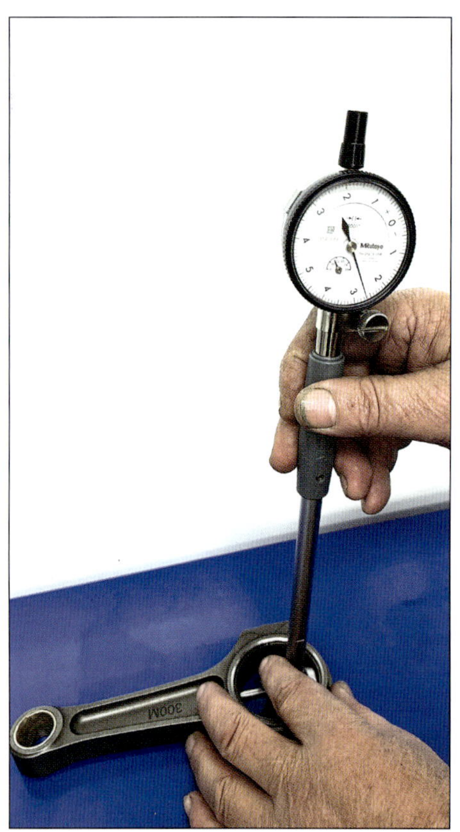

Check rod-journal dimensions to confirm sizing before going any further. You don't want to assemble piston-and-rod assemblies only to learn that dimensions are not within the correct limits. QMP Racing stresses doing this before assembly.

Check the piston-ring end gaps before installation. The end gap is dependent upon how you intend to use the engine and also ring location. The top ring will have the largest gap due to the extreme heat on top. The secondary ring will have a slightly smaller end gap. Ring gaps should be positioned 45 degrees apart.

rotary motion. Each and every bore commands your close attention. The cylinder walls must be clean and properly finish-honed with a uniform crosshatch pattern for good cylinder sealing and oil control.

Piston-ring seating with the cylinder wall determines sealing and oil distribution. Representatives from Federal-Mogul, which manufactures Speed-Pro and Sealed Power piston rings, told me that piston rings form a dynamic, sliding seal—of which rings are but one part of the cylinder sealing package. Ring grooves support the rings for improved piston-ring function.

The Ford Coyote engine employs three rings. The top (compression) ring seals the chamber. The second ring carries oil away from the combustion chamber and assists the top ring's sealing efforts. The bottom ring package (wiper rings and expanders) is an oil-control ring. It wipes the cylinder wall clean and returns oil to the

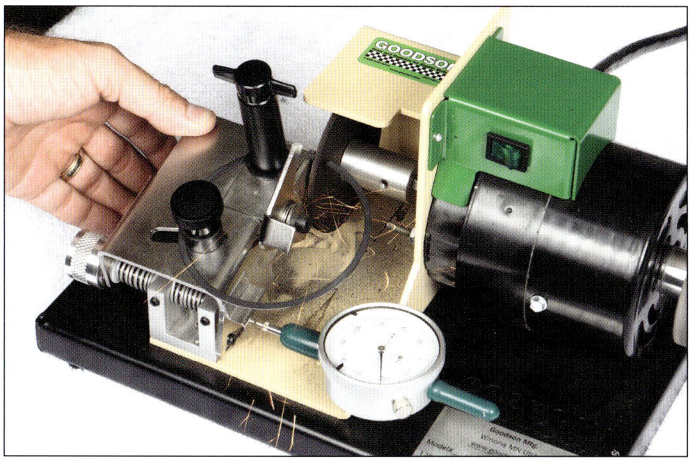

Always nice to have a piston-ring grinder handy. However, for the rest of us, this step means carefully filing ring ends a little at a time until you get it right. File, dress the corners, and check the gap. (Photo Courtesy Wes Duenkel)

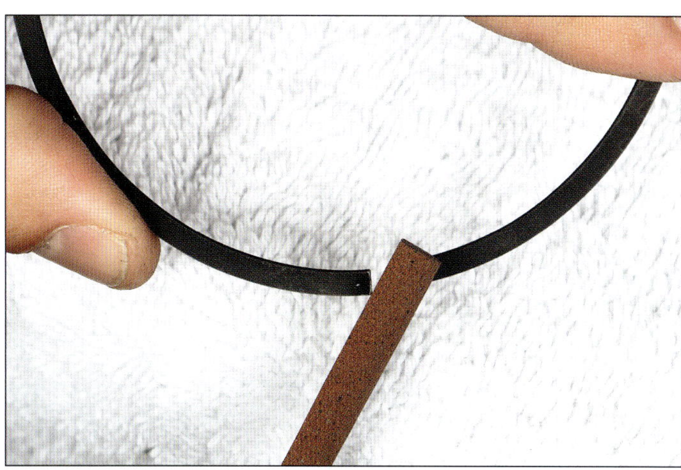

Dress the ring ends with a file (as shown) and make sure that you've removed the rough edges. Rough edges can cause cylinder wall and piston damage. (Photo Courtesy Wes Duenkel)

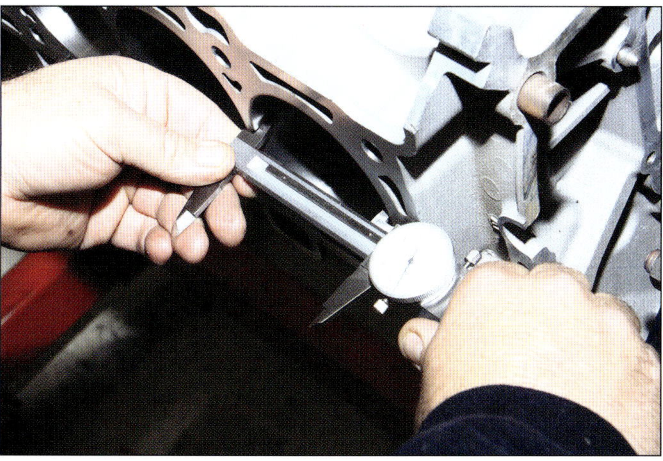

Measure the bore diameter in three locations from top to bottom in each bore and log the dimensions of each location. I suggest measuring three locations two ways to confirm any bore irregularities. You need these numbers to compare with piston dimensions specific to each cylinder bore. Your machine shop should have recorded these numbers on the build sheet. Reputable engine builders do this. See how your numbers compare.

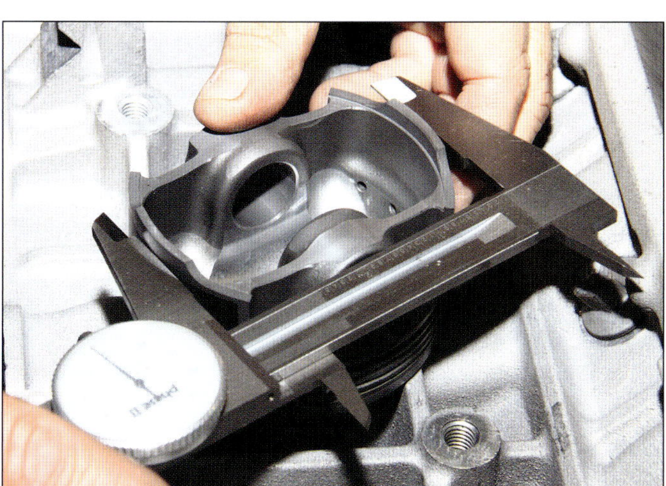

Use calipers to check the piston dimensions and record the dimensions for each piston. The piston dimensions are compared with bore dimensions to learn piston-to-cylinder wall clearances. Check dimensions in two directions.

pan. There's also an element known as oil fog, which is created with the rapid motion of moving parts connecting with engine oil heading in all directions. This also contributes greatly to lubrication.

Another potential issue is what's known as scuff wear. Because today's engines operate at high temperatures, they can get hot spots between the rings and cylinder walls. These hot spots form weld marks as the piston dwells at top dead center (the dwell time depends upon the rod ratio). These welds will separate as soon as the piston begins its journey to the bottom of the bore, which leaves coarse spots on the cylinder walls. These spots can damage piston rings.

Before I go any further, I need to address ring material. Because the top rings tend to be ductile iron in most circumstances, they tend to break down at about 2,250°F. Chromoly can withstand roughly 3,450°F. Molybdenum rings shouldn't break down until 4,800°F. Moly rings are preferred by engine builders and manufacturers due to their porous surface, which holds oil, minimizing ring and cylinder-wall wear.

Ductile-iron top rings are preferred by builders because they do better than cast. Ductile iron's greatest virtue is flexibility, which allows it to stand up to extremely high cylinder pressures. Molybdenum is typically a coating on ductile-iron rings for durability. Oil-control rings offer chrome coated steel scraper rails and a stainless-steel expander to get oil back to the pan.

As rings are compressed into the piston-ring grooves upon installation, rings press against the cylinder

Proper Ring Installation

The top two rings tend to be referred to as compression rings. However, only the top ring is a true compression ring. The top ring is there to contain cylinder pressure in the combustion chamber, which includes compression, combustion, exhaust scavenging, and intake vacuum. The secondary ring acts as a backup sealing ring that helps to contain cylinder pressure that escapes past the top ring. At the same time, the secondary ring also acts as an oil controller to keep oil away from the chamber.

Oil control is important to keep oil out of the combustion chamber—not only to limit oil consumption but also so that it will not adversely affect air/fuel ratio, which affects combustion. Oil contamination in the chamber reduces power and can cause detonation by affecting compression. The other side of this coin is that if excessive amounts of oil are removed from the cylinder walls, the pistons and rings will not get enough lubrication, which causes scuffing. Another purpose that rings have is heat transfer from the piston to the cylinder wall, where it can be absorbed into the coolant. This is especially true for the top ring, which encounters the greatest heat. ■

Get everything laid out on a clean work surface with each piston and with each rod numbered. It is critical to make sure that each piston, rod, and ring pack is with the crank journal on which it was dynamically balanced. Confirm rod and piston indexing with both of them set up correctly to the crank journal. Pistons have "FRONT" arrows on top in reference to the block. Connecting-rod chamfers (the large end) and journal fillets go together, with the flat part of the rod journal against the opposing rod.

Never be shy about the use of engine assembly lube. Lube the pins, pistons, and small end of the rod. Lube the ring grooves. Some engine builders prefer to use assembly lube specific to pistons, rods, and cylinder walls.

Slide the pin in and get it against the retainer on the opposite side. You can expect either a spiro lock or a wire lock to secure the pin. Make absolutely sure that the retaining rings are secure. I've seen too many that weren't secure due to severe cylinder wall damage.

walls, which is known as "diametric tension." Cylinder pressure, ring twist, and the shape of the rings are major factors in cylinder sealing. Rings are bevel-cut to twist in their journey up and down the bore.

To provide an idea of how ring function works, the top ring is generally beveled on top at its edge, which allows a positive twist and better sealing. By contrast, the secondary ring's bevel is located in the lower inside edge of the ring, which creates a negative twist to press the outside edge of the ring against the cylinder

Never force or distort the spiro/wire lock during installation. Make sure that the pin is properly centered against the opposite lock and that the lock is firmly seated in the groove.

Double-check the security and seating of the piston-pin locks.

Rotate the rings to where you have the end gaps 180 degrees apart at 12 and 6 o'clock. Check the rings for freedom of movement and any rough edges. The bottom oil-control rings and expander should be checked for freedom of movement and expander installation.

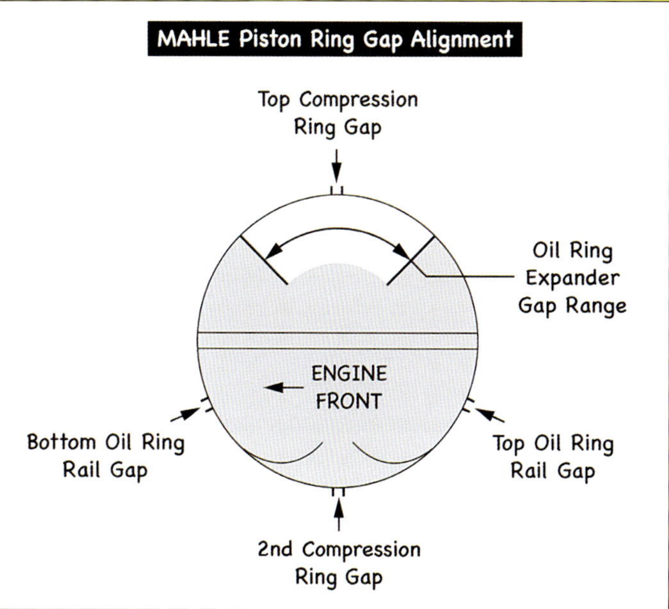

This Mahle illustration demonstrates proper ring end-gap indexing. The top two ring end gaps must be 180 degrees opposite. Take note of the oil rail gaps and where they are indexed. (Photo Courtesy Mahle)

Engine builders have various approaches to cylinder-wall treatments prior to installation. There are cylinder-wall-specific engine assembly lubes. There are also builders who use SAE 30-weight conventional oil on the walls and pistons. I like drowning the piston skirts, rings, grooves, and cylinder walls in either assembly lube or engine oil to ensure a slippery, wet start-up with zero scuffing.

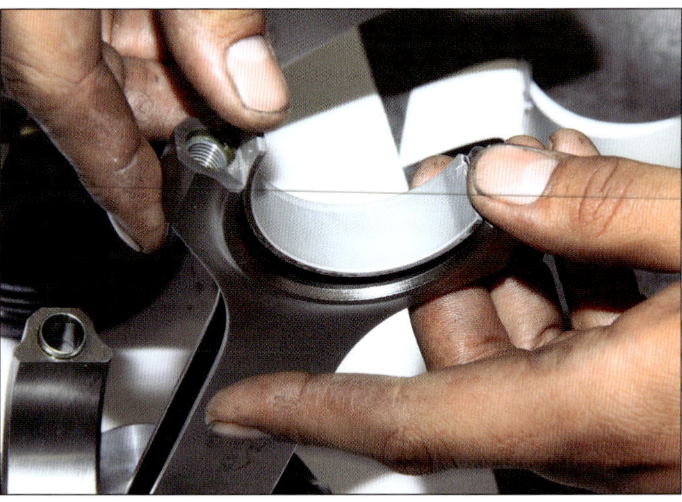

Seat the rod bearings with the tangs properly aligned and then lubed.

In this image, we're at L&R Engines in Los Angeles using an adjustable ring compressor to get these slugs installed. When adjusting the ring compressor, watch ring compression closely and make sure that all are flush with the ring lands.

Make the ring compressor flush against the deck (as shown) and gently press the piston into the bore. Prevent the large end of the rod from hitting the journal below. Place your hand between the rod and journal below to prevent rod-journal damage.

wall. This allows the secondary ring to "wipe" oil away from the top ring.

When end-gapping the rings, understand that the top ring will have the greater gap due to the temperature extremes on top. The secondary ring will have a smaller gap due to less heat and expansion issues. Ring end gaps need to be dressed smooth with a file to where they won't score grooves on the cylinder walls.

With all of this in mind, you must be focused on ring installation, taking your time and making sure that each of the rings is installed per the manufacturer's instructions. As each ring is installed, inspect the installation and double-check your work. Checking your work two to three times means not having to go back and do it all over again.

Coyote performance and durability depend upon the job that is done assembling the engine. Because the Coyote's cylinder walls are paper thin (or plasma sprayed in the case of the Gen 3 Coyote), extra care must be taken. If you're building an all-out racing engine, I am pretty convinced that you've sleeved the block to withstand the extremes of racing.

Regardless of the path taken with your Coyote engine, be methodical in your approach to ring prep and installation. Ring end gaps must be matched to each bore because no two bores are going to be the same dimensionally and for their entire length. You want to see a good cross-hatch pattern from deck to skirt, contributing to ring seating.

There's always debate on which approach to ring installation is best: a ring expander or carefully rolling rings on. I prefer using a ring expander, which limits and prevents distortion. A seasoned engine builder also knows how to roll rings on cautiously without consequences.

Ring gaps should be positioned at 45 degrees around the piston's circumference. This gets them started well away from each other, though they will rotate during operation.

When setting ring end gaps, get the gap set and file the rough edges. Always confirm that you have the top rings installed per the manufacturer's instructions. Double-check your work before stuffing bores. Improper

Lube the rod bolts with engine oil or assembly lube to ensure smooth, accurate torque. Hand-snug these bolts and then apply torque with a torque wrench. (Photo Courtesy Wes Duenkel)

The rod's large end features both a chamfered side and a non-chamfered side. The non-chamfered side of the rod faces the opposing rod from the opposite bank. The chamfered side faces the crank's rod-journal fillet. This is the non-chamfered side.

Torque the connecting-rod bolts to 60 ft-lbs and do so in one-third values. Hand-snug these bolts and observe the rod cap orientation. Then, tighten alternately in one-third values.

Connecting-rod side clearances should be 0.010 to 0.020 inch (per Manley Performance). This applies to both stock and aftermarket rods. (Photo Courtesy Wes Duenkel)

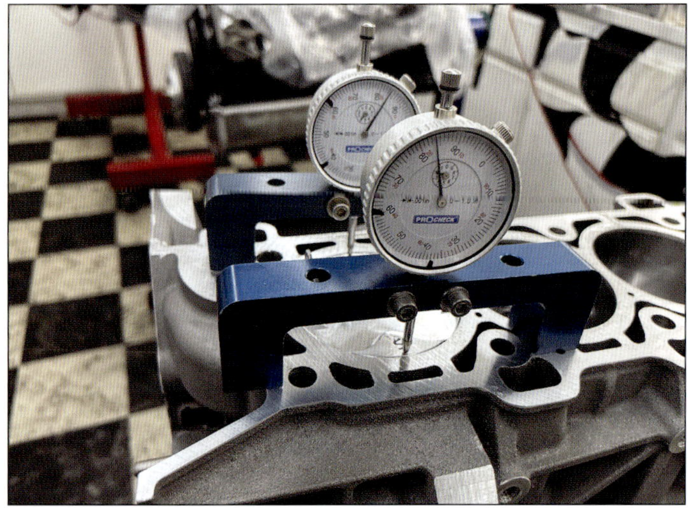

True top dead center is confirmed with two dial indicators, although you can get away with one. This lays the foundation for accurate camshaft degreeing because if you don't confirm true TDC, cam timing events will never be accurate. QMP Racing Engines uses two dial indicators to provide more accurate results.

The short-block is fully assembled with all of its rotating/reciprocating mass ready for final assembly. These are domed pistons in a naturally aspirated Coyote with 11.0:1 or 12.0:1 compression.

ring installation will rear its ugly head in lost power and increased oil consumption.

When assembling pistons and rods, make sure that the rod is indexed in the right direction. I've witnessed engine failures where the rods were indexed backward, which made cranking the engine impossible. The connecting-rod chamfer (beveled side) at the large end should face the fillet radius in the rod journal. By the same token, pistons are typically indexed by following the arrow on the dome, which means "front" facing.

Rod and main bearing tangs are used for reference purposes (not to prevent bearing spin). They help the builder index the bearing properly. Bearing "crush" and dry contact surfaces between the bearing and rod or the bearing and saddle secure the bearings. When installing bearings, observe oil-hole locations and alignment. Always confirm that you have the correct bearings for your application. I've seen bearings mispackaged or mismarked on several occasions, which can lead to severe engine damage.

If you're going to dress the crankshaft snout and/or flange to eliminate burrs and irregularities, do this before the crankshaft is installed. Dress the crank on the bench and thoroughly wash it with soap and hot water. Then, spray it down with brake cleaner, eliminating debris and drying quickly.

Lubrication

Although this has been addressed earlier in this book, always opt for a high-volume oil pump with hardened-steel internals because the standard sintered-metal rotor may not stand up to the extremes. This may seem like overkill for a mild-mannered street engine, but you will never have to wonder about the oil pump. You don't always need a high-volume pump. The most important issue is pressure.

Check Rotation As You Go

As you install the piston and rod assembly in each bore, check the crank rotation for freedom of movement. Tighten the rod bolts to the correct specifications and check rotation. By doing this one cylinder at a time, a problem with clearance/fitment will be found immediately without having to wonder where the trouble is. ■

I presume that you've assembled an appropriate oil system for the type of driving you intend to do with your Coyote. Through the years, I've looked to the expertise of terrific engine builders and racers as well as aftermarket manufacturers who've performed extensive research into what works and what doesn't. Based on experience, Melling is the most reputable manufacturer of

I suggest the use of hardened oil-pump steel rotors for durability, even when building a stocker. (Photo Courtesy Wes Duenkel)

You can't just slide the oil pump onto the crankshaft and run the bolts down. The pump must be centered on the crank to where there's no side load on the pump rotors, which can cause unnecessary rotor and housing wear.

Hardened-steel crank timing gears are also good engine insurance. When installing the oil pump, adjust the pump's positioning where there's no side load on the pump rotor and the pump is centered.

Make sure that all block plugs have been properly installed using Teflon sealer or anti-seize to prevent leakage or a plug being permanently frozen in the block from corrosion.

oil pumps and lubrication systems for high-performance engines. I've had the best performance from its products.

Melling's high-pressure Coyote oil pump (part number 10396) features a hard-coat, anodized aluminum housing and cover, which is better than the factory pump. The Melling pump is fitted with a high-pressure spring for an additional 5 psi of oil pressure. Melling also includes a standard oil-pressure relief-valve spring. The key here is to maintain enough oil pressure to keep an engine safe at high RPM.

If you've opted for an aftermarket oil pan for road or drag racing, it should be a compatible oil pickup. The sump and pickup combination should ensure a robust oil supply at high RPM. The nice thing about today's engines is that oil pumps are driven right off of the crankshaft for a connection between the pump and crank.

Fill the pump cavity with engine assembly lube, whether it is a new pump or an existing pump with hardened internals. When installing the oil pump, make sure that it slides onto the crank smoothly and with no binding. Loosely install the pump and gently hand-crank the engine to ascertain smoothness and detect binding. Then, tighten the fasteners and position the crank keyway at 12 o'clock in preparation for installing the timing components.

Ford went to a different pump and pickup design with the Gen 3 Coyote engines, where the pump called for a pressed-in pickup, which was part of the pan assembly. This means using a compatible pump and pickup. Moroso created a special pickup that will work without having to replace the Gen 3 pump. It came up with a special pickup with a billet end that presses into that pump. When installing the pan, be it composite or cast aluminum, check the pickup-to-pan clearances and ensure that there's plenty of space in between.

Top End

If you've never worked with the Modular or Coyote engines, you will find the cylinder heads to be quite involved. With the Coyote, cylinder heads are a complex maze of 32 valves, springs, and related parts, including the rocker arms and lash adjusters. There's always the issue of whether to replace the valves or reface them. Replace the valves and reface the seats in the interest of durability and saving money. If the exhaust valve seats are badly worn, I suggest replacing them. Your machine shop will know the best course of action. By this time, all cylinder-head work should have been completed, with cylinder head installation being the only task left.

For our money, Fel-Pro and SCE Gaskets are the best gasket sources

Valve-spring pressure needs to coincide with the cam profile. I suggest having the machine shop do the head work, where they have the equipment to check spring pressure and installed height.

This is the valve seal that Ford uses in OEM Coyotes. The very best valve seals are Viton and are available from Summit Racing Equipment.

In the interest of valvetrain security, I suggest using titanium valve keepers and race-ready retainers to ensure valvetrain integrity. Titanium retainers and keepers are good performance modifications that offer better valvetrain security for racing engines and modified street engines. Because titanium is lighter, it allows higher revs without the consequences of weight.

out there, although everyone has their favorites. Gasket technology has improved by leaps and bounds, which means that only a few locations require Permatex's "The Right Stuff" for leak prevention. Apply

Use ARP Bolts

Because cylinder-head bolts are torque-to-yield, it is my hope that you have acquired those prior to assembly. Because Ford parts, such as fasteners, tend to be quite expensive, I suggest using ARP cylinder head bolts (or studs). If you plan to use boost or nitrous, stud the heads instead of using bolts. Studs provide unequaled security on top. ARP fasteners are not torque-to-yield. ∎

The Coyote uses composition multilayer head gaskets for good, positive sealing. Make sure that all contact surfaces are free of debris. I suggest using ARP head bolts or studs for maximum security. (Photo Courtesy Wes Duenkel)

The Right Stuff only at gasket joints where the heads meet the timing cover and block below where the oil pan meets the timing cover.

All contact surfaces must be hospital-clean prior to cylinder-head installation. I cannot stress this enough. Even the tiniest grain of sand can cause leakage. Seal grooves in the timing cover, cam covers, and oil pan must receive a final cleaning with brake parts cleaner prior to assembly, and all must be closely inspected for debris. Cylinder-head and block-deck surfaces call for close inspection. Check intake and exhaust ports for any stray debris that might have been ingested.

With the cylinder heads seated and bolts torqued in their proper order, it is time for the cams and valvetrain. Use generous amounts of assembly lube on the journals and cam lobes. I suggest soaking the rocker arms and lash adjusters in synthetic engine oil before installation to ensure deep needle bearings and internal lubrication. Give cam phasers the same treatment.

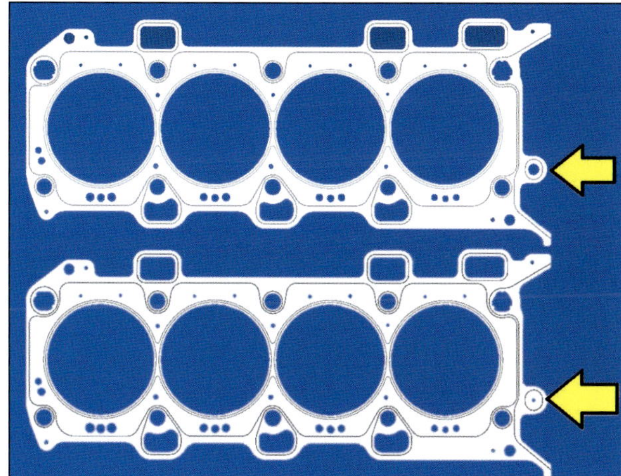

The difference between the 2011–2014 and 2015–2017 head gaskets is shown here. On top is the 2015–2017 head gasket with a revised VCV oil galley passage (arrow), which is larger. Bottom is the 2011–2014 gasket with a pinhole-sized galley passage (arrow). (Photo Courtesy Ford Performance Parts)

If running stock cylinder-head bolts, follow the torque-to-yield approach to tightening with the proper torque specifications. Then, torque-angle the fasteners a specific number of degrees in the proper order. Bolts should be torqued in one-third values, meaning one-third of the total value, then two-thirds, then torque-angle. If you're running ARP bolts or studs, follow ARP's torque specifications, which are included with the fasteners. (Photo Courtesy Wes Duenkel)

Cam Timing

The greatest challenge of engine assembly is valve timing. This is a phase where you must inspect your work repeatedly by hand, cranking the engine several times to ensure that all timing marks fall into place.

Cam timing begins at the crankshaft, with the keyway positioned at 12 o'clock (straight up). Once the crank is set with the keyway at 12 o'clock, you're ready to install cams, phasers, chains, guides, and tensioners. The first order of business is cams, which must be carefully set in the journals and capped.

Each of the four camshafts has "D" slots, which are timing marks that mandate careful, attentive positioning. Once the D slots are positioned, it is a matter of getting the black and dark blue anodized timing chain links properly positioned at the crank and cam phasers/sprockets to achieve proper valve timing.

The first order of business is to get the cam phasers and secondary chains aligned/timed with the camshafts with a test fit. Remember that intake phasers get the double link, while exhaust phasers get the single link. This applies to both heads.

The roller finger followers and lash adjusters (lifters) are next and should be soaked in either 5W30 engine oil or engine assembly lube before installation.

Factory camshaft journal bolts work very well in mild street to moderate performance applications. ARP fasteners offer additional security.

Lubricate the camshaft journals with engine assembly lube and then carefully set the camshafts in place.

First, snug camshaft journal caps in the proper order and check the cams for freedom of rotation before going any further. Torque the journal caps to 53 in-lbs. Then, torque-angle 45 degrees in proper order (per the appendix).

Passenger-side cylinder-head cams are installed and timed per this image. These D-shaped timing marks must be positioned as shown at 5 o'clock (exhaust cam) and 2 o'clock (intake cam). When cam phasers are installed, they should line up. If they do not, the cams and phasers need to be rotated until they do. Again, some adjustment of the cams and/or crank is required to achieve perfect cam/sprocket alignment.

The exhaust cam phaser (left) is driven by the primary chain (black arrow). The intake phaser (right) is driven by the secondary chain. The Coyote has just two types of phasers for both banks (intake and exhaust), which can interchange from side to side. Secondary chains have two types of timing links: single (exhaust) and double (intake). The double secondary chain link goes on the intake cam phaser. Single links are located at the exhaust cam phasers. Timing marks (white arrows) are indicated on each phaser.

Intake and exhaust phasers are reversible from bank to bank.

Once the cam phasers/sprockets are properly aligned, connect the primary chains from the crankshaft. With the secondary chains/sprockets/phasers timed, install the primary chains and get the timing links lined up with the crank and phaser sprockets. The crank sprockets get a single timing link.

From here on out, assembly is a process of installing components, including sensors, the timing cover, the water pump and coolant manifold, the harmonic damper, the intake manifold, and a host of other components. The crank sensor and trigger wheel are installed

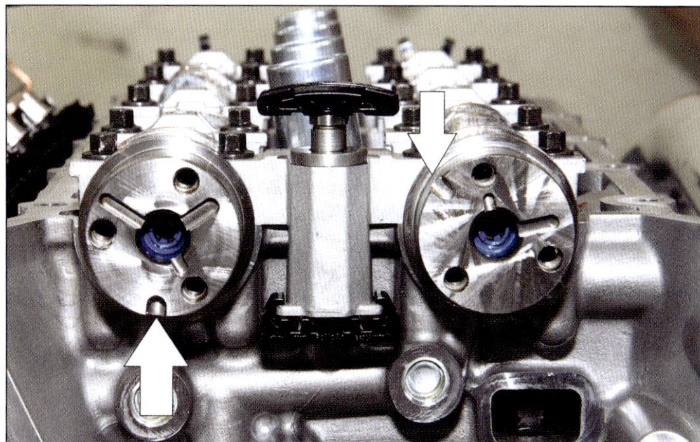

Driver-side cylinder-head cams are installed and timed like this. These D-shaped pockets are timing marks. The intake cam "D" is located at approximately 6 o'clock. The exhaust cam "D" is at approximately 10 o'clock. When the cam phasers are installed, some adjustment is required to get cams and sprockets lined up.

Position the cams as shown for initial setup.

Although a special cam-holding tool can be used to secure the cams, using an adjustable Crescent wrench allows you to save money.

The cam phasers have timing marks (shown here) where dark timing-chain links align for proper timing. The dark links are timing-mark links.

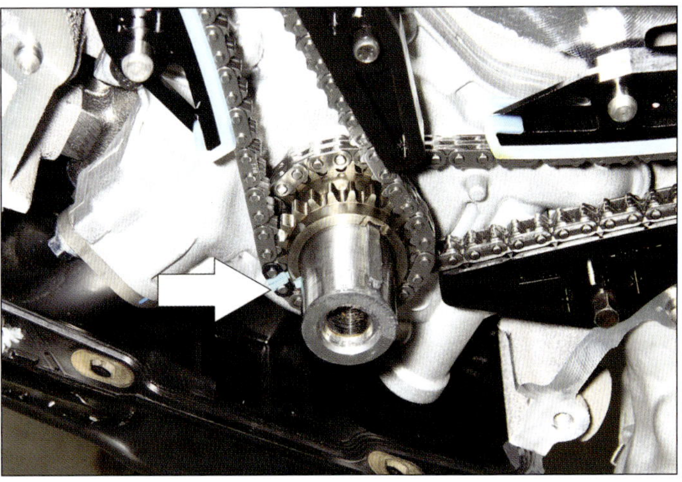

Let's walk through the timing-component sequence. The crankshaft-sprocket timing mark and chain link line up like this.

The passenger-side exhaust cam phaser/timing sprocket mark and chain link line up like this.

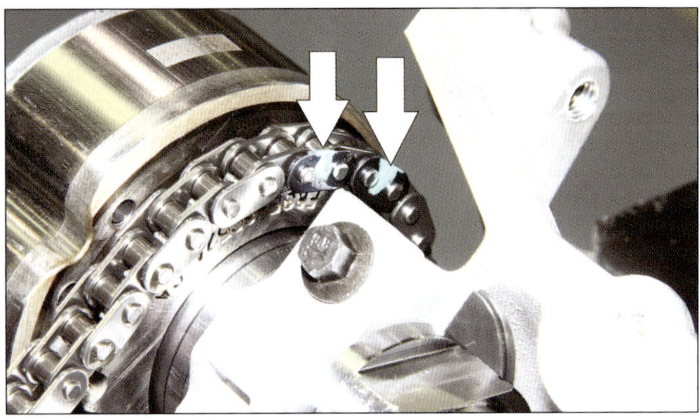

Line up the driver-side intake cam phaser and sprocket with the two dark links aligned on the appropriate tooth. The timing mark is not visible here.

The driver-side exhaust phaser sprocket's timing mark lines up with the primary chain link from the crankshaft (dark in color for identification).

Here are the cam phasers/sprockets and secondary timing chain joining the two. The Coyote has two types of cam phasers: intake and exhaust. Secondary chains have darkened timing links. The double link goes on the intake cam phaser and timing mark. Single links are located at the exhaust cam phaser and timing mark. Note that the double link is on the left (intake), and the single link is on the right (exhaust). The exhaust phaser/sprocket is driven by the primary chain from the crankshaft on each side.

with the aft block cover, which requires special care because it includes the one-piece rear main seal. Do not lubricate the rear main seal and make sure that the seal lip is turned toward the crankshaft.

The timing cover needs the inner and outer silicone seals carefully seated in the grooves. These seals do not call for sealer. Room temperature vulcanizing (RTV) sealant is required where seals come together at the cam

Once the primary timing chains are secured and all timing marks are properly indexed, install and release the timing-chain guide tensioners that are modulated by oil pressure. This is the passenger-side tensioner. (Photo Courtesy Wes Duenkel)

The passenger-side timing chain guide is against the chain. Pull the tensioner pin to release the tensioner and apply pressure to the chain.

The driver-side tensioner pin is pulled and released against the guide and chain. (Photo Courtesy Wes Duenkel)

covers and oil pan. The seal lip and garter spring face the crankshaft (the engine). The timing cover includes the cam phaser solenoids and seals located at the top of each side of the timing cover.

The garter spring's job is to hold the seal lip against the crank. If the garter spring pops out during installation, the seal will leak. Pack the garter-spring pocket with engine assembly lube. This will reduce the risk of spring loss during seal installation. This seal is installed before the timing cover is installed. Inspect the garter spring for security at the seal lip. Apply Permatex's The Right Stuff sealer sparingly where the timing cover, cam covers, and oil pan meet. You don't need a lot of it.

The water-pump O-ring seal should have plenty of lubricant for ease of installation. Slowly press the water pump into place, line up the bolt holes, and install the fasteners. I hope that you remembered to photograph bolt and stud positions during disassembly. The coolant manifold, which includes the thermostat and housing, is next.

When installing the harmonic damper, use RTV where the damper joins the crankshaft. This keeps oil

Timing-chain routing should have the primary chains routed over the guides (as shown) and up to the cam phasers. Primary timing chains drive the exhaust cams. Smaller secondary chains from the exhaust-cam sprockets drive the intake cams.

The front crankshaft seal requires special care during installation. Lube this seal with engine assembly lube and make sure that the garter spring-loaded lip is pointed inward toward the crank. Pack the seal cavity with assembly lube to keep the garter spring secured.

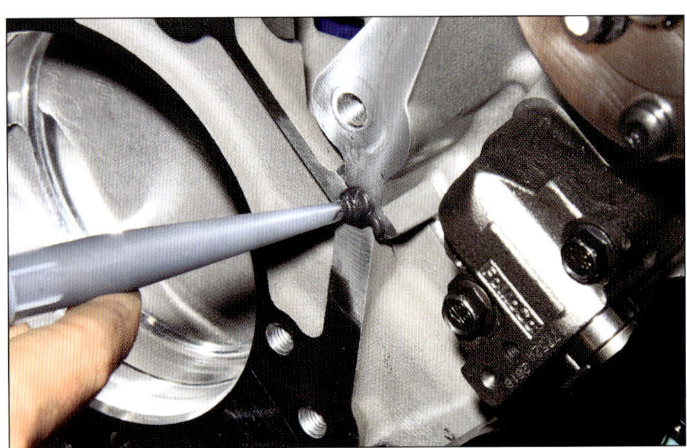

Use Permatex's The Right Stuff RTV to seal the locations where the cam covers and timing cover meet and where the timing cover meets the oil pan. Be conservative with the use of sealant, as you need very little.

After installing the timing-cover seal, carefully align and position the timing cover over the crank, the heads, and the block. These arrows indicate the joints where RTV should be applied.

Water pump installation is next. Make sure that the O-ring seal is lubricated for easy installation and that it is properly positioned in the water-pump groove. Gently press the pump into the block cavity. Snug these bolts and then torque them to 15 ft-lbs and an additional 60 degrees.

Next is installation of the cooling manifold and thermostat housing, where coolant flows into the engine from the radiator, known as cross-flow cooling. Coolant flows into the engine (instead of out) via an open two-valve thermostat.

Next is the harmonic damper, which can be installed with a specialized tool or by tightening the bolt and running the damper onto the crankshaft until it seats. Use RTV (silicone) between the damper and the crankshaft to prevent oil leakage.

Never use a hammer or a mallet to install the harmonic damper. The installation tool can be a specialized tool available at Harbor Freight, or you can use a long bolt and washers to run the damper down. (Photo Courtesy Wes Duenkel)

Today's gasket technology is better than it has ever been in the past. Cam covers are easy to install and secure. Make sure that seals are seated firmly in the valve cover and free of distortion. Examine the seals around the phaser solenoids and spark plug wells for fitment. I have seen aftermarket cover gaskets that are too large.

inside the engine and eases installation. Do not hammer the damper onto the crankshaft. Use an installation tool or the crank bolt to run the damper down.

Cam cover installation is easy. Inspect the condition of cam-cover seals, which are one-piece affairs and don't require sealer anywhere but at the joints that are shared with the timing cover and oil pan.

Oil-pickup and pan installation is straightforward. Gen 1 and Gen 2 engines have a steel oil-pan pickup, which bolts to the oil pump in front. This should be installed before the timing components. Gen 3 engines have an oil pan that includes a pressed-in plastic pickup, which presses into the oil pump. The windage tray and pan gasket are one

For a Gen 3 Coyote with dual fuel injection, be mindful of the high-pressure injection pump in the passenger-side cylinder head. Make sure that the pump cam has plenty of lubrication before installing the cam cover.

The Gen 3 Coyote has this high-pressure direct-injection manifold beneath the intake manifold. This is where the Gen 3 differs from Gen 1 and Gen 2.

These high-pressure direct-injection lines are one-time-use parts and cannot be reused. They are available from Ford.

The rear block cover is sealed with The Right Stuff from Permatex. It does not employ a gasket.

Do not lubricate the Coyote's one-piece crank seal before installation. Lubricating the seal lip can lead to leakage.

integral unit. Expect to see either a cast pan or a composite. Depending upon the generation Coyote, the oil-to-water cooler oil filter is next and involves installing the proper filter/cooler on the engine block.

Intake manifold installation is likely the easiest phase of installation because it sits right on top of the intake ports. Inspect the port seals for proper seating and lay the manifold in place. Follow the proper bolt-torque sequence beginning with snugging the bolts and then following the proper tightening sequence.

Finishing Touches

At this juncture in an engine build, you've gone the distance and are nearing the finish line. There's always a certain amount of apprehension when you're ready to fire a fresh engine. It is a religious moment when you hear the starter and combustion for the first time. There is fear coupled with anticipation. However, don't let these emotions slow you down. The build should continue much as it already has (in a methodical step-by-step manner) until the last fastener has been torqued.

There are important steps to take. The oil-to-coolant cooler, which is one of the final phases, may need to be replaced. If the Coyote experienced engine failure, replace the cooler, which may be contaminated with debris.

When building a Gen 3 Dual-Injection Coyote, the high-pressure direct injection requires special care. I was surprised to learn from Ford that the two high-pressure injection lines are for one-time use only. Once disconnected, they must be replaced.

The rear block cover is worthy of mention because it is so important. Use Permatex's The Right Stuff on the rear block cover. It does not employ a gasket. The rear main seal also requires special care. It must be carefully pressed into place in the cover. Do not lubricate the seal lip. Install it dry because it will leak if lubed. I've been told this by several engine builders. If you are building a Gen 4 Coyote, be advised that the Gen 4 is fitted with a redesigned rear block cover.

This O-ring seal is installed and lubricated where the pickup joins the oil pump in front with Gen 1 and Gen 2 Coyote engines. When installing this pickup, make sure to have the O-ring seal installed and generously lubricated. The Gen 3 Coyote's oil pickup is part of the pan and is press-fitted into the oil pump.

The Coyote's oil pickup is routed from the crank-driven oil pump to a deep (8-quart) oil sump. This pickup can handle the volume. The factory windage tray and pan gasket combination are one part. Confirm which Coyote engine (Gen 1, Gen 2, or Gen 3) is being used, and confirm that there is a pan, pickup, and windage tray. Gen 3 has a pickup-and-pan combination.

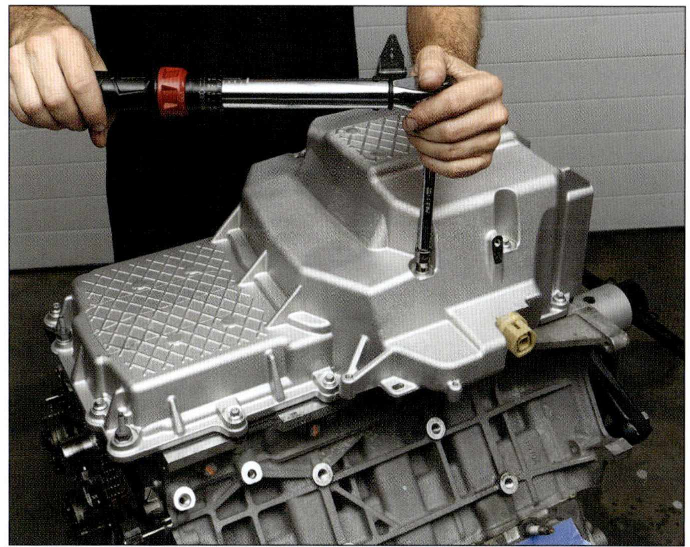

Coyotes are fitted with either a cast or a composite oil pan with the same type of embedded seal at the timing and cam covers. Use The Right Stuff at the joints in modest amounts and secure the pan. (Photo Courtesy Wes Duenkel)

FINAL PREPARATION, BREAK-IN, AND TUNING

With a freshly rebuilt Coyote engine, you will have a combination of anxiety and anticipation. However, before you can fire the engine safely and successfully, it is important to ensure the engine and all of its support systems are ready.

Have you adequately prepared the engine for that first start-up? Does the engine have an adequate cooling system? What about the headers and exhaust system? Are you confident of the ignition and fuel systems? Is the driveline in good condition? Can the vehicle's driveline handle the amount of power that you now have? Have you thought about brakes, suspension, wheels, and tires? It all has to work together cohesively to be enjoyable and safe.

With thoughts of vehicle condition aside, there's a lot to think about with the engine alone. You're not working with an old-school engine. Instead, this is Ford's Coyote is a precision high-tech mill. Get ready— you're about to hear it for the first time. Let's get started on prep.

Lubrication

It is often debated which oil to use in the Coyote. This engine's design specification calls for 5W20 synthetic, which is what the majority of Coyote engine builders and racers use. I prefer Mobil 1 synthetic, although Lucas and Amsoil synthetics are also excellent choices.

Ford recommends 5W20 oil primarily with the National Highway Traffic Safety Administration's Corporate Average Fuel Economy (CAFE) standards in mind. However, I suggest the use of 5W30 to control oil consumption and improve lubricity once the break-in is complete.

If your budget allows, invest in a professional dyno tune and break-in. Breaking in an engine on a dyno allows a controlled break-in with a hard pull at high RPM to seat the rings and bearings once the engine reaches operating temperature. Once the break-in is complete, power pulls and tuning follow.

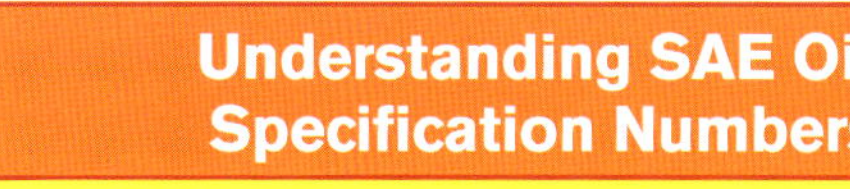

TECH TIP

Understanding SAE Oil Specification Numbers

Ever wondered what SAE viscosity numbers mean? For example, take "5W20." The "5" indicates what the oil does when it is cold. The "W" stands for winter. The "20" indicates what the oil does when it is hot.

Reputable engine-oil brands have at least three different types of certification information on the container. At least one of those certification standards will apply to Ford engines. Expect to see "SC," "SM," "GF-4," and "GF-5" along with the API donut logo.

Sulfur was once used in engine oil to reduce friction. Today, oil companies use molybdenum, which tends to make the oil black through time and use. Black oil isn't always a bad thing. By the way, there's no magic in the latest wave of high-mileage-engine-type oils. These oils have seal conditioners designed to reduce or eliminate seal leak issues. They don't improve ring seating or quiet noisy pistons and bearings. ■

Only use synthetic lubrication for the Coyote engine. For my money, Mobil 1 5W20 is good for the break-in. Then, give it a steady diet of 5W30 for a good oil wedge and lubricity.

Amsoil offers a complete line of synthetic lubrication for the Coyote engines. Perform your break-in with 5W20, and follow that with 5W30 for the following oil and filter changes.

When it comes to oil filters, opt for Wix, Motorcraft, or K&N filters. Where possible, fill the filter with as much oil as possible before installation.

To ensure a good, slippery start-up, secure an oil-pressure pot or pump connected to the oil galleries to pre-lube the moving parts. Yes, this should be done even though everything has already been coated with assembly lube. If a pressure pot is not available, remove the spark plugs and spin the engine for a good 30 seconds on the starter to get the oiling system saturated with the oil in the pan and filter. Where possible, fill the oil filter with the same oil that is in the pan and then spin the engine.

Finally, install a filter magnet on the oil filter to catch any ferrous metal debris. Change the oil and filter right after the break-in. Then, change the oil and filter again at 1,000 miles.

Oil Filter

Although most engine oil filters look the same externally, there are big differences inside. With oil filters, you get what you pay for. Here's what you need to know about oil filters.

There needs to be plenty of filter material, high burst pressure, and good drainback qualities in an oil filter. The Society of Automotive Engineers (SAE) has specific tests it conducts to determine engine oil filter quality and function. These tests are known as J806 and J1858. The SAE is looking for:

- Drainback, anti-drainback issues
- The point at which the filter becomes so blocked that the bypass unseats and oil becomes unfiltered

- True filtering capacity
- High burst pressure

SAE testing is conducted to determine whether engine oil filters meet a manufacturer's specifications or not. Although all engine oil filters must pass the J806 test, there's a tougher test that tells us even more: the J1858 test. The J806 test is little more than running the filter and seeing how much it traps along with its bypass and drainback qualities. The tougher J1858 test gets into the nitty-gritty of what a filter traps and for how long. Go to the SAE's website (sae.org) for more information.

The drainback valve in an engine oil filter is nothing more than a rubber or a urethane flapper valve, which allows the flow of oil in one direction but not the other (a simple check valve). Some of them are metal-on-metal affairs that don't always keep oil in the filter.

According to Russ W. Knize, who conducted an extensive independent study of dozens of oil filters on his own time and at his own expense, drainback valves don't always work as designed. Knize's study tells it like it is based on his findings. Oil filters tend to be a shell game produced by a small group of manufacturers.

There aren't as many oil-filter types as you might think. For example, a Motorcraft oil filter is "Motorcraft" in brand name only because this same exact filter is shared with other brand names. This isn't necessarily a bad thing because the Motorcraft filter that Knize tested performed quite well in the comparison.

Knize's study ran the gamut of brands and filters. He cut each filter open and shared his findings. He looked at all of the same things that the SAE does, including the amount of filter material, the density of the filter-ing material, drainback issues, etc. He suggested choosing an oil filter based on filtering material and a thoughtful combination of good drainback and bypass qualities. His first order of business was filtering material. He looked at how much filtering material was there to capture dirt particles.

"Cellulose media (basically paper), can trap fewer particles and can flow less oil per square inch because there are fewer passages through it," Knize said.

Knize added that some filters have a combination of cellulose and synthetics, which does a better job of filtration.

"More pleats in the elements does not necessarily mean more surface area," Knize said. "Too many pleats can end up restricting flow because there's not enough area in between to allow oil to flow."

Aside from filtering material, good drainback, and bypass qualities, you want a filter with high burst pressure. You won't find high-burst-pressure capability in a cheap oil filter.

Another issue that I would like to address here is the use of an oil-filter magnet to catch stray metal (iron) particles that can cause engine damage. I suggest using an oil-filter magnet for the life of the Coyote engine. Several brands make filter magnets.

Filter Magnets	
Brand	**Contact Information**
Magna-Guard	619-284-7608, magna-guard.com
Magneclean	Available at Amazon.com
MagnaFilter	866-643-5877, 734-424-0487; bossproducts.com
Filter Plus	Filter-plus.com
Filter Mag	800-FILTERMAG; filtermag.com

Oil filter magnets are not a cure-all for oil-system issues. However, the more ferrous metals that can be kept out of circulation, the better. Filter magnets can help improve engine life, but not significantly. Much depends on how often the oil is changed and the kind of oil that is used. Filter magnets will not keep non-magnetic particles (such as brass, copper, aluminum, or dirt/dust) from doing engine damage. This is what a filter is supposed to do.

Cooling System

The Coyote's cooling system pays close attention to exhaust-valve cooling as well as other high-heat areas of the engine. Ford calls this cross-flow cooling, which is different from conventional engine cooling. Cross-flow cooling routes coolant up through the block, where it enters cylinder heads at the exhaust valves for excellent heat transfer and reduced operating temperatures.

Coolant runs through a long manifold cast into the cylinder head at the exhaust-valve seats for exceptional cooling. Then, it flows toward the spark plugs, the intake manifold, and the block before heading back to the radiator. This keeps detonation issues to a minimum and keeps durability high.

When studying the Coyote's cooling system, it gets confusing. There are what looks like two thermostat housings: one on top of the intake manifold on the driver's side and another at the driver-side cylinder head in front. However, there is but one thermostat, which is located at the driver-side cylinder head, where coolant flows from the radiator into the block.

The Ford Coyote operates with a two-valve/two-stage thermostat. The two-valve function is designed to precisely regulate coolant flow and temperature, yet it works conventionally. What makes it different is its location at the inlet to the engine instead of the outlet. Flow is achieved through extensive computational flow dynamics and thoughtful engine architecture. This is a revised cooling approach called "cross-flow" cooling, where heads get cooling priority.

In a conventional cooling system, coolant flows into the block from the radiator. The thermostat controls the flow out of the engine. With the Coyote, coolant flow

The Coyote's thermostat is located where coolant from the radiator enters the engine's water jackets at the cylinder heads, where cooling is needed most.

remains from the radiator through the bottom hose. However, the thermostat controls flow *into* the engine instead of *out* of it.

It is important to get a fresh engine started with a new radiator with the use of a coolant filter on the return side to trap impurities. A coolant filter is designed to capture rust and aluminum particles that can come loose and end up in a new radiator. During the first few miles, check the coolant filter and make sure that it is clear. A clogged coolant filter will

create the same kind of overheating issues as a clogged radiator. Once there are at least a thousand miles showing, remove the coolant filter.

A new thermostat is needed in the interest of durability. A thermostat's operating temperature is determined by the spring pressure in the thermostat. The greater the spring pressure, the higher the operating temperature. For example, a 195°F thermostat has more spring pressure than a 160°F or a 180°F thermostat. Thermostats fail when wax leaks

Never run straight water in the Coyote cooling system unless you're on the dyno or going racing. Racers should use a corrosion inhibitor at the very least. Service the cooling system with a 50-50 mix of antifreeze and distilled water. Do not use tap water.

A fresh approach to coolant protection is Evans Non-Aqueous coolant, which is 100-percent coolant with no water added. Evans feels oily to the touch and, as a result, prevents corrosion and improves heat transfer. However, you need to completely purge all water and antifreeze from the cooling system to service it with Evans. This can be challenging with the Coyote block, which has insufficient drainage access. Evans coolant never has to be changed, and it yields a higher boiling point than conventional coolant.

from the thermostat actuator and it will not open.

The Coyote calls for a 210°F thermostat, which is important for proper electronic engine control function. Some Coyote performance types prefer 160°F, which is not always a good idea. I've been told by tuners and builders alike to have the tune adjusted to where the electric fans will turn on earlier to take advantage of cooler operating temperatures, which means more power. I am not certain that I agree with this approach because it affects when the ECM/PCM goes closed loop. The Coyote was designed to operate at the higher 210°F temperature range.

Electric cooling fans are designed to do their job primarily when the vehicle is sitting still. They don't serve much of a purpose when the vehicle is in motion. Electric cooling fans have to be chosen with some level of common sense. Not all of them are designed to cool as effectively as manufacturers want you to believe. I am of the belief that factory cooling fans work best. Choose a fan based on cubic feet of air a minute (CFMs).

Electric fans should encompass 100 percent of the radiator's surface area. The objective is to keep air flowing across the tubes and fins at all times, which draws heat from the coolant inside. I've been told by professional tuners that a minimum of 300 cfm from a radiator-cooling fan is needed to maintain temperature.

Opt for a 50-50 mixture of ethylene glycol and water. Use the Water Wetter coolant additive to improve coolant surface tension and eliminate corrosion. Some fill the cooling system with straight water, which is never a good idea unless you're running a good corrosion inhibitor and are going racing.

Evans non-aqueous coolant is the best coolant that is available, and it works well by itself without water. Do not use Evans coolant with water. Because Evans coolant is priced at approximately $60 to $80 a gallon, it can get expensive. However, Evans is a very effective coolant because it transfers heat better than water or ethylene glycol. Because it does not mix with water, there is no corrosion. In addition, Evans never has to be changed.

Amsoil Dominator Coolant Boost is a good corrosion inhibitor that can be used with water or the 50-50 antifreeze/water mix. It improves coolant surface tension and reduces corrosion. Surface tension is how much of the coolant is in direct contact with the block and heads. High surface tension causes three-dimensional balls or bubbles, creating a gap between the aluminum and coolant. Low surface tension causes the coolant to spread out across the surface, eliminating or minimizing the gap.

Although there is a wide variety of aftermarket electric cooling fans for Coyote applications, the factory cooling fans are very effective for street and race applications.

A new radiator is a good investment in engine longevity. Go for the greatest capacity that is available for your F-150 or Mustang.

Fresh engines and radiators need a coolant filter to keep impurities out of the cooling system. Summit Racing Equipment stocks a wide variety of coolant filters, including its own brand of filters, Gano, and the Trap coolant filters. Use a coolant filter on a fresh engine to trap metal particles during the break-in process. Then, remove the filter.

Although some engine builders provide the "stop leak" chemical additive as a leak preventer, never use a leak inhibitor for any reason. Arm yourself with a leak-tight cooling system and never cut corners. If you have a leaky cooling system, replace the affected components.

Ready to Fire

Before firing your Coyote, consider investing in a good dyno session with a reputable tuner. The best way to break in an engine is under the load of a dyno, which helps seat rings and bearings. Once the engine fires, let it run at 2,500 rpm for 30 minutes for good oil splash and pressure lubrication. Allow it to come to operating temperature (around 150 to 200°F coolant temperature).

Once the engine has had a chance to warm up, examine the coolant for discoloration. Check the oil (which should be dark from assem-bly lube) and check for leaks. The rear main seal area should be free of leakage. Closely inspect freeze plugs, intake-manifold gaskets, valve-cover gaskets, and front timing cover for leakage.

After the break-in, change the oil and run 5W30 synthetic engine oil with a Wix or a Motorcraft oil filter. After 1,000 miles, perform another fluid inspection. Pull the dipstick and examine the oil. It should be free of debris and be relatively clear. If it is milky and resembles turkey gravy, there is coolant in the oil. The cause of coolant leakage must be deter-mined and corrected immediately.

At 1,000 miles, check the spark plugs. They should be off-white to snow white in color. Black and sooty spark plugs indicate a rich fuel mix-ture. Snow white with dots of alumi-num is cause for concern, as it results from a lean condition with piston damage. Spark plugs that are oily are the result of piston-ring leakage or excessive valve-guide wear.

While you are under the hood, listen to the engine at idle. Do any noises stand out, such as a stand-alone clicking? This would indicate an oil-starved or dam-aged rocker arm or a collapsed lash adjuster. Do these noises happen cold or hot? Use a long-handle screw-driver or a mechanic's stethoscope to listen for noise and determine its location. Remove cam covers and watch the valvetrain at idle. Ascer-tain the source of the clicking. In addition, look for oil starvation.

If there is a knock, especially in the bottom end, this is a reason to be more concerned about assem-bly issues, clearances, etc. If there is a knock in rhythm with the crank-shaft, disconnect the coil leads one at a time and listen closely. If the knock

Did You Burp It?

Engines need coolant in con-tact with every square inch of cooling passage for effective heat transfer to the coolant. When servicing an engine's cooling system with the correct mix of antifreeze and water or Evans coolant, keep the heater hose or temperature sender loose to allow air to escape from the water jackets before firing the engine. Leaving a hose or a sender loose at the top of the engine allows air to escape, which eliminates air pockets (hot spots) in the engine.

Use Water Wetter, which improves the coolant's surface ten-sion (contact with iron and aluminum surfaces inside the water jackets). The better the surface tension, the better the heat transfer. Water Wetter is also a terrific corrosion inhibitor. ■

vanishes on one bore, the problem mandates a teardown and inspection.

Ignition

There isn't much to think about with the Coyote's coil-on-plug igni-tion system. The factory ignition coils work quite well regardless of how much power you intend to make. The stock Ford ignition coils can handle more than 1,000 hp. The aftermarket offers plenty of ignition-system options from MSD, Accel, Ford Performance, and Perfor-mance Distributors.

Steve Davis of Performance Dis-tributors said that the new Coyote "Sultans of Spark" (SOS) ignition coils offer updated, high-output technol-ogy, which has allowed a significant

I've been told by seasoned engine builders that the Coyote's factory Motorcraft ignition coils can handle in excess of 1,000 hp and 7,000-plus rpm without breaking a sweat. MSD ignition coils are affordable and deliver a hotter spark than the stock coils. If you are running a mild street/strip Coyote, Motorcraft/Ford Performance coils are more than adequate. If you are running boost, you need the more powerful spark that you get from good aftermarket performance coils, such as those from MSD.

When connecting ignition coils, sensors, and other electronic engine control devices, make sure to have a solid connection. A marginal connection can cause issues that can adversely affect performance. Give connectors a shot of contact cleaner, which dries quickly and will protect the connectors. Ignition coils, for example, need dielectric compound at the spark-plug terminals to prevent corrosion.

Always Use Synthetic Oil

There has been a lot of debate through the years about the use of synthetic engine oil in all types of engines. The Ford Coyote is all about synthetic lubrication, which should always be used. Do not run conventional engine oil in this engine.

During the initial fire-up and break-in period, use Mobil 1 5W20 or 5W30 weight engine oil along with a new Wix or Motorcraft filter. Although I mentioned 5W30, I suggest 5W20 for the break-in, which is what Ford recommends for Coyote engines. Coyote engines call for low-viscosity oil because tolerances are tight and Ford having to meet tough Environmental Protection Agency (EPA) fuel-consumption standards. ∎

increase in voltage for each coil from 25,000 to 40,000 volts under load. This means that there are 15,000 more volts per coil. This added voltage under load increases spark intensity for a more complete burn, which is important when you're running boost. This enables you to gap plugs to 0.055 inch.

MSD, of course, doesn't need an introduction with performance enthusiasts. The MSD Blaster coils incorporate a new patented winding design in a direct replacement. As you might expect from MSD, improved spark energy and voltage, combined with MSD durability, make these coils an industry standard. They perform very well with the Coyote's high-revving demeanor.

Exhaust System

You can improve performance by installing the right exhaust system on your F-150 or Mustang GT. There are two basic types of exhaust systems: engine-back and catback. Engine-back systems include all catalytic converters and associated exhaust plumbing. A catback system includes everything from the catalytic converters back. Catalytic converters not only clean up emissions but also reduce noise levels significantly.

For the daily driver, look for mufflers that will deliver a soft, throaty bark at the tailpipes without damaging your hearing. I am often asked, "Which is better: X-pipe or H-pipe?" It has been proven through dyno testing that X-pipes are the better choice when it comes to high-RPM power. I've been told by some tune shops the H-pipe delivers better low-end torque. However, for high-RPM horsepower, nothing beats the X-pipe.

Manufacturers call H- and X-pipes without catalytic converters "off-road" pieces because running them on the street is illegal from coast to coast. All registered street-driven vehicles must have catalytic converters, which is not only a state mandate but also a federal law for all 50 states. When shopping for catalytic converters, look for low-restriction, all-metal cats that will improve exhaust scavenging.

Opt for a low-restriction muffler that will breathe. Unless you're determined to make a lot of noise, opt for that soft throat I was talking about earlier. One of my favorite mufflers is the venerable Flowmaster three-chamber Series 50 Delta Flow, which offers excellent scavenging and that legendary Flowmaster throaty sound without being

The Coyote's factory shorty headers are adequate for street applications. They were well thought-out during the Coyote's development. They offer minimal restriction and good scavenging. However, when power is increased, more header capacity is needed, either as shorties or long-tube headers. To be street-legal in 50 states, you need to retain the catalytic converters. In fact, keep the catalytic converters in any case.

L&M Engines Suggested Start-Up and Break-In

Michael Rauscher, the owner of L&M Engines, is very knowledgeable regarding engine break-in and knows what has worked for him over the span of more than 50 years of engine building.

"We use a break-in procedure that goes against the myths that exist," Rauscher said. "Due to the smooth cylinder finish in today's engines, we run the engine immediately to seat the rings (grind the ring) to the cylinder before the cylinder becomes a mirror. We have a limited amount of time to do this before the roughness disappears. Imagine a piece of sandpaper that gets dull, and if you keep sanding, it doesn't cut but just gets hot. Well, the sandpaper is the honed cylinder finish and the ring is the piece of wood.

"Before engine start, all fluids are topped off, and the car is ready to run. We usually supply engine break-in oil, which can be purchased through our website. The engine must be set up to start immediately without a lot of false starts and excessive cranking. The coolant system must be purged of air before starting. Using a vacuum coolant refiller works best. The intercooler system must be purged and circulating fluid.

"Start the car, but do not crank the engine to prime the oil pump. The engine will have immediate oil pressure on start. Let the car run to cycle the thermostat and fan, check for leaks, etc. When warming up to cycle the thermostat, observe the temperatures of the top and bottom hoses. If both hoses are cool/warm and the temperature gauge is rising or you expect the temperature gauge to rise and it's not, then there is a cooling-system malfunction that must be fixed immediately. The hose temperature differential on a warmed-up engine should be 50 to 75 degrees. Avoid excess idle or very low load operation.

"Do not conduct deceleration operations. Deceleration is an extremely low load condition and reduces ring pressure to the cylinder to zero, polishing the cylinder and removing the roughness. Low-speed and baby throttle operation just polishes the rings. We need combustion pressure to push the ring against the cylinder wall and seat in the ring, which is accomplished by medium to high load.

"Do not over-fuel," Rauscher continued. "An excessively rich condition dilutes the thin film of oil on the cylinder walls, causing accelerated ring wear. We have seen rings with 100 miles of wear look like they have 300,000 miles of wear with the resulting excess oil consumption.

"Beware of crankcase vacuum pumps. Many cases of extreme ring wear are caused by poor vacuum-pump-system engineering. Never use a vacuum pump on a boosted application because it increases the pressure differential across the rings, increasing ring contact pressure and poor lubrication. Incorrect positive crankcase ventilation (PCV) engineering has also acted as a vacuum pump, destroying rings and cylinder walls by removing the thin film of oil, causing excess pressure differential across the ring.

"One more thing—the most common thing is not to overheat the ring," Rauscher continued. "That is done by allowing a few minutes for the ring to cool down, such as flashing the PCM. After thermostat cycling and a leak check, get it on the dyno and start making wide-open-throttle (WOT) pulls, with the first one being 5,000 to 5,500 rpm and subsequent pulls 5,800 to 6,000 rpm. After that, the break-in will be 50- to 75-percent complete. Then, finish your tuning session and go race!" ■

BBK Performance ceramic-coated shorty headers are good for 10 to 15 additional hp and comparable torque. More remarkable was their performance against long-tube headers. The numbers were similar to the long-tube headers. For street use, the BBK shorties work just as well for low-to-midrange torque.

too overwhelming. There is no resonance from the Delta Flow. One of the best mufflers available for good all-around performance and sound is the DynoMax muffler, which offers excellent scavenging without overwhelming cabin noise.

Like the engine on which these are installed, stock exhaust manifolds and shorty headers give the Coyote engine everything they were designed to give. Most of us want attractive tubular exhaust headers. Ideally, you will choose shorty headers that bolt on without modification.

What makes aftermarket shorty headers better than factory manifolds is improved scavenging because the tubes are generally larger. Because most of these headers are ceramic coated, they do reduce underhood heat. Long-tube headers don't make much sense for stock applications. It is challenging to operate catalytic converters with long-tube headers.

Calculating Fuel-Line Size

Few things are more important than proper fuel-line sizing. What works on the street likely will not work on the racetrack and vice versa.

Street and racing are two completely different elements. Fuel-line sizing for carburetion is different from that for fuel injection. This is because the duty cycle is typically 20 to 30 percent at idle and 15 to 20 percent in normal driving. The percentages are for fuel system capacity.

Then comes the subject of pressure and return line sizing. Pressure lines, typically 3/8 inch, are adequate for the kind of street/strip performance expected. As your expected power increases, go to 7/16 inch or even 1/2 inch on the pressure side, depending on the power that is anticipated. As a rule, this means 125- to 150-percent fuel delivery at wide-open throttle.

Keep in mind that fuel turbulence (foaming) in the pressure line will adversely affect performance. This is why there must be enough pressure-line size to handle demand and fuel flow. The return line is there to cycle any unused fuel to the tank. This is why there must be a return line or a self-returning pump in the fuel tank to handle return flow. The fuel-pressure regulator is there to control fuel pressure on the pressure side. This minimizes the chance of

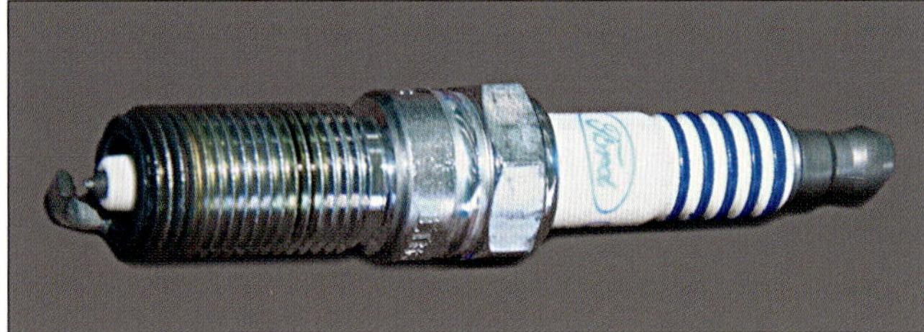

It is critical to inspect spark-plug firing tips after each dyno pull and tune. If you're going to perform the break-in for the vehicle, do a plug reading at 350 to 500 miles. The firing tips should be a light tan to white.

Injector Sizing Selector

Ford's 5.0L and 5.2L Coyote/Voodoo engines have always been fitted with EV-14 injectors, dating back to this engine's introduction in 2011. The injector size chosen depends on the power expected. Here's a breakdown of stock applications:

Application	Injector Size
2011–2017 Mustang GT	34 lbs/hr
2016–2020 GT350	34 lbs/hr
2011–2017 F-150	34 lbs/hr
2018–2023 Mustang GT with Dual Injection	28 lbs/hr
2018–2023 Mach 1	28 lbs/hr
2020–2022 GT500	62 lbs/hr
2018–2023 F-150	28 lbs/hr

any issues between the pump and the injectors.

If you're thinking in AN specifications, a 3/8-inch inside-diameter (ID) hose converts to -6 sizing, and -8 is for 5/8-inch ID. I'd never go smaller than -6, which is the 3/8-inch just mentioned. The main thing to remember with fuel-line sizing is having enough fuel-line diameter to meet the demand and a large enough return line to handle the excess.

You also have a choice of line types: steel or stainless-steel tubing, high-pressure hose and braided hose, and push-to-lock (as the factory uses). Summit Racing Equipment has all of these types and can meet the need. As a rule, flexible rubber hose is rated at 300 psi of maximum pressure. You will also want hoses that can stand up to E85 fuels and California fuels with harsh additives.

If you're going with steel/stainless-steel lines, which are the most durable choice, metal fittings must be paired with hoses from the same manufacturer for compatibility reasons. Mating a hose to steel can be difficult, but it is necessary because you want security in the connection. Push-to-lock, factory-style tubing and fittings are also a best-case scenario in the interest of safety and security.

Selecting Injector Size

Engines must have a specific fuel flow rate in pounds per hour (lbs/hr), which is measured in brake specific fuel consumption (BSFC). BSFC refers to how much fuel is required per hour per each brake horsepower (bhp) that the engine produces. What this means is that if a Coyote

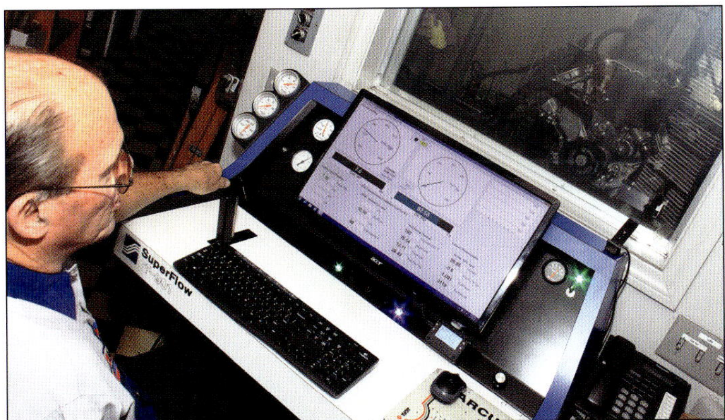

Dyno testing has never been cheap, but it is money well spent considering what has been invested in an engine build. Dyno testing involves a series of pulls under load not only to determine power output but also to properly break in a Coyote engine for ring and bearing seating. Dyno sessions are approximately $600 to $1,000 per day.

is rated at 500 bhp, the total maximum fuel consumption can be confirmed with the fuel-flow requirement = BHP x BSFC.

Another way to confirm is maximum safe horsepower = injector size (lbs/hr) x 8 injectors x maximum duty cycle gets you BSFC. View the following table from Ford Performance and Late Model Restorations.

Injector Flow Rate	Naturally Aspirated HP (at 0.50)	Forced Induction HP (at 0.65)
19 lbs/hr	258 hp at 85-percent duty cycle	199 hp at 85-percent duty cycle
24 lbs/hr	326 hp at 85-percent duty cycle	241 hp at 85-percent duty cycle
30 lbs/hr	408 hp at 85-percent duty cycle	314 hp at 85-percent duty cycle
32 lbs/hr	435 hp at 85-percent duty cycle	335 hp at 85-percent duty cycle
34 lbs/hr	452 hp at 85-percent duty cycle	356 hp at 85-percent duty cycle
36 lbs/hr	490 hp at 85-percent duty cycle	377 hp at 85-percent duty cycle
38 lbs/hr	516 hp at 85-percent duty cycle	398 hp at 85-percent duty cycle
39 lbs/hr	530 hp at 85-percent duty cycle	408 hp at 85-percent duty cycle
42 lbs/hr	571 hp at 85-percent duty cycle	439 hp at 85-percent duty cycle
44 lbs/hr	598 hp at 85-percent duty cycle	460 hp at 85-percent duty cycle
47 lbs/hr	639 hp at 85-percent duty cycle	492 hp at 85-percent duty cycle
60 lbs/hr	816 hp at 85-percent duty cycle	628 hp at 85-percent duty cycle
72 lbs/hr	979 hp at 85-percent duty cycle	753 hp at 85-percent duty cycle
80 lbs/hr	1,088 hp at 85-percent duty cycle	837 hp at 85-percent duty cycle
98 lbs/hr	1,333 hp at 85-percent duty cycle	1,025 hp at 85-percent duty cycle

NOTE: This table is from Ford Performance and Late Model Restorations. These calculations go under the assumption there is at least 39.15 psi of fuel pressure. If the fuel pressure is raised and the pump has the capacity (flow rate), these maximum numbers will increase.

Ford Performance said that going with larger fuel injectors alone will not provide additional horsepower. The decision to go to larger injectors was made for the instance of when a Coyote engine has exceeded the horsepower capacity of its injectors. So, go with a larger injector when you have more horsepower than the current injectors can handle.

Ford Performance confirmed that nominal fuel pressure for most Ford electronic fuel injection (EFI) systems is 39.15 psi, meaning fuel manifold system pressure. It takes this logic a step further by saying that fuel injectors are always rated at 39.15 psi. With that being said, fuel-injector sizing discussions will naturally assume fuel pressure is at least 39.15 psi "delta."

Ford said that there are some exceptions to the nominal injection pressure of 39.15 psi. In recent years, EPA regulations have become so strict that the government is now regulating the emissions that vehicles are allowed to produce even when the engine is shut down. These EPA issues are evaporative emissions and unburned hydrocarbons (fuel vapors) emitting into the atmosphere from the fuel tank, lines, injectors, and intake manifold when the engine is off.

Ford explained that this is the reason for the charcoal canister and hydrocarbon trap in the air box on newer vehicles. It is also the reason that Ford switched to the returnless fuel systems (RFS) that are found in new production vehicles today. This means that there is only a pressure line from the pump and no return line back to the tank.

It becomes complicated with tougher EPA standards. Evaporative emissions means fuel vapors that come as fuel temperature increases in the tank or anywhere in the fuel system. Since the engine gets hot, this heats up the fuel and thus increases evaporative emissions. As a result, Ford went from a return-line fuel

system to what's known as an electronic returnless fuel system (ERFS) and mechanical returnless fuel system (MRFS). The mechanical returnless system is the simpler of the two and controls the engine's fuel rail to a constant pressure via a regulator in the tank, which is normally set to around 60 psi, according to Ford Performance.

Ford further explained that the powertrain control module (PCM) calculates the pressure across the injectors either by inferring or measuring manifold pressure and subtracting from what it knows is the rail pressure set point.

According to Ford, ERFS doesn't have a mechanical regulator. Instead, it has a fuel-rail pressure transducer (FRPT), which is a variable resistor mounted on the fuel rail that measures fuel-rail pressure relative to manifold pressure and feeds that information back to the PCM.

The PCM controls the fuel-pump-driver module (FPDM), which, in turn, varies voltage to the fuel pump (thereby controlling pump output) in the tank to supply the correct pressure and flow rate to the injectors. This is a very precise system of controlling both emissions and fuel flow. As stated earlier, this pressure is maintained at 39.15 psi delta, but when the fuel temperature rises, this pressure can be boosted to delay the onset of boiling the fuel.

The bottom line is that if fuel injectors are chosen based on a pressure of 39.15 psi delta (which is the pressure Ford specifies), the injectors will be correctly sized regardless of which fuel system is used. This also shows that fuel pressure on ERFS vehicles changes based on multiple conditions but primarily temperature.

Ford adds that when trying to compare injector flow rates with the flow data at one delta pressure, injector flow rate at a different delta pressure can be calculated as follows:

Flow rate at new delta pressure = (flow rate at old pressure) x (new pressure ÷ old pressure)

For example, what is the flow rate for an injector at 43.50 psi if it is rated at 60 lbs/hr at 39.15 psi?

Flow rate at 43.50 psi delta = 60 x (43.5 ÷ 39.15) = 66.6 lbs/hr

Use this information to properly determine what size injectors are needed for the application you have. For example, we're talking a naturally aspirated 5.0L V-8 engine making 450 hp. This is flywheel power known as brake horsepower (bhp)—not the "at-the-rear-wheels" horsepower that is measured on the dyno.

Coyote engines require a fuel flow rate measured in pounds per hour (lbs/hr) that can be calculated via the knowledge of brake-specific fuel consumption (BSFC). BSFC means how much fuel (in-lbs) is required per hour per each brake horsepower that the Coyote produces. Most naturally aspirated production gasoline engines generally operate on a 0.42 to 0.52 lb/hp-hr BSFC at wide-open throttle (WOT), according to Ford Performance.

High-performance gasoline engines (with 12.5:1 compression ratio and higher) are extremely efficient and can sometimes have a BSFC as low as 0.38 to 0.42, according to Ford. This means that if you have a gasoline engine that makes 450 bhp, its total maximum fuel requirement in lbs/hr can be calculated as follows:

Ray McClelland of Full Throttle Kustomz of Fillmore, California, performs a professional dyno tune to achieve reliable operation and to get the most power possible safely. Here, McClelland makes digital adjustments to ignition timing and fuel curves.

Fuel flow requirement = (bhp) x (BSFC)

For example, a 450-hp naturally aspirated Coyote V-8 requires what size fuel injector? Begin with a BSFC of 0.50 lbs/hr and injection pressure of 39.15 psi across the injector.

450 hp x 0.50 lbs/hp-hr = 225 lbs/hr

Because this is total fuel flow, divide this by the number of injectors being used to determine the flow rate that is necessary for each injector. The flow rate is needed to select the correct injector size from the Ford Performance catalog. In this example, we have a Coyote V-8 engine using one injector per cylinder, which gives us: 225 lbs/hr ÷ 8 injectors = 28.125 lbs/hr per cylinder.

So, technically, the engine only needs a 28 lbs/hr fuel injector to support 450 hp. However, this will require the injector is at nearly a 100-percent duty cycle to achieve this horsepower level. The duty cycle is how long the injector needs to be open (flowing fuel) to supply the required fuel.

If the injector calls for a 100-percent duty cycle at a particular engine speed and load to inject sufficient amounts of fuel, that means it is open 100 percent of the time. Normally, fuel is injected when the intake valves are closed, which helps with fuel atomization and efficiency. If the injectors need to be on 100 percent of the time to supply fuel, this means that some fuel is being injected when the intake valves are open.

Depending on valve overlap, some of this unburned fuel can be blown right past the exhaust valve, which makes for a less-efficient combustion process. More importantly, operating a fuel injector between a roughly 85- and 99-percent duty cycle does not give the injector sufficient time to close before it has to open again. This can cause an overly rich mixture.

Similar issues can be expected at the low end of the flow region at low duty cycles. However, this is highly dependent upon the type and flow rate of each injector. When this happens, the injector does not have enough time to fully open before it has to close again, which can cause a lean condition.

Based on Ford's advice, I recom-mended choosing an injector with a flow rate that is high enough that it will not be required to exceed an 85-percent duty cycle. To figure out what size of fuel injector will result in an 85-percent duty cycle, divide the original result by 0.85: 18.75 lbs/hr ÷ 0.85 = 35.0 lbs/hr. Since the next most popular injector size is 36 lbs/hr, this is the correct size injector to choose for this application.

Keep in mind that this is based on the assumption that the fuel pump, lines, and regulator are sufficient to be able to maintain at least 39.15 psi across the injector group at all engine speeds and loads (even under boost). Now that an injector has been selected, the calibration (or tune) in the PCM must either be adjusted or a different mass airflow (MAF) sensor must be used. This calculation can also be reversed to give the maximum safe amount of horsepower that a set of injectors can support.

Maximum safe horsepower = injector size x total number of injectors x max duty cycle = BSFC

Fuel Pump

Most EFI fuel pumps are 12 volts and 40 psi. Ford, more specifically, says that its fuel pumps produce 39.15 psi. As a rule, the more voltage that you feed a fuel pump, the faster it runs, which results in higher fuel output from the same pump. As previously mentioned, engines require a certain amount of fuel, not a certain volume of fuel per hour per horsepower. This gets confusing, considering that most fuel pumps are rated by volume and not by mass.

To determine the fuel pump required, use the following information. There are 3.785 liters in 1 U.S.

gallon, and 1 gallon of gasoline (0.72 specific gravity at 65°F) weighs 6.009 pounds. In addition, considering the BSFC specific gravity of the fuel being used is very important.

The fuel feeding a Coyote should be obtained from a source that supplies fuel intended strictly for an automobile. Some people make the mistake of using aviation fuel (avgas), thinking that the higher octane may offer a gain in performance. The reality is that true avgas has a much lower specific gravity (normally as low as 0.62 to 0.65) than automotive fuels, which are 0.72 to 0.76.

An engine calls for a certain mass of fuel per hour per horsepower. One gallon of aviation gasoline has a lower mass than 1 gallon of automotive gasoline. Since the specific gravity of aviation gasoline is only about 90 percent of automotive gasoline, an engine will run approximately 10-percent lean using aviation gasoline.

Be sure to take the specific gravity and stoichiometric ratio of your preferred fuel into consideration when sizing the fuel pump and injectors. Ford suggests applying a safety element for items such as pump-to-pump variability, voltage loss between the pump and the battery, etc. Ford recommends multiplying the final output of the fuel pump by 0.90 to determine the capacity of the fuel pump at 90-percent output to be safe.

As mentioned earlier, all injector flow rates are determined based on a pressure of 39.15 psi across the injector. However, what does "across the injector" mean exactly? It is first important to address the three different methods of measuring fuel pressure.

The first method is absolute pressure, which is defined as the pres-

injector size, compression ratio, etc. Think of the Coyote engine as a package deal. Any single modification isn't going to make much of a difference.

sure relative to a complete vacuum. For example, atmospheric pressure is normally around 14.7 psi at sea level, depending on temperature and weather conditions.

An engine that has an intake-manifold vacuum signal of 12 inches means that the absolute pressure in the intake manifold is 12 in Hg less than the atmospheric pressure. When you subtract the 12 inches from the atmospheric pressure of 29.93 inches of mercury (inHg) or 14.7 psi, you are left with a positive pressure of 17.93 inHg, or roughly 9 psi absolute compared to a complete vacuum (zero pressure).

Sometimes, absolute pressure in psi is written as "PSIA," which stands for pounds per square inch absolute. This is called gauge pressure, which is pressure relative to atmospheric pressure. Instrument pressure is what most of us are familiar with because it is what is measured when checking the air in tires or when connecting a fuel-pressure gauge to the fuel rail.

An engine that makes 6 psi of boost at sea level is actually equivalent to 20.7 psia (14.7 psi + 6 psi = 20.7 psi). Gauge pressure in psi may be written as "PSIG" (pounds per square inch gauge). This third form of pressure is called delta pressure, and it is very much like gauge pressure but instead of being relative to atmospheric pressure. In fact, it can be relative to any other pressure, such as pressure in the intake manifold.

Sometimes delta pressure in psi is written as "PSID" (pounds per square inch differential). When we address pressure "across the injector," what we are really referring to is the delta pressure (or difference) between the fuel-rail pressure and the intake manifold pressure or vacuum.

Ford said that on most EFI systems (non-MRFS), this is the pressure that the system controls, either using a mechanical regulator as referenced to the intake manifold (in a traditional or "return" system) or by the use of the FRPT and the PCM (in ERFS). What this means is that if a fuel-rail pressure gauge is connected to the fuel rail on one of these systems, the fuel pressure will vary, depending on intake manifold pressure/vacuum (known as negative pressure). This happens because the gauge is measuring gauge pressure

Cold-air induction can make a difference in power, especially when there is less restriction. The Coyote's factory air cleaner takes in cooler air from outside. This aftermarket BBK cold-air system is less restrictive, which is important.

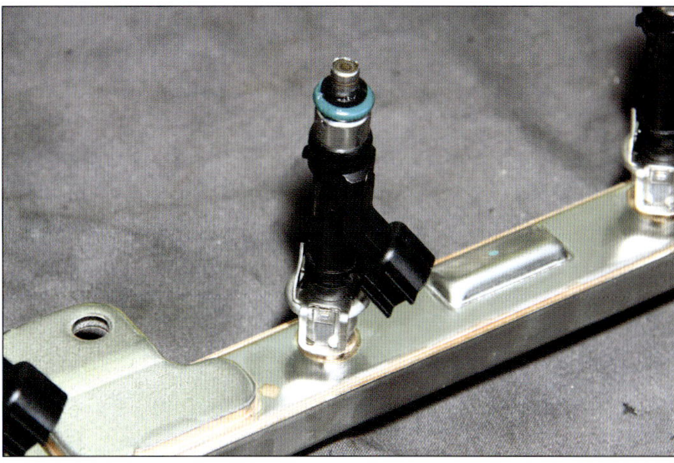

The best advice that I can offer is to seek the input of a professional tuner who can help you select the most compatible injector size for your combination of cams, throttle-body size, intake manifold, compression ratio, and boost (or no boost). If dished pistons and a lower compression ratio have been selected in anticipation of boost, power isn't going to be impressive until there is boost.

relative to atmospheric, but the EFI system is controlling the fuel-rail pressure relative to the intake manifold's negative pressure, which changes depending upon engine load.

On a naturally aspirated Coyote engine, the manifold's vacuum at idle is typically around 10 psia. Manifold pressure at wide-open throttle (WOT) will be atmospheric, so normally at the fuel rail you will see approximately 30 psig at idle and at least 39.15 psig at WOT, depending on whether or not you have ERFS and whether or not it is boosting pressure. On a forced-induction (boosted) engine, the highest manifold pressure that the engine can reach will be atmospheric plus the maximum boost that your forced-air system can obtain. This means that to keep 39.15 psid across the injector, the gauge pressure will have to increase by the same amount as the maximum boost. A couple of examples should make these concepts more clear. First, consider a naturally aspirated conventional (non-ERFS, non-MRFS) EFI system with a mechanical regulator set at the stock pressure setting.

The system will try to maintain pressure across the injector at 39.15 psid regardless of engine load. If a fuel-pressure gauge is attached to the fuel rail, there will be a maximum pressure of 39.15 psig at WOT if the system is doing its job properly. With a forced-induction Coyote making a maximum of 10 psig of boost with a conventional EFI system and mechanical regulator set to the stock pressure setting, the system will still try to keep the pressure across the injector at 39.15 psi. Your fuel-pressure gauge attached to the rail should read a maximum of 39.15 + 10 = 49.15 psig. If it never gets to 49.15 psig at WOT, your fuel system is inadequate for your engine.

It is necessary to either increase the capacity of the fuel pump, minimize the voltage loss between the pump and the battery, or decrease the pressure loss between the pump and the engine through the use of larger lines and test again. Ford strongly discourages trying to tune around this type of fuel delivery problem. It will hurt in the long run and can result in hard-to-diagnose problems all the way to engine failure.

Note that at WOT, the fuel pump in a forced-induction Coyote must supply fuel at a higher pressure than with the naturally aspirated engine. As already mentioned, this means that the fuel pump that is supplying the forced-induction engine will have a lower maximum flow rate capability than the fuel pump supplying the naturally aspirated engine.

E85

There has been a lot of chatter about the use of E85 ethanol-based fuels and engine failure. It is time to talk about this and get the facts straight. E85 is often believed to be

85-percent ethanol and 15-percent gasoline. This has never been true. According to ASTM D5798-11, which is the "Standard Specification for Ethanol Fuel Blends for Flexible-Fuel Automotive Spark-Ignition Engines" the "85" in E85 indicates that the maximum allowable ethanol content is 85 percent and the rest is unleaded gasoline in various blends, depending on where you live. California and other environmentally oriented states have custom blends for oxygenating gasoline to reduce hydrocarbons. Understand that you're not always going to get the same blend from pump to pump.

The benefit of ethanol over petroleum (gasoline) is its heat of vaporization, which is when ethanol turns from a liquid to a vapor or a gas. Because ethanol behaves differently than gasoline, it delivers less heat energy (BTUs) than gasoline. This charge cooling allows a greater mass to be introduced. This allows for more aggressive ignition timing, which can yield greater power over gasoline.

Although this sounds good in theory, it also has its disadvantages. Ethanol calls for more fuel mass per each combustion cycle. This all by itself reduces fuel efficiency because you have to lean harder on the throttle to get the same power. Ethanol, like mineral brake fluid, is hygroscopic, which means that it can absorb moisture that causes compatibility issues with fuel-system components, gaskets, rubber, and silicone. It can adversely affect fuel injectors, pumps, and O-ring seals— not to mention tubing and even fuel rails. I have seen unexpected corrosion issues with engine parts, such as valves and cylinder walls. This happens most with seasonal race cars that sit for months and sometimes years.

If the fear is engine failure due to ethanol, consider the following. Because there is a false sense of security with ethanol, racers tend to push the engine harder, which can cause excessive combustion temperatures and destructive pressures that lead to blown-out cylinder walls, damaged pistons, cylinder heads, and blown head gaskets. Before filling up with E85, ascertain octane. Know what you're pumping. There is Street E85 and there is Race E85. They are not the same octane.

One other important issue with E85 (and gasoline) is the spark-plug heat range, which can drive combustion temperatures sky high. Engine failure comes from not having full knowledge of both octane and spark-plug heat range. Heat range is important because the spark-plug firing tip must cool down before the next combustion cycle. Hot spots in the chamber and early ignition timing can cause destructive preignition and detonation. We don't take spark knock seriously enough as it is happening. This is especially true with boosted engines, where things can wrong in a nanosecond at high RPM.

Get familiar with spark-plug heat ranges before starting on tuning. The minute that you get into boost and nitrous, be thinking ahead of the engine and what's going to happen at full throttle at high RPM. Finally, some engine builders I've spoken with have addressed Spiro locks that manage to work their way out of the piston, tearing up cylinder walls in the process. I'm not sure who discovered this phenomenon first or why it happens, but I've been told that it is a dynamic of E85 and extreme oscillation caused by the energy of combustion. Wire-style locks have proven to perform better than the Spiro locks.

The most important thing to remember about ethanol fuels is that they are alcohol, plain and simple. Being alcohol, E85, as mentioned earlier, is hygroscopic. It likes to suck moisture out of the air just like mineral-based brake fluid. If you live where relative humidity levels are high, E85 will absorb even more moisture. The first thing you will notice is corrosion issues. The fuel system, especially the tank, will exhibit corrosion. Consider stainless fuel-system components where they can be found.

One more thing. A vehicle/engine running E85 street or race fuel cannot sit for extended periods in storage. All fuel must be drained, and the system allowed to dry out. Use every drop of the E85 and get the system dry. Remember, areas with high humidity levels make this problem even worse.

Mass Airflow Sensor

The mass airflow (MAF) sensor is the single most important sensor on the engine for determining the correct air/fuel ratio. The downside is that it is also one of the most misunderstood sensors on a Coyote engine. Few of us get this right. The engine's air-to-fuel ratio and spark advance are determined by the PCM primarily from the input received from the MAF sensor in the intake. This is also why there cannot be any air leaks (defined as air entering the intake stream between the MAF and the combustion chamber) in a MAF-based system. Air leaks will cause a check-engine light, rough idle, stalling, spark knock, drivability issues, and engine failure (in extreme cases).

As with fuel injectors, changing the MAF alone will not result in more horsepower on an otherwise-stock engine. A different MAF sensor should only be considered after an engine modification, which either causes the stock sensor to become a flow restriction or when the stock MAF-sensor electronics are insufficient to measure the airflow that a modified engine is capable of ingesting.

This latter point is critical in understanding when a MAF sensor needs to be replaced. It is possible to have two MAF sensors that are equal in size but capable of different maximum power levels. This is because the electronics of each MAF sensor is different and measures different maximum airflow levels. For example, you can have two different 90-mm MAF sensors but one will be capable of measuring 60 lbs/min of air, while the other may measure 100 lbs/min of air.

Both MAF sensor assemblies present the same airflow restriction, but they are not interchangeable. With that being said, how do you know how much air your MAF needs to be capable of measuring?

According to Ford, the two main methods of dealing with the installation of a new MAF sensor and injectors is to either "trick" the PCM by carefully selecting injectors and a matched MAF sensor or to change the calibration in the PCM to match the MAF and injectors that you've selected. The first method requires

When swapping cams, have a professional tune in the interest of engine safety. With significant changes (cam, throttle body, manifold, and header changes), the tune has to match the changes. Consult with a professional tuner whenever making significant changes.

a MAF sensor that has been curved to a certain injector flow rate. For instance, let's say that the engine originally came with 34 lbs/hr injectors and they were replaced with 39 lbs/hr injectors. A MAF sensor is needed with electronics that have been modified in such a way that it will output a signal proportional to an airflow that is 19/39 times as great as the stock MAF. This will result in the PCM delivering the correct amount of fuel despite the injector size change.

The downside to this method is that many other variables, such as spark advance, are determined from the MAF sensor through a parameter known as "load." For a given engine RPM, as load increases, the required spark advance decreases. By using this method, the MAF sensor outputs a signal that is lower than the stock MAF, which means that the calculated load will also be lower. This also means that the commanded spark advance will be higher than it should be, which can lead to spark knock.

The factory Ford catalytic converters are not that restrictive, and they are necessary for proper function and cleaner emissions. There is little or no logic in removing them believing you're going to make more power. One other sticky issue is smog laws. It is illegal to remove them. Aftermarket catalytic converters may be less restrictive.

I suggest testing the new calibration on a dynamometer to ensure that the engine receives the correct air-to-fuel ratio at all speeds and loads. Provided that this is performed by a competent and experienced professional tuner using proper equipment, this is by far the best method and will result in the best part-throttle drivability and idle. This means less trouble with check-engine lights, returnless fuel, electronic throttle monitors, transmission shifting, etc.

Prior to tuning on a dyno, be certain that the grounds for the EFI system are solid. Doing this will help ensure that the calibration your tuner develops on the dyno will also work when you're on the road. I cannot stress enough that all vacuum leaks and electrical and fuel issues must be resolved prior to the vehicle being dyno tuned. Correcting any issues before heading to the dyno will always be cheaper than paying for dyno time while correcting these problems during dyno time.

Dyno Tuning Provides Power and Reliability

Whether opting for the factory coils or high-output aftermarket coils, protocol for start-up, break-in, and testing is the same. Consider consulting with a professional tuner to make the most of your Coyote build. I suggest investing in dyno testing and tuning by an experienced and proven tune shop with a great reputation.

There are two choices when it comes to dyno testing and tuning: an engine break-in and tuning session on an engine dyno or having it tested and tuned in the vehicle. Whatever you decide to do, it should receive the break-in and tune by a proven professional. Professional tune shops typically charge anywhere from $600 to $1,200 a day for tuning, depending on where it is tuned.

A word of caution: check references and credentials when shopping for a tune shop. Anyone can hang up a shingle and call themselves a tune shop using off-the-shelf mail-order tuning programs. This logic can cost you an engine. Few things are riskier than a bad tune with excessive timing and a lean mixture just to get bigger numbers. You want both power and durability in an engine that will last. Tuning should dovetail into the kind of driving that you do most of the time.

Although dyno tuning tends to come off as a speed and performance thing, it is also about proper tuning for power and reliability. Even when a Coyote engine is built exclusively for street use, the electronics should be in proper tune. Today's electronically controlled engines have to be thought of differently. Instead of swapping jets and adjusting idle/air mixture screws in a carburetor, we have to sit down with a laptop computer and hone our ECM programming skills. This process is not for the novice. Coyote tuning is strictly for the professional.

The dyno-tuning professional will put the Ford vehicle on the chassis dynamometer and run it under wide-open-throttle conditions as well as normal driving to get fuel and ignition curves dialed in. If there weren't any major changes to your Coyote engine, dyno tuning almost isn't required. However, when you want to be certain of fuel and ignition curves, dyno tuning is a good idea.

Dyno tuning becomes mandatory whenever we change camshafts, heads, fuel injectors, throttle body size, or anything else changing the engine's basic personality. When upgrading to hotter cams or high-performance heads, it becomes necessary to upgrade fuel injectors, the throttle body, and the intake manifold. This means changes to fuel and spark curves as well. A professional tune is money well spent and a good investment.

ENGINE MATH

Successful engine building is primarily about math. It is needed for machining dimensions, compression and rod ratios, bore sizes, stroke, journal diameters, fuel-injector and port sizes, dynamic balancing, tolerances, etc. You simply cannot successfully build an engine without math knowledge.

Displacement

Displacement is the area above the piston when it is at bottom dead center (BDC) multiplied by the number of cylinders in the engine. When the piston rises to top dead center (TDC), it displaces the volume above the dome. The formula for cylinder volume (displacement) is:

Pi (ϖ) x Radius^2 x Stroke = Cylinder Volume

Pi (ϖ) is a mathematical constant that is equal to 3.14159. A cylinder's radius is half of its diameter. With a cylinder bore, the diameter is a measurement from one side of the cylinder to the other. The stroke is the distance that the piston will travel in one direction.

Bore x Bore x Stroke x 0.7854 = Cylinder Volume

Multiply single-cylinder volume by the total number of cylinders to learn displacement:

Bore x Bore x Stroke x 0.7854 x Total Number of Cylinders

Let's put this formula to work using a 5.0L Coyote engine with a 3.630-inch bore and 3.650-inch stroke:

3.630 inches x 3.630 inches x 3.650 inches x 0.7854 x 8 = 302.1948 ci

Ford rounded 302.1948 to 302 ci of displacement. If we bore this engine 0.005-inch oversize to 3.635 inches, we get:

3.635 inches x 3.635 inches x 3.650 inches x 0.7854 x 8 = 303.022787 ci (303 ci)

Calculating Compression Ratio

An engine's compression ratio is the difference between two volumes:

a cylinder's volume with the piston at BDC and the remaining volume with the piston at TDC. If only compression were this easy to calculate. There's more to this than just BDC bore volume and TDC remaining volume. To know an engine's true compression ratio, know the following volumes:

- Combustion-chamber volume
- Compressed head-gasket volume (thickness)
- Piston deck height
- Piston dish/dome volume
- Cylinder volume

When the piston is at BDC, the total cylinder volume becomes all of these volumes added together. When the piston is at TDC, volume becomes all of these elements except cylinder volume. Add it up, and it should look like this:

Cylinder Volume + Piston Deck Height + Compressed Head Gasket Volume + Chamber Volume + Piston Dish ÷ Dome Volume

Piston Deck Height + Compressed Head Gasket Volume + Chamber Volume + Piston Dish ÷ Dome Volume

The bottom number is divided into the top number to achieve compression ratio.

Combustion-Chamber Volume

Combustion-chamber volumes are available from manufacturers when dealing with aftermarket cylinder heads or if port work has been done. To be absolutely sure of chamber volume, measure it yourself using a graduated cylinder with a valve, burettes, and a plastic deck plate. The machine shop can do this too.

Converting Cubic Inches to Cubic Centimeters and Liters

Combustion-chamber volume and piston-dish/dome volume are normally measured in cubic centimeters (not cubic inches). To convert cubic centimeters (cc) to cubic inches (ci), divide the measurement by 16.4:

$$\text{Cubic Centimeters} \div 16.4 = \text{Cubic Inches}$$

If we have a 54.6-cc combustion chamber, divide 54.5 by 16.4 to get 3.3231707 ci. If you want to convert 54.5 cc to liters, remember that 1,000 cc is 1.0 liter. This makes 54.5 cc equal to 0.0054 liter (or 54.5-percent of 1 liter).

Compressed Head-Gasket Volume

Compressed head-gasket volume is cylinder volume in the compressed gasket. Think of it as a very shallow cylinder bore. We compute compressed head-gasket cylinder volume the same way we do cylinder volume:

$$\text{Bore x Bore x Gasket Thickness x } 0.7854 = \text{Compressed Head-Gasket Volume}$$

Let's say that our compressed head-gasket thickness is 0.040 inch:

$$3.630 \text{ inch x } 3.630 \text{ inch x } 0.040 \text{ inch x } 0.7854 = 0.4139654 \text{ ci}$$

Piston/Deck-Height Volume

Piston/deck-height volume is the small volume amount that is left when the piston reaches TDC (not taken up by swept volume). Measure piston/deck height with a dial indicator with the piston at top dead center and measure the distance from the piston dome to the block deck. Expect to see anything from 0.008 to 0.025 inch. For example, if a block deck has been milled 0.010 inch, the deck height will be considerably less. Don't ever be surprised by a zero deck with the piston flush, which calls for a thicker head gasket.

As with compressed head-gasket thickness, think of deck height like you would a very shallow cylinder bore and compute it like this:

$$\text{Bore x Bore x Deck Height x } 0.7854 = \text{Deck Height Volume}$$

Let's play with this formula together, basing it on a typical 5.0L Coyote:

$$3.630 \text{ inch x } 3.630 \text{ inch x } 0.010 \text{ inch x } 0.7854 = 0.10349137 \text{ ci}$$

Piston Dish/Dome Volume

This information is needed when computing compression ratio because it positively will affect compression. Because dishes and domes are never dimensionally the same from piston to piston, each piston should be measured. The same can be said for valve reliefs where equipped. Since Coyote combustion-chamber size varies very little, don't expect much variation across head castings. Measure piston dish volume like this:

$$cc/16.4 = \text{cubic inches}$$
$$\text{or}$$
$$10 \text{ cc}/16.4 = 0.609756 \text{ ci}$$

How Does This Affect Compression Ratio?

Let's look at a typical Coyote engine and measure compression ratio. Assume that it has a 54.5 cc chamber, compressed head-gasket thickness of 0.040 inch, and a piston/deck height of 0.0.4139654 ci (0.010 inch). Here's how it computes:

$$37,77433 \text{ ci} + 2.5609 \text{ ci} + 0.382508 \text{ ci} + 0.609756 \text{ ci} + 0.0080528 \text{ ci} = 41.336 \text{ ci}$$
$$0.0080528 \text{ ci} + 0.382508 \text{ ci} + 2.5609 \text{ ci} + 0.609756 \text{ ci} = 3.5612168 \text{ ci}$$

When you divide 41.336 ci by 3.5612168 ci, you arrive at 11607.268 (11.6:1 compression).

Calculating Horsepower and Torque

Horsepower gets too much airtime when it comes to street engines. The real hero on the street is torque. Torque is way more significant than horsepower because horsepower doesn't count until high RPM. Think of torque as the power that gets you moving and horsepower as what keeps you going at wide-open throttle.

I have seen hundreds of dyno pulls through the years and observed how engines make power. One element always remains true: horsepower and torque always pass each other at 5,250 rpm.

$$\text{Horsepower} = \frac{\text{RPM x Torque}}{5,252 \text{ rpm}}$$

Here's another way to look at it:

$$\text{Torque} = \frac{5,252 \text{ rpm x Horsepower}}{\text{RPM}}$$

Power-to-Weight Facts

A good rule of thumb when planning a street Coyote planning is: 10 hp for every 100 pounds of vehicle weight, including you, your fuel, and all fluids. The magic number there is 300 hp for a 3,000-pound vehicle. If your vehicle weighs 3,500 pounds, you need 350 hp. A heavier vehicle, say 4,000 pounds, needs 400 hp to impress the crowds.

Estimating Horsepower at the Drag Strip

A Coyote engine's approximate horsepower and torque can be determined with a single quarter-mile pass at the drag strip. Begin by weighing the vehicle. Scales can be found at most farmers' co-ops, truck stops, and truck weigh stations along the interstate. Make several quarter-mile passes, understanding that you will lose power once you get beyond 2 to 3 passes. Average out your time slips. Then, do the following calculation:

$$\text{Horsepower} = \frac{\text{Weight x 0.4 x 1/4-mile mph}}{282}$$

Let's assume that your Ford weighs 3,500 pounds and your average quarter-mile trap speed was 100 mph. If you plug in those numbers, we get:

$$\frac{3,000 \text{ pounds x 0.4 x 100 mph}}{282} = 425.53191 \text{ hp}$$

If you know what RPM your engine is turning when you pass through the traps, you can also closely figure out torque.

$$\frac{5,252 \text{ x 425 hp}}{6,000 \text{ rpm}} = 372 \text{ ft-lbs of torque}$$

These calculations aren't foolproof, but they are close enough to provide some idea about power. Of course, there are an untold number of tuner shops that are eager to help to determine power output and super tune your engine to help it reach its greatest potential.

*A*PPENDIX

Coyote Engine Specifications (Gen 1 and Gen 2)	
Displacement	4.957L (302 ci)
Bore	92.2 mm (3.629 inches)
Stroke	92.7 mm (3.649 inches)
Firing Order	1-5-4-8-6-3-7-2
Spark Plug Gap	1.25–1.35 mm (0.049–0.053 inch)
Oil Pressure at Idle	10 psi–15 psi
Oil Pressure at 2,000 rpm	30 psi–40 psi
Compression Ratio	11.0:1; 9.5:1 (Supercharged FRP applications)
Engine Weight	431 pounds

Cylinder Heads	
Combustion Chamber Volume	54.5–57.5 cc
Intake Valve Stem Diameter	6.015–6.044 mm (0.2368–0.2379 inch)
Exhaust Valve Stem Diameter	6.015–6.044 mm (0.2368–0.2379 inch)
Intake Valve Stem-to-Guide Clearance	0.020–0.069 mm (0.008–0.0027 inch)
Exhaust Valve Stem-to-Guide Clearance	0.045–0094 mm (0.0018–0.0037 inch)
Intake Valve Head Diameter (2011–2014); Intake Valve Head Diameter (2015–2017)	37.0 mm (1.450 inches)
Exhaust Valve Head Diameter (2011–2014); Exhaust Valve Head Diameter (2015–2017)	31.0 mm (1.220 inches)
Valve Face Runout	0.05 mm (0.019 inch)
Valve Face Angle	3-angle
Intake Valve Seat Width	1.3–1.5 mm (0.051–0.059 inch)
Exhaust Valve Seat Width	1.4–1.6 mm (0.059–0.063 inch)
Valve Seat Runout	0.04 mm (0.016 inch)
Valve Seat Angle	121/91/61 degrees
Intake Valve Spring Free Length	51.32 mm (2.020 inches)
Exhaust Valve Spring Free Length	51.32 mm (2.020 inches)
Intake Valve Perpendicularity	3.0 mm (0.118 inch)
Exhaust Valve Perpendicularity	3.0 mm (0.118 inch)
Intake Valve Spring Compression Force	650 n
Exhaust Valve Spring Compression Force	650 n
Intake Valve Spring Installed Height	40 mm (1.5748 inches)
Exhaust Valve Spring Installed Height	40 mm (1.5748 inches)
Intake Valve Installed Force	265 n
Exhaust Valve Installed Force	265 n
Roller Rocker Ratio	2:1
Head Gasket Surface Flatness	0.025 mm (0.001 inch) in any 25 mm (1.000 inch); 0.050 mm (0.002 inch) in any 150 mm (6.000 inches) x 150 mm (6.000 inches); 0.1 mm (0.004 inch) overall

Hydraulic Lash Adjuster	
Hydraulic Lash Adjuster Diameter	12 mm (0.472 inch) Intake/Exhaust
Bore Clearance	0.018–0.050 mm (0.0007–0.0019 inch)
Hydraulic Lash Adjuster Leakdown	0.45–3.0 seconds Intake/Exhaust
Collapsed Lash Adjuster Gap	0.35–0.85 mm (0.0137–0.0334 inch)

Camshafts	
Intake Lobe Lift	5.963 mm (0.2348 inch)
Exhaust Lobe Lift	5.488 mm (0.2160 inch)
Cam Journal Diameter	28.620 mm (1.1267 inch)
Cam Journal Bore Diameter	28.682–28.657 mm (1.1292–1.1282 inch)
Cam Journal to Bearing Clearance	0.025–0.075 mm (0.001–0.002 inch)
Camshaft Runout	0.04 mm (0.0016 inch)
Camshaft Endplay	0.15 mm (0.0059 inch)

Cylinder Block	
Cylinder Bore Diameter	92.200–92.220 mm (3.6299–3.6307 inch)
Cylinder Bore Taper	0.013 mm (0.0005 inch)
Cylinder Bore Maximum Out-Of-Round	0.010 mm (0.0004 inch)
Main Bearing Bore Inside Diameter	72.400–72.424 mm (2.850–2.851 inch)
Head Gasket Surface Flatness (Block)	0.0254 mm (0.001 inch) across any 38.1 mm (1.500 inch) surface

Piston and Connecting Rod	
Piston Diameter	92.161–92.175 mm (3.6283–3.6289 inches)
Piston-to-Cylinder Wall Clearance	0.025–0.059 mm (0.0009–0.0023 inch)
Piston Ring End Gap (Top)	0.15–0.25 mm (0.0059–0.0098 inch)
Piston Ring End Gap (Middle)	0.30–0.55 mm (0.0118–0.0216 inch)
Piston Ring End Gap (Oil Control)	0.15–0.45 mm (0.0059–0.0177 inch)
Piston Ring Groove Width (Top)	1.220–1.250 mm (0.0480–0.0492 inch)
Piston Ring Groove Width (Middle)	1.220–1.240 mm (0.0480–0.0488 inch)
Piston Ring Groove Width (Oil Control)	2.530–2.560 mm (0.0996–0.1003 inches)
Piston Ring Width (Top)	1.17–1.19 mm (0.0460–0.0468 inch)
Piston Ring Width (Middle)	1.17–1.19 mm (0.0460–0.0468 inch)
Piston Ring-to-Groove Clearance (Top)	0.030–0.080 mm (0.0019–0.0031 inch)
Piston Ring-to-Groove Clearance (Middle)	0.030–0.070 mm (0.0019–0.0028 inch)
Piston Pin Bore Diameter	22.004–22.010 mm (0.8663–0.8665 inch)
Piston Pin Diameter	22.004–22.010 mm (0.8649–0.8661 inch)
Piston Pin Length	60.7–61.0 mm (2.3897–2.4015 inches)
Piston Pin-to-Bore Fit (Clearance)	0.004–0.013 mm (0.0002–0.0005 inch)
Connecting Rod-to-Pin (Clearance)	0.003–0.018 mm (0.0001–0.0007 inch)
Connecting Rod Pin Bore Diameter	22.003–22.015 mm (0.8663–0.8667 inch)
Connecting Rod Length (Bore-to-Bore)	150.7 mm (5.933 inches)
Connecting Rod Maximum Allowable Bend	0.038 mm (0.0015 inch)
Connecting Rod Maximum Allowable Twist	0.050 mm (0.0019 inch)
Connecting Rod Bearing-to-Crankshaft Clearance	0.028–0.069 mm (0.0011–0.0027 inch)
Connecting Rod Side Clearance at Crank	0.325 mm (0.0128 inch) Standard Play; 0.500 mm (0.0197 inch) Maximum Play

Crankshaft	
Main Bearing Journal Diameter	67.481–67.505 mm (2.657–2.658 inches)
Main Bearing Journal Maximum Taper	0.004 mm (0.0002 inch)
Main Bearing Journal Maximum Out-Of-Round	0.006 mm (0.0002 inch)
Main Bearing Journal-to-Main Bearing Clearance	0.025–0.045 mm (0.0009–0.0016 inch)
Connecting Rod Journal Diameter	52.983–53.003 mm (2.086–2.087 inches)
Connecting Rod Journal Maximum Taper	0.004 mm (0.0002 inch)
Crankshaft Maximum Endplay	0.28 mm (0.011 inch)

Cooling System	
Coolant	Motorcraft Orange Antifreeze/Coolant

Lubrication	
Engine Oil	Motorcraft SAE 5W20 Synthetic; Motorcraft SAE 5W20 Premium Blend; Never use conventional engine oil

Coyote Engine Specifications (Gen 3 and Gen 4)	
Displacement	4.957L (302 ci)
Bore	92.2 mm (3.660 inches)
Stroke	92.7 mm (3.650 inches)
Firing Order	1-5-4-8-6-3-7-2
Spark Plug Gap	1.25–1.35 mm (0.049–0.053 inch)
Oil Pressure at Idle	10–15 psi
Oil Pressure at 2,000 rpm	30–40 psi
Compression Ratio	12.0:1
Engine Weight	431 pounds

Cylinder Heads	
Combustion Chamber Volume	55.0 cc
Intake Valve Stem Diameter	6.015–6.044 mm (0.2368–0.2379 inch)
Exhaust Valve Stem Diameter	6.015–6.044 mm (0.2368–0.2379 inch)
Intake Valve Stem-to-Guide Clearance	0.020–0.069 mm (0.008–0.0027 inch)
Exhaust Valve Stem-to-Guide Clearance	0.045–0094 mm (0.0018–0.0037 inch)
Intake Valve Head Diameter	37.0 mm (1.450 inches)
Exhaust Valve Head Diameter	31.0 mm (1.259 inches)
Valve Face Runout	0.05 mm (0.019 inch)
Valve Face Angle	3-Angle
Intake Valve Seat Width	1.3–1.5 mm (0.051–0.059 inch)
Exhaust Valve Seat Width	1.4–1.6 mm (0.059–0.063 inch)
Valve Seat Runout	0.04 mm (0.016 inch)
Valve Seat Angle	121/91/61 degrees
Intake Valve Spring Free Length	51.32 mm (2.020 inches)
Exhaust Valve Spring Free Length	51.32 mm (2.020 inches)
Intake Valve Perpendicularity	3.0 mm (0.118 inch)
Exhaust Valve Perpendicularity	3.0 mm (0.118 inch)
Intake Valve Spring Compression Force	650 n
Exhaust Valve Spring Compression Force	650 n
Intake Valve Spring Installed Height	40 mm (1.5748 inches)
Exhaust Valve Spring Installed Height	40 mm (1.5748 inches)
Intake Valve Installed Force	265 n
Exhaust Valve Installed Force	265 n
Roller Rocker Ratio	2:1
Head Gasket Surface Flatness	0.025 mm (0.001 inch) in any 25 mm (1.000 inch); 0.050 mm (0.002 inch) in any 150 mm (6.000 inches) x 150 mm (6.000 inches); 0.1 mm (0.004 inch) overall

Hydraulic Lash Adjuster	
Hydraulic Lash Adjuster Diameter	12 mm (0.472 inch) Intake/Exhaust
Bore Clearance	0.018–0.050 mm (0.0007–0.0019 inch)
Hydraulic Lash Adjuster Leakdown	0.45–3.0 seconds Intake/Exhaust
Collapsed Lash Adjuster Gap	0.35–0.85 mm (0.0137–0.0334 inch)

Camshafts	
Intake Lobe Lift	5.963 mm (0.2348 inch)
Exhaust Lobe Lift	5.488 mm (0.2160 inch)
Cam Journal Diameter	28.620 mm (1.1267 inches)
Cam Journal Bore Diameter	28.682–28.657 mm (1.1292–1.1282 inches)
Cam Journal to Bearing Clearance	0.025–0.075 mm (0.001–0.002 inch)
Camshaft Runout	0.04 mm (0.0016 inch)
Camshaft Endplay	0.15 mm (0.0059 inch)

Cylinder Block	
Cylinder Bore Diameter	92.200–92.220 mm (3.6299–3.6307 inches)
Cylinder Bore Taper	0.013 mm (0.0005 inch)
Cylinder Bore Maximum Out-Of-Round	0.010 mm (0.0004 inch)
Main Bearing Bore Inside Diameter	72.400–72.424 mm (2.850–2.851 inches)
Head Gasket Surface Flatness (Block)	0.0254 mm (0.001 inch) across any 38.1 mm (1.500 inches) surface

Piston and Connecting Rod	
Piston Diameter	92.161–92.175 mm (3.6283–3.6289 inch)
Piston-to-Cylinder Wall Clearance	0.025–0.059 mm (0.0009–0.0023 inch)
Piston Ring End Gap (Top)	0.15–0.25 mm (0.0059–0.0098 inch)
Piston Ring End Gap (Middle)	0.30–0.55 mm (0.0118–0.0216 inch)
Piston Ring End Gap (Oil Control)	0.15–0.45 mm (0.0059–0.0177 inch)
Piston Ring Groove Width (Top)	1.220–1.250 mm (0.0480–0.0492 inch)
Piston Ring Groove Width (Middle)	1.220–1.240 mm (0.0480–0.0488 inch)
Piston Ring Groove Width (Oil Control)	2.530–2.560 mm (0.0996–0.1003 inch)
Piston Ring Width (Top)	1.17–1.19 mm (0.0460–0.0468 inch)
Piston Ring Width (Middle)	1.17–1.19 mm (0.0460–0.0468 inch)
Piston Ring-to-Groove Clearance (Top)	0.030–0.080 mm (0.0019–0.0031 inch)
Piston Ring-to-Groove Clearance (Middle)	0.030–0.070 mm (0.0019–0.0028 inch)
Piston Pin Bore Diameter	22.004–22.010 mm (0.8663–0.8665 inch)
Piston Pin Diameter	22.004–22.010 mm (0.8649–0.8661 inch)
Piston Pin Length	60.7–61.0 mm (2.3897–2.4015 inch)
Piston Pin-to-Bore Fit (Clearance)	0.004–0.013 mm (0.0002–0.0005 inch)
Connecting Rod-to-Pin (Clearance)	0.003–0.018 mm (0.0001–0.0007 inch)
Connecting Rod Pin Bore Diameter	22.003–22.015 mm (0.8663–0.8667 inch)
Connecting Rod Length (Bore-to-Bore)	150.7 mm (5.933 inch)
Connecting Rod Maximum Allowable Bend	0.038 mm (0.0015 inch)
Connecting Rod Maximum Allowable Twist	0.050 mm (0.0019 inch)
Connecting Rod Bearing-to-Crankshaft Clearance	0.028-0.069 mm (0.0011–0.0027 inch)
Connecting Rod Side Clearance at Crank	0.325 mm (0.0128 inch) Standard Play; 0.500 mm (0.0197 inch) Maximum Play

Crankshaft	
Main Bearing Journal Diameter	67.481–67.505 mm (2.657–2.658 inches)
Main Bearing Journal Maximum Taper	0.004 mm (0.0002 inch)
Main Bearing Journal Maximum Out-of-Round	0.006 mm (0.0002 inch)
Main Bearing Journal-to-Main Bearing Clearance	0.025–0.045 mm (0.0009–0.0016 inch)
Connecting Rod Journal Diameter	52.983–53.003 mm (2.086–2.087 inches)
Connecting Rod Journal Maximum Taper	0.004 mm (0.0002 inch)
Crankshaft Maximum Endplay	0.28 mm (0.011 inch)

Cooling System	
Coolant	Motorcraft Orange Antifreeze/Coolant

Lubrication	
Engine Oil	Motorcraft SAE 5W20 Synthetic; Motorcraft SAE 5W20 Premium Blend; Never use conventional engine oil

Engine Fastener Torque Specifications				
Fastener Type	**First Pass**	**Second Pass**	**Third Pass**	**Final Pass**
Main Caps	In Proper Numerical Order; 177 in-lbs	Outer Only; 30 ft-lbs	Inner Only; 48 ft-lbs	All – 90 Degrees Torque-Angle
Main Caps; Cross Bolts	89 in-lbs	22 ft-lbs	N/A	60 Degrees; Torque-Angle
Connecting Rods	N/A	N/A	N/A	60 ft-lbs
Cylinder Heads	In Proper Numerical Order; 18 ft-lbs	30 ft-lbs	Plus 90 Degrees; Torque-Angle	90 Degrees; Torque-Angle
Camshaft Journal Caps	In Proper Numerical Order; 53 in-lbs	N/A	N/A	45 Degrees; Torque-Angle
Camshaft Mega Journal Caps	53 in-lbs	N/A	N/A	45 Degrees; Torque-Angle
Timing Chain Guides	N/A	N/A	N/A	89 in-lbs
Oil Pump Bolts	89 in-lbs	N/A	N/A	60 Degrees; Torque-Angle
Oil Pump Tube-to-Pump	89 in-lbs	N/A	N/A	45 Degrees; Torque-Angle
Oil Pump Pickup Tube Strap	N/A	N/A	N/A	89 in-lbs
Oil Pan Bolts	89 in-lbs	N/A	N/A	89 in-lbs
Piston Cooling Jets	89 in-lbs	N/A	N/A	45 Degrees; Torque-Angle
VCT Phaser Assembly Bolts	133 in-lbs	N/A	N/A	90 Degrees; Torque-Angle
VCT Solenoid Bolts	70 in-lbs	N/A	N/A	30 Degrees; Torque-Angle
Front Timing Cover Bolts	18 ft-lbs	N/A	N/A	60 Degrees; Torque-Angle
Cam/Valve Cover Bolts	N/A	N/A	N/A	89 in-lbs
Engine Oil Pressure Sensor	124 in-lbs	N/A	N/A	90 Degrees; Torque-Angle
Camshaft Position Sensor	N/A	N/A	N/A	89 in-lbs
Harmonic Damper Bolt	103 ft-lbs	Back Off 1/4 Turn	N/A	74 ft-lbs
Flywheel Bolts	177 in-lbs	N/A	N/A	60 Degrees; Torque-Angle
Clutch Pressure Plate Bolts	46 ft-lbs	N/A	N/A	60 Degrees; Torque-Angle
Water Pump Bolts	177 in-lbs	N/A	N/A	60 Degrees; Torque-Angle
Bellhousing Bolts	N/A	N/A	N/A	35 ft-lbs
Intake Manifold Bolts	100 in-lbs	N/A	N/A	30 Degrees; Torque-Angle
Fuel Rail Bolts	89 in-lbs		N/A	90 Degrees; Torque-Angle
Exhaust Manifold Bolts	18 ft-lbs	N/A	N/A	26 ft-lbs

(Specifications Courtesy Summit Racing Equipment)
NOTE: Clean all fastener threads and lubricate threads with engine oil. Do not bottom out the studs. Leave some space in the bolt hole below the stud to prevent cracking the casting.
NOTE: The harmonic damper must be fully seated before tightening the bolt.
NOTE: Torque-angle means torque-to-yield in an additional number of degrees of torque. Torque-to-Yield is the type of fastener. Torque-angle is the torque procedure. You're using a "Torque-to-Yield" fastener and the method is "Torque-Angle."

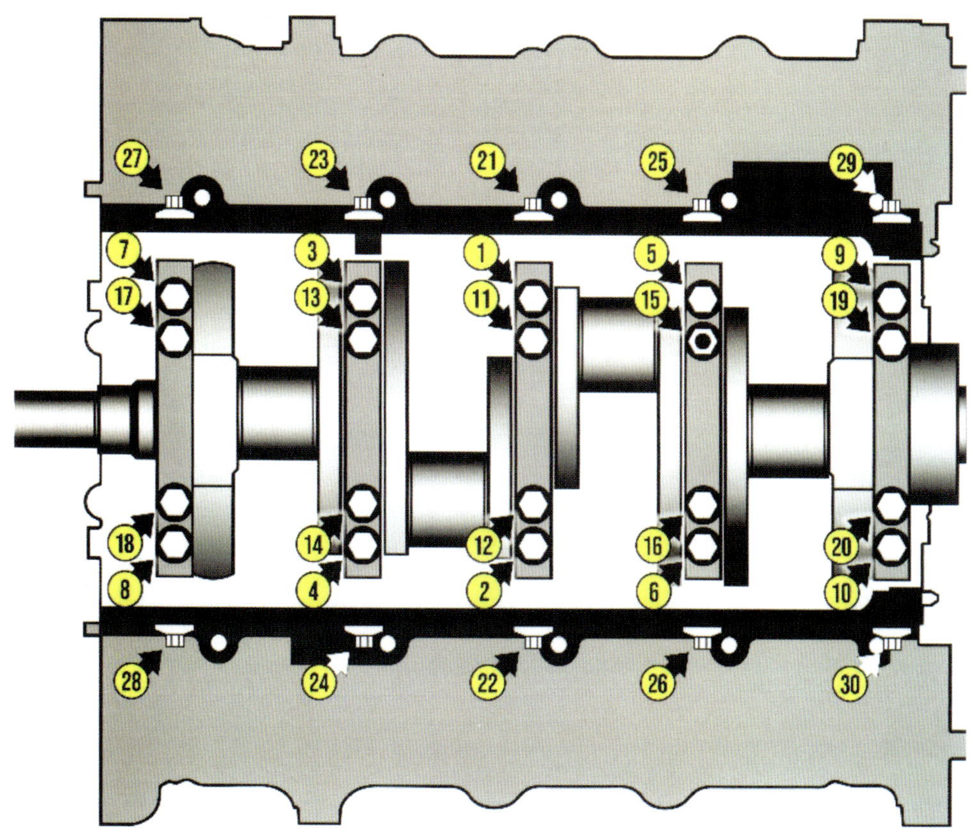

This is the main cap torque sequence. (Image Courtesy Summit Racing Equipment)

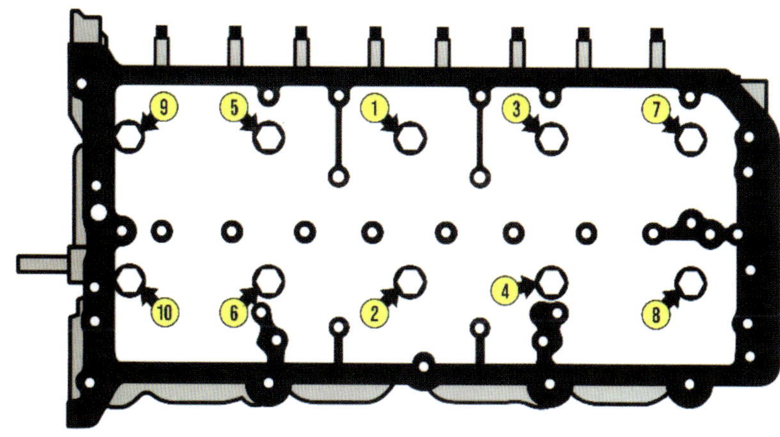

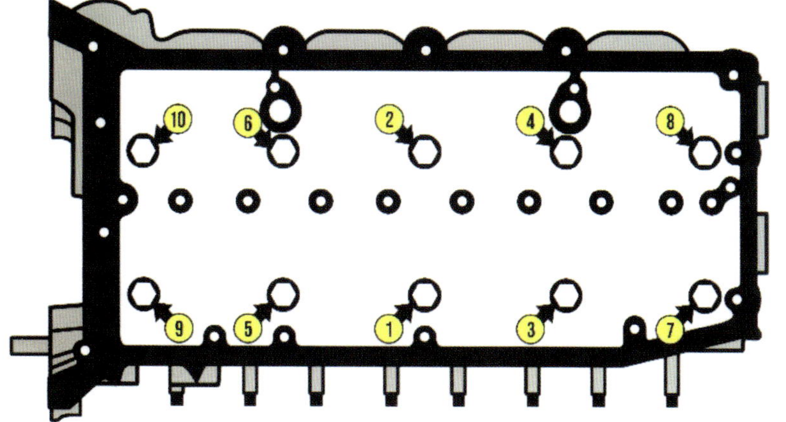

The cylinder-head bolt torque sequence is shown. (Image Courtesy Summit Racing Equipment)

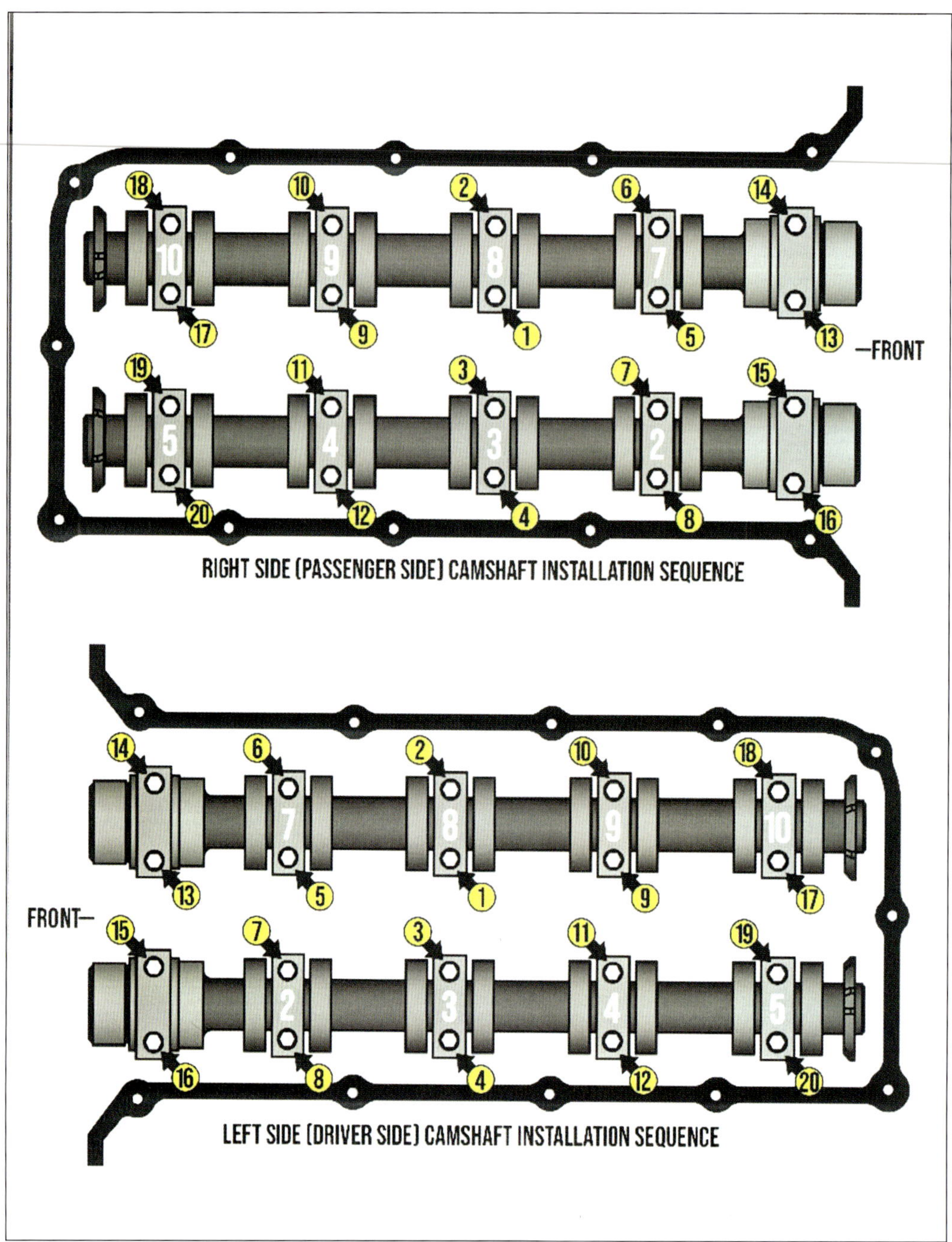

This is the camshaft journal cap bolt torque sequence. (Image Courtesy Summit Racing Equipment)

Work-A-Long Sheet Also available at www.cartechbooks.com

DISASSEMBLY

Project Statistics

Your Name ____

Today's Date _______________ Vehicle Engine Removed From __________________

Engine Year _______________ CI _________ Block Casting _____________ ☐ 2 barrel ☐ 4 barrel ☐ Fuel Injection

Accessories Attached to Used Engine

☐ A/C Pump   ☐ AIR Pump   ☐ AIR Distributor Lines and Hoses   ☐ Water Pump
☐ Flywheel   ☐ Clutch   ☐ Flexplate   ☐ Transmission
☐ Starter   ☐ Fuel Pump   ☐ Exhaust Manifolds   ☐ All Pulleys; Except _______________
☐ Alternator   ☐ Distributor   ☐ Coil   ☐ Carburetor
☐ Motor Mounts   ☐ Motor Mount Attaching Brackets   ☐ Spark Plug Heat Shields
☐ EGR Valve   ☐ Dipstick Tube   ☐ All Bolts; except _______________
☐ _______   ☐ _______   ☐ _______   ☐ _______   ☐ _______

Operational Notes

Oil consumption _______________________   Compression check pressure variation _______________ psi

Leak-down percent _____________________   Other observations _______________________

Disassembly Notations

Crank uses centerbolt   ☐ Yes   ☐ No
Heat riser restricted on   ☐ Left   ☐ Right   ☐ Both
Head gaskets   ☐ Steel shim   ☐ Composition
Worn/damaged lifters   ☐ No   ☐ Yes;   where _______________

Vibration damper pulley screws   ☐ 3/8-NC   ☐ 3/8-NF

Location of timing-pointer attaching points: _______________

Oil filter adapter type:
☐ Spin-on
☐ Long cartridge (late)
☐ Short cartridge (early)

Type of rear main seal:
☐ Rubber—two piece
☐ Rubber—one piece (late)
☐ Rope (early)

INSPECTION

Initial Parts Inspection Observations

Block OK   ☐ Yes   ☐ No; describe problem _______________________
Heads OK   ☐ Yes   ☐ No; describe problem _______________________
Crank Ok   ☐ Yes   ☐ No; describe problem _______________________
Bearings OK   ☐ Yes   ☐ No; describe problem _______________________
Pistons OK   ☐ Yes   ☐ No; describe problem _______________________
Cam/lifters OK   ☐ Yes   ☐ No; describe problem _______________________
Damper OK   ☐ Yes   ☐ No; describe problem _______________________
Intake manifold OK ☐ Yes   ☐ No; describe problem _______________________
Exhaust manifold OK ☐ Yes   ☐ No; describe problem _______________________
Oil pump OK   ☐ Yes   ☐ No; describe problem _______________________

Oil pump/rear main cap mating surfaces damage/abnormalities   ☐ No   ☐ Yes
Identifying mark you placed on all parts:

____

AT THE MACHINE SHOP

Parts Delivered to the Machine Shop

☐ Block	☐ Main Caps	☐ Crankshaft	☐ Oil Pump	☐ Oil Pump Pickup
☐ Connecting Rods	☐ Pistons	☐ Piston Rings	☐ Camshaft	☐ Lifters
☐ Vibration Damper	☐ Main Bearings	☐ Rod Bearings	☐ Cam Bearings	☐ Rod Bolts
☐ Gasket Set	☐ Push Rods	☐ Rockerarms	☐ Head Bolts	☐ Main Bolts/Studs
☐ Miscellaneous Nuts/Bolts/Brackets for Cleaning			☐ _________	
☐ Water Pump	☐ Timing Cover	☐ Oil Pan	☐ Flywheel/Flexplate	
☐ Clutch	☐ Exhaust Manifolds	☐ Motor Mounts	☐ Motor Mount Attaching Brackets	
☐ Assembled Heads	☐ Disassembled Heads with: ☐ Valves	☐ Springs ☐ Retainers ☐ Keepers		
☐ _________	☐ _________		☐ Rocker Balls and Nuts ☐ _________	
☐ Intake Manifold	☐ With Heat Riser Shield	☐ Installed ☐ Not Installed		
☐ _________	☐ _________	☐ _________	☐ _________	☐ _________
☐ _________	☐ _________	☐ _________	☐ _________	☐ _________
☐ _________	☐ _________	☐ _________	☐ _________	☐ _________
☐ Other Accessories _________				

Special Instructions for Machine Shop

☐ Bore block	☐ Use torque plates	☐ Desired piston-to-wall clearance: 0. _______ -inch
☐ Grind crank	☐ Rod bearing clearance: 0. _______ -inch	☐ Main bearing clearance: 0. _______ -inch
☐ Deck to clean	☐ Surface heads	☐ Install cam bearings ☐ _________ ☐ _________
☐ _________	☐ _________	
☐ _________	☐ _________	

Is pilot bushing to be installed in crankshaft (required for manual transmission)?   ☐ Yes   ☐ No
Are intake manifold heat shield holes to be tapped for 8-32 screws?   ☐ Yes   ☐ No

After You Pick Up Your Parts

☐ Yes	☐ No	Threaded holes reconditioned/chased	☐ Yes	☐ No	Drilled holes and edges chamfered
☐ Yes	☐ No	head/block dowels properly installed	☐ Yes	☐ No	Are cam bearings properly installed
☐ Yes	☐ No	Galleries tapped for screw-in plugs	☐ Yes	☐ No	Add 0.030-inch hole in gallery plug
☐ Yes	☐ No	Add 0.030-inch hole in thrust face	☐ Yes	☐ No	Core plugs properly installed
☐ Yes	☐ No	Retaining straps on core plugs	☐ Yes	☐ No	Crank keys properly installed
☐ Yes	☐ No	Manifold heat-shield holes tapped for 8-32 screws			

PRE-ASSEMBLY FITTING

Measured and Recorded During Pre-Assembly Fitting

☐ Yes	☐ No	Do all valveguides have proper clearance? If no, which are correct _________
☐ Yes	☐ No	Do all valveseats meet dimensional specs? If no, which are faulty _________
☐ Yes	☐ No	Do all valveseats hold solvent? If no, which leak _________
☐ Yes	☐ No	Have all valveguides been machined concentric for press-on seals?

Retainer to Valveguide clearance 0. _______ -inch; adequate on all valves?   ☐ Yes   ☐ No   If no, which valves have insufficient clearance? _________

Recommended valvespring seat pressure _______ psi at _______ -inches installed height.

Measured valvespring installed height:

1 _________	3 _________	5 _________	7 _________
2 _________	4 _________	6 _________	8 _________

Spring shims used to obtain correct installed height:

1 _______________ 3 _______________ 5 _______________ 7 _______________
2 _______________ 4 _______________ 6 _______________ 8 _______________

Measured valvespring solid height __________ -inches

Calculated compressed spring clearance:

1 _______________ 3 _______________ 5 _______________ 7 _______________
2 _______________ 4 _______________ 6 _______________ 8 _______________

Connecting rod bore OK?	☐ Yes ☐ No;	Which rods are defective _______________
Crank straightness OK?	☐ Yes ☐ No	Runout on center main of O. __________ -inch
Main bearing clearance OK?	☐ Yes ☐ No	Measured clearance O. __________ -inch
Crank thrust OK?	☐ Yes ☐ No	Measured clearance O. __________ -inch
Main bearing clearance OK?	☐ Yes ☐ No	Measured clearance O. __________ -inch
Camshaft bearing fit OK?	☐ Yes ☐ No;	Describe problem _______________
Block required clearance grinding for upper sprocket?	☐ Yes ☐ No	
Pin end clearance OK?	☐ Yes ☐ No	Measured clearance O. __________ -inch
Piston-to-wall clearance OK?	☐ Yes ☐ No	Measured clearance O. __________ -inch
		Pistons with incorrect clearance _______________

Measured ring end gap:

1 Top ______ 2nd ______ 3 Top ______ 2nd ______ 5 Top ______ 2nd ______ 7 Top ______ 2nd ______
2 Top ______ 2nd ______ 4 Top ______ 2nd ______ 6 Top ______ 2nd ______ 8 Top ______ 2nd ______

Rod bearing clearance OK?	☐ Yes ☐ No	Measured clearance O. __________ -inch
Rod side clearance OK?	☐ Yes ☐ No	Measured clearance O. __________ -inch
Piston-to-head clearance OK?	☐ Yes ☐ No	Measured clearance O. __________ -inch
		Cylinders with incorrect clearance _______________

Offset bushings/key used: ☐ + – 2° ☐ + – 4° ☐ + – 6° ☐ + – 8° ☐ + – 10° ☐ + – 12°

Rotating assembly clearance OK?	☐ Yes ☐ No;	Cause of interference _______________
Crank index OK?	☐ Yes ☐ No	Maximum ______ ° out of index on journal no. __________
Cylinder-to-cylinder deck height accurate?	☐ Yes ☐ No	Maximum O. ______ -inch variation.
Rocker geometry OK?	☐ Yes ☐ No;	Describe problem _______________
Rocker-to-stud clearance OK?	☐ Yes ☐ No	Maximum O. ______ -inch (Intake); O. ______ -inch (Exhaust);
Piston-to-valve clearance OK?	☐ Yes ☐ No	Maximum O. ______ -inch (Intake); O. ______ -inch (Exhaust);
Oil pump drive clearance OK?	☐ Yes ☐ No	Measured clearance O. __________ -inch
Intake manifold end-rail clearance OK?	☐ Yes ☐ No	Measured clearance O. __________ -inch
Manifold surface parallel with head?	☐ Yes ☐ No;	Describe problem _______________
Pulleys/accessories aligned?	☐ Yes ☐ No;	Describe problem _______________

____
____

Accufab
909-930-1751
accufabracing.com

American Muscle
877-887-1105
americanmuscle.com

Automotive Racing Products (ARP)
800-826-3045
805-339-2200
arp-bolts.com

BBK Performance
386-624-0025
bbkperformance.com

Brian Roche Racing Engines
410-285-7250

Comp Cams
901-795-2400
compcams.com

Crower Cams & Equipment
619-661-6477
crower.com

CJ Pony Parts
800-888-6473
717-657-9252
cjponyparts.com

Coyote Direct
806-414-0369
coyotedirect.com

DRiVParts
drivparts.com

Ford Performance Parts
800-FORD-788
313-621-0771
performanceparts.ford.com

Full Throttle Kustomz (Performance Dyno Tuning)
805-200-5500
fullthrottlekustomz.com

Holley Performance
866-464-6553
holley.com

JBA Performance Exhaust (PerTronix Brands)
913-808-2376
pertronixbrands.com

JGM Performance Engineering
661-257-0101
Email: jbjperformance@sbcglobal.net

Justin's Performance Center (JPC)
410-729-0005
jpcracing.com

Late Model Restoration
866-507-3786
lmr.com

Lethal Performance
877-416-9986
561-753-8105
lethalperformance.com

Livernois Motorsports & Performance
313-723-2466
livernoismotorsports.com

MAK Performance
305-822-9272
makperformance.com

Modular Motorsports Racing (MMR)
805-383-4130
modularmotorsportsracing.com

MSD Ignition
866-464-6553
holley/brands/msd.com

National Parts Depot (California)
800-235-3445
805-654-0468
npdlink.com

National Parts Depot (Florida)
800-874-7595
352-861-8700
npdlink.com

National Parts Depot (Michigan)
800-521-6104
734-397-4569
npdlink.com

National Parts Depot (North Carolina)
800-368-6451
704-331-0900
npdlink.com

Quarter Mile Performance (QMP)
818-576-0816
qmpracing.com

Real Street Performance
407-695-7223
realstreeperformance.com

Roush Performance
800-59-ROUSH
roushperformance.com

Stage 3 Motorsports
623-434-5277
stage3motorsports.com

Summit Racing Equipment
800-230-3030
330-630-3030
summitracing.com